A Tradition of Excellence
THE SESQUICENTENNIAL HISTORY OF THE UNIVERSITY AT ALBANY
1844 to 1994

The Class of 1879, the oldest extant group photograph of a graduating class.

A Tradition of Excellence

THE SESQUICENTENNIAL HISTORY OF THE UNIVERSITY AT ALBANY STATE UNIVERSITY OF NEW YORK

1844 to 1994

By Kendall A. Birr,
Professor Emeritus of History

Editor: Vincent P. Reda, '74
Photo editor: Robert Peagler, MFA, '92
University Archivist: Geoffrey Williams
Project Director: Sheila A. Mahan

THE DONNING COMPANY PUBLISHERS
20TH ANNIVERSARY

The Normal School and College had always included science in its curricula. Professor Cook's geology class was photographed on a field trip to the Van Rensselaer Bank Moraine. (Cook photo from The *Echo*, 1906.)

Copyright © 1994 by The University at Albany, State University of New York
All rights reserved, including the right to reproduce this work in any form
whatsoever without permission in writing from the publisher, except for brief
passages in connection with a review. For information, write:

The Donning Company/Publishers
184 Business Park Drive, Suite 106
Virginia Beach, VA 23462

Steve Mull, General Manager
Debra Y. Quesnel, Project Director
Tracey Emmons-Schneider, Project Research Coordinator
Elizabeth B. Bobbitt, Editor
Eliza Midgett, Designer

Library of Congress Cataloging-in-Publication Data:
Birr, Kendall.
A tradition of excellence : the sequicentennial history of the University at
Albany, State University of New York, 1844 to 1994 / by Kendall A. Birr.
p. cm.
Includes index.
ISBN 0-89865-889-6
1. State University of New York at Albany—History. I. Title.
LD3839.B57 1994   94-2894
378.747'42—dc20   CIP
Printed in the United States of America

CONTENTS

Acknowledgments	7
Chapter I	11
Beginnings, 1844 to 1848	
Chapter II	25
The Normal School, 1848 to 1890	
Chapter III	45
From Normal School to College for Teachers, 1890 to 1915	
Chapter IV	63
The College for Teachers in Wars and Depression, 1915 to 1945	
Chapter V	93
The Apogee of Teacher Education, 1945 to 1962	
Chapter VI	119
Creating a University in the 1960s	
Chapter VII	155
Weathering a Turbulent Era, 1969 to 1976	
Chapter VIII	177
The Emergence of a Mature Public Research University, 1976 to 1994	
Appendix	218
Index	219
About the Author	224

ACKNOWLEDGMENTS

Footnotes did not seem appropriate for a volume of this kind. Those readers interested in the sources used are referred to an annotated copy of the text deposited in the University Archives. The text for the first four chapters is based heavily on two sources: William Marshall French, '29, and Florence Smith French, '33, *College of the Empire State* (1944), the centennial history of the College, and W. Paul Vogt, *The State University of New York at Albany, 1844-1984: A Short History* (1984), an unpublished manuscript. Geoffrey Williams, *Chronological History of the University at Albany, SUNY, 1844-1992* (revised, 1992) and fragments of an uncompleted manuscript on the history of the University by the late John Maguire were also useful.

Several other works proved helpful. Frederick Rudolph, *The American College and University* (1962) and Helen Lefkowitz Horowitz, *Campus Life: Undergraduate Cultures from the End of the Eighteenth Century to the Present* (1987) provided valuable background. John McEneny, *Albany: Capital City on the Hudson* (1981), David W. Martin, *The Liberal*

(Opposite) The faculty from a program in "domestic science," in 1914. Seated: Florence D. Frear and Edna Avery. Front: Emma P. Garrison, Marion L. Van Liew, and Eva Wilson. Back: Cora A. Steele and Eunice Perine (the first art teacher). (Alumni Memorabilia Collection.)

Arts in the Curricula for the Preparation of Teachers at the State University of New York at Albany (Ph.D. dissertation, University of Connecticut, 1967), and Robert Connery and Gerald Benjamin, *Rockefeller of New York: Executive Power in the Statehouse* (1979) were helpful for their particular topics.

The text is otherwise based heavily on research in the University Archives. Archivist Geoffrey Williams was an essential resource in locating material; Dorothy Christensen, head of Special Collections, and Mary Osielski, '64, were helpful in many ways. Elizabeth Buss did a great deal of the research, particularly on student life. Thomas Pullyblank checked the facts. (Needless to say, the author takes sole responsibility for any errors, factual or interpretive.) Vincent Reda of University Relations edited the copy. Several people—Paul Vogt, Lewis Welch, Harold Hanson, '63, Warren Roberts, and Arthur Collins, '48,—read and critiqued the manuscript in whole or in part. Locating and choosing photos was a joint effort on the part of the author, Geoffrey Williams, Vincent Reda, '74, and Robert Peagler, MFA, '92. Liza Frenette, '91, '93, wrote some of the sidebars. Edward Wozniak of University Graphics gave skillful attention to preserving and duplicating photographs.

Sheila Mahan, Senior Assistant to the President, presided over the entire operation from conception to publication. She provided essential resources, critiqued the manuscript at various stages, wrote photo captions, and generally played an essential role in making certain that the project was pushed to completion.

Thanks, too, to the many alumni(ae) and friends of Albany—the College and the University—who have donated their photographs and other memorabilia to the University Archives Alumni Memorabilia Collection.

My thanks to everyone who helped make this volume possible.

September 30, 1993

Kendall Birr

[*A note about photographs: we have made every effort to identify the source, the photographer, and the subjects in all photographs, based on the information available. Our apologies for any errors or omissions that may appear here. All photos not otherwise described are from University Archives.*]

(Opposite) *The Daily Graphic* for January 27, 1885, illustrated President-elect Grover Cleveland's attendance at the mid-year closing exercises of the Normal School. Cleveland had been Governor of New York from 1883 to 1885 and was inaugurated as President about five weeks after this event.

PRESIDENT-ELECT CLEVELAND AT THE CLOSING EXERCISES OF THE STATE NORMAL SCHOOL, ALBANY.

CHAPTER I
Beginnings
1844 to 1848

On December 18, 1844, twenty-nine students from around the State of New York, two instructors, and a group of educational and civic dignitaries gathered in an abandoned railroad depot on the north side of State Street between Lodge and Eagle streets in Albany. With workers hammering in the background making last-minute changes in the building, dignitaries, faculty and students officially opened the newly authorized New York State Normal School.

The speaker for the occasion was Col. Samuel Young, Superintendent of Common Schools, and one of the people principally responsible for the creation of the school. His remarks, replete with the oratorical flourishes characteristic of the age, extolled the high calling of teaching, described the new curriculum, advised the students to develop good health habits, and urged them to "diffuse throughout the state a . . . fund of moral and intellectual wealth." A half century later, William Phelps, one of those original students, characterized himself

(Opposite) David Perkins Page, the Normal School's visionary founding Principal.

Gideon Hawley, lawyer, businessman, and educator, had been New York's first superintendent of public instruction. In 1844, as a member of New York's Board of Regents, he was instrumental in the founding of the Normal School, and became a member of its first Executive Committee.

and his cohorts as "young people who had left their rural homes in distant parts of the State and journeyed to the capital to gather, if possible, some inspiration of the new gospel of education . . . They were teachers actuated by a high and noble ambition."

Immediately after the ceremonies, Principal David Page and faculty member George Perkins divided the twenty-nine students into two sections and conducted the first drills in reading and arithmetic. The new Normal School was officially launched.

The New York State Normal School was New York's response to the universal American enthusiasm for common school education in the 1830s and 1840s. Public expectations matched the public enthusiasm. Community leaders never tired of emphasizing the importance of an educated electorate in a democracy. "The schools are the pillars of the republic," asserted one author. Such schools were expected to eradicate almost every vice in American society: crime, vagrancy, unemployment, alcoholism, prostitution, and political radicalism, to name a few. Ultimately, said one observer, the schools were "the grand lever, which is to raise up the mighty mass of this community . . ."

In New York the Legislature in 1795 began offering matching funds to communities willing to tax themselves to maintain common schools. Between 1812 and 1814, lawmakers created a complex system for sharing the costs of supporting these schools. School districts provided buildings, towns hired and paid the teachers, and the state distributed funds from a "permanent school fund." The principal result: attendance burgeoned, and by 1844 nearly two-thirds of New York's children under age nineteen were enrolled in schools for at least part of the year.

Most teachers in the common schools were temporary, ill-paid, and ill-prepared by any standard. In rural upstate New York, common-school education was a seasonal activity. Older students attended during the winter months when there was little farm work to do, and men did much of the teaching in these "winter schools." Younger children often attended during the summer and were frequently taught by women, since the male teachers, like their students, often farmed in the summer. Many teachers, often barely older than their students, had little more than a few years of common school education, often gained in the very school in which they taught. Male teachers generally viewed ill-paid teaching positions as a form of temporary employment until "something better" came along. Women, with fewer career alternatives, stayed longer but after marriage often left teaching for "another line of work." The rapid turnover of teachers had become a serious problem by the 1840s.

Those who saw the common schools as the salvation of the nation concluded that something must be done to better prepare teachers for their important task. Some turned to existing private secondary academies. These were basically college preparatory schools, but the Regents in 1828 saw them as "fit seminaries . . . for the training of teachers." From 1834 to the end of the century, some academies received state funds for teacher education, but many supporters of the common schools believed that teacher training was only an afterthought for the academies and turned instead to the idea of a normal school devoted solely to that purpose. Not until the 1840s, however, did they achieve success.

The principal champion of a state-supported normal school was Colonel Young, an experienced politician who became state superintendent in 1842, won support from two successive governors, William Seward and William C. Bouck, and found a powerful ally in Calvin T. Hulburd, the chair of the Assembly Committee on Colleges, Academies and Common Schools.

Soon after taking office, Young began his campaign at a meeting of common schools officials in Utica. There he assembled a collection of educational notables from within the state as well as such national figures as Horace Mann of Massachusetts. Mann argued passionately that professional preparation was necessary for successful teaching and that New York should follow Massachusetts' example by establishing one or more normal schools. The gathering followed Mann's lead and approved a resolution in favor of such a move.

In 1844 the effort moved into the Legislature. There, Hulburd's committee issued a seventy-seven-page report on New York's common

(Top) Alonzo Potter, a member of the Executive Committee and a professor at nearby Union College, shared the vision for common school education and teacher training espoused by Horace Mann, lawyer and Massachusetts educational reformer (bottom). Mann encouraged the organization of the Albany State Normal School and recommended David Page as its first Principal, a recommendation endorsed by Potter. (Potter photo courtesy of the College Archives, Schaffer Library, Union College.)

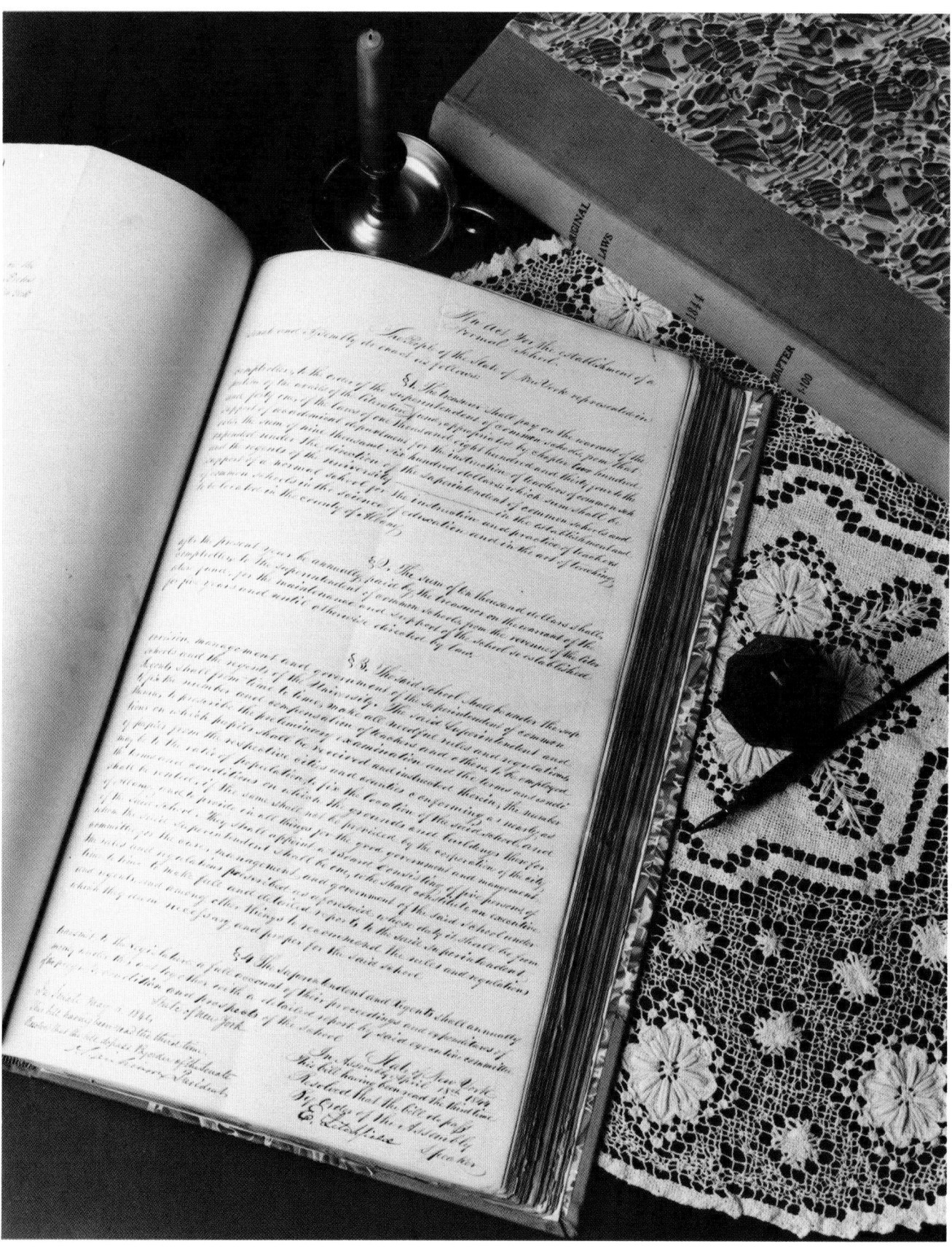

schools and introduced a bill to establish a state normal school at Albany. After some political maneuvering, a substitute bill was passed on May 7, 1844, and promptly signed by Governor Bouck. The final measure provided for the establishment and support of a normal school in Albany "for the instruction and practice of teachers of common schools in the science of education and in the art of teaching." To support the new school the bill provided $9,600 to be followed by five annual appropriations of $10,000. Supervision was the joint responsibility of the Regents and the Superintendent of Common Schools, but immediate oversight of the new school fell to a five-person local Executive Committee which included the superintendent.

Why Albany? Curiously, there seems to have been little competition for the school. Many of the most important advocates for the Normal School were from Albany or the immediate vicinity. But the most compelling argument for the Albany location was political. The Normal School was, in a sense, an experiment. Locating it within easy view of the Legislature could generate political support for its continuation. In addition, Normal School supporters pointed to the educational advantages of training common school teachers where they could observe the operations of the American republic in the halls of state government.

In any event, Albany in 1844 seemed to be a suitable site. Its rapidly-growing population was approaching 50,000. Westward-moving Yankees with their traditional respect for education still dominated the city, but there were also varying numbers of the older Dutch, newly arrived Irish and Germans, Jews, and African-Americans. Ninety percent of the population lived within a half mile of the city center at State and Pearl streets.

Of course, the students who arrived in the 1840s could hardly have been impressed with the urban amenities: there was no sewage system, streets were ill-paved, and the inhabitants had to depend on inadequate, privately owned water systems. Hogs running loose in the city streets often outnumbered the people!

Yet Albany was an extraordinarily prosperous city by the 1840s. It was a major transportation hub. The Hudson River and the Erie Canal gave Albany superb access to the expanding west as well as New York

Friend Humphrey was mayor of Albany from 1843 to 1845; the city provided use of the first building occupied by the Normal School. (Photo reproduced from Cuyler Reynolds, *Albany Chronicles*: Albany, 1906.)

(Opposite) The final legislation establishing the Normal School as New York's first public institution of higher learning. It was approved by the New York State Legislature on May 7, 1844, and promptly signed by Governor Bouck. (Photo by Gary Gold, '70, of original document in the New York State Archives.)

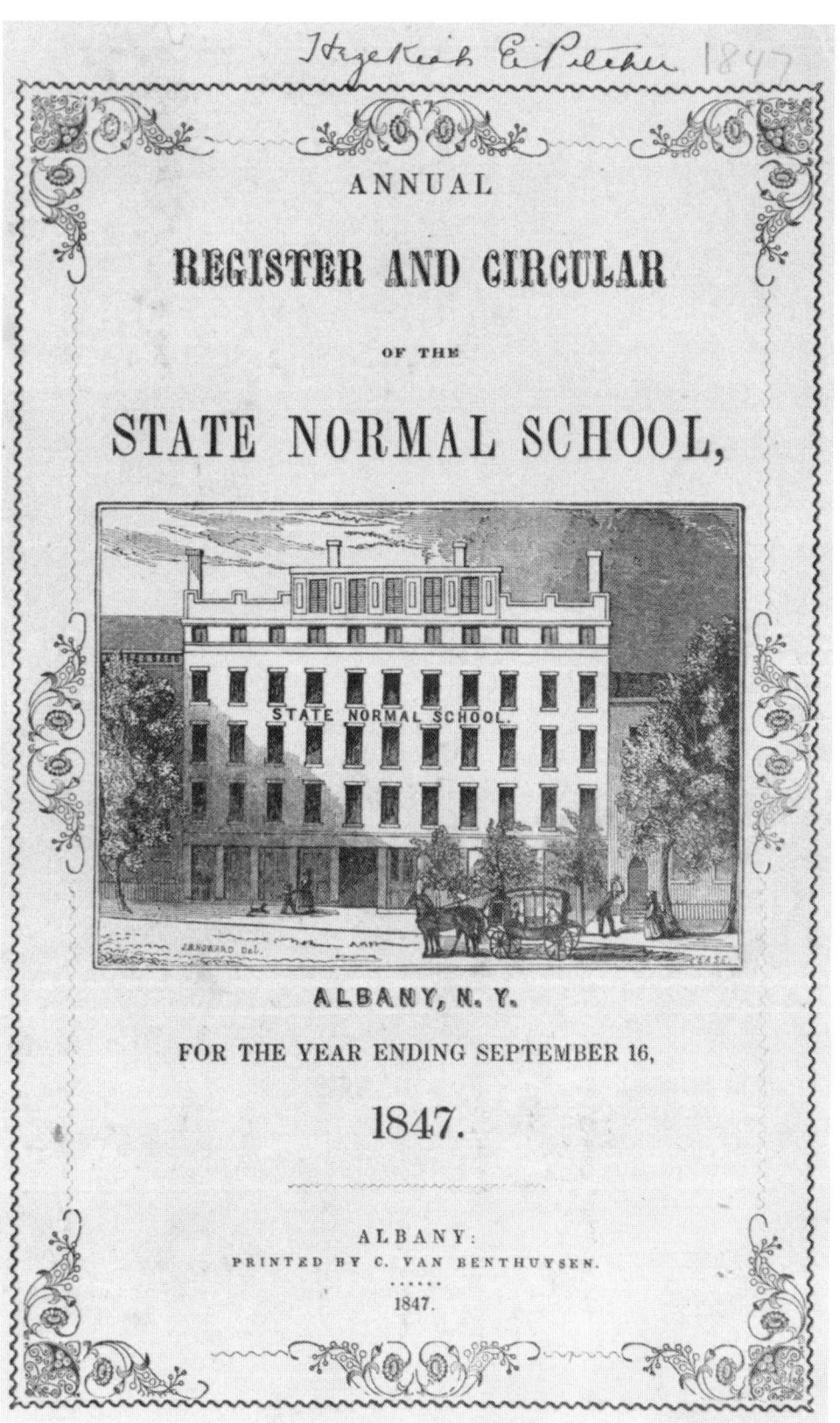

The cover of the *1847 Annual Register and Circular* showing the School's building, a former train depot at 115-121 State Street.

City and its overseas trade, and by 1842 Albany had rail connections both to Buffalo and Boston. The city bustled with activity. Goods passed through Albany headed for the west or for New York City and overseas destinations; immigrants headed into the interior to carve out farms. Wealthy merchants such as the first Erastus Corning expanded into banking and manufacturing. Workers manufactured iron stoves and rails, brewed beer, printed books, and sawed logs into lumber.

Albany was politically powerful as well. It was the capital of the most populous state in the Union, but its political influence reached into the entire nation through the Democratic party faction known as the "Albany Regency," dominated by Martin Van Buren.

Yet New York's capital was not solely concerned with the nitty gritty of economic existence or political power; it was also interested in the "higher things" of human life. The community counted some twenty-five churches of nine denominations to conduct its religious life. The Albany Institute of History and Art had begun its distinguished esthetic and historical career in the 1790s. The pages of the *Albany Argus* showed numerous advertisements for "amusements," including theater, museums, a circus, and art exhibitions.

Albany also had a long tradition of interest in education. The Albany Academy was chartered in 1813 and by the time of the establishment of the Normal School had already seen its physics professor, Joseph Henry, conduct his path-breaking experiments in electro-magnetism. The Albany Academy was joined by its female counterpart in 1814, the Albany Medical College in 1838, and the Albany Law School in 1851. The newspapers were filled with notices of private schools, and Albany's common school system was beginning to grow.

Starting a new normal school from scratch was no easy task, but in the Summer and Fall of 1844 the Executive Committee energetically attacked the problem. The City of Albany proposed in August that the new school occupy the upper floors of a building in the heart of the city on State Street which had been used as a railroad depot by the Mohawk and Hudson Railroad from 1833 to 1841. The Executive Committee promptly agreed. The city paid the $1,200 annual lease fee for five years, provided $500 more to rehabilitate the building, and later paid another $3,000 for the use of land adjoining the structure. Nearby well-to-do residents paid for painting the State Street side of the building. The first home of the Normal School contained eight rooms: two study rooms accommodating about one hundred students each, four recitation rooms, a lecture hall seating about 350, and a room for the library and storage of apparatus.

Meanwhile, Francis Dwight, the secretary of the Executive Committee, prepared a list of necessary apparatus based on an examination of the nation's first normal school in Massachusetts. A primitive library was built from two sources. School book publishers gave the Normal School sets of textbooks, and by 1846 the textbook library had over 5,000 volumes. James L. Wadsworth donated nearly 600 additional volumes; it was the School's first

William Franklin Phelps

Like many of the early Normal School students, William Phelps, '45, had experience as a teacher when he began his studies in Albany. Phelps began teaching at age sixteen in Auburn, New York, and his exceptional reputation as a pedagogue spread across Cayuga County. It earned him a spot as one of the county's first two students at the new Albany Normal School.

Recognizing Phelps' abilities, David Page entrusted him with the task of starting the School's practice teaching program. Phelps believed that a superior teacher emerged from a blend of scholarship, methodology, and theory. In accord with this, he designed Albany's experimental program around the mastery of academic subject matter, observation of expert teachers at work, and teaching experience. Phelps' successful model school program became an integral part of the Albany Normal School curriculum.

Due to ill health, Phelps resigned as head of Albany's model school in 1852, but his career as an educator had only begun. He went on to serve as the president of three state normal schools in New Jersey and Minnesota. Recognized as an expert in the design of normal schools, his patterns were imitated by other state teachers' institutions.

In addition, writing a widely acclaimed book on teaching practice, authoring numerous articles, and serving as president of two national teachers' organizations, Phelps earned himself an international reputation as an educational theorist. His book, *The Teacher's Hand-Book*, was translated into Spanish. In 1879, he was awarded a silver medal at the Paris Exposition for his accomplishments as an educator.

Though quick-tempered and sometimes uncompromising, Phelps strove throughout his career to insure that future generations of students would not experience the teacher incompetency he had endured as a young student in western New York.

philanthropic experience. Subsequent reports of the Executive Committee suggest that while textbooks were periodically replaced, the entire collection grew very little over the years.

A school, however, needed faculty and students. The principalship fell to a thirty-four-year-old Massachusetts teacher, David Perkins Page. Page was one of five candidates for the position and came highly recommended by Horace Mann. The Executive Committee dispatched one of its members, Union College professor and Episcopal clergyman Alonzo Potter, to Newburyport to interview the young man. Potter was so impressed that he immediately reached an agreement with Page to appoint him Principal at an annual salary of $1,500. It proved to be an admirable decision.

Page had been born and raised on a prosperous New Hampshire farm, and his father for many years pressed him to remain at home to operate it. But the young man developed a strong taste for education. He attended district school and, over the objections of his father, spent about a year at Hampton Academy, teaching during the winter to help pay for his education. Page's formal education was very limited, but he developed a lifelong enthusiasm for self-education.

For about fifteen years, Page taught, first in a small district school in Newbury, Massachusetts, then in a private school and in the Newburyport High School. By age thirty-four he had become a successful classroom teacher. When he left for Albany his students in a letter to the *Newburyport Herald* observed that Page's "loss will be greatly felt in town both as a man and a christian [sic]." But it was the delivery of several lectures before the Essex County Teachers' Association that brought Page to Horace Mann's attention (and ultimately to the attention of Albany's Executive Committee). Mann was so impressed with the lectures that he printed and distributed some of them at his own expense.

Page shaped both the curriculum and educational practices of the new Normal School, and they would change little for several decades. The School began operating with winter and summer terms of twenty and twenty-two weeks with vacations in April and October when teachers' institutes were normally held. By 1850, however, summer heat caused the School to switch to a calendar comparable to the modern semester system with two terms of twenty-one and twenty weeks beginning in late September and late February. The principal classes were

Daily class schedule for the Winter 1847-48 term. Note the division of classes into senior, middle, and junior levels and the instructors for each class.

(E.)
PROGRAME,
For a portion of the Term, commencing November 1, 1847.

Time.	Exercises.	Teacher.
From 9 to 9.30 minutes, A. M.	Opening exercises. Lecture Room.	
From 9.30 to 10.15 minutes,	Senior, No. 1, Natural Philosophy,	Mr. Clark.
	do 2, Geometry,	Mr. Eaton.
	Middle, No. 1, Grammar,	Mr. S. T. Bowen.
	do 2, Higher Arithmetic,	Mr. Webb.
	do 3, Algebra,	Prof. Perkins.
	do 4, Drawing,	Miss Ostrom.
	Junior, No. 1, Grammar,	Mr. T. H. Bowen.
	do 2, Geography,	Miss Hance.
From 10.15 to 10.20 minutes,	Change of classes.	
From 10.20 to 11.5 minutes,	Senior, No. 1, Geometry,	Mr. S. T. Bowen.
	do 2, Natural Philosophy,	Mr. Clark.
	Middle, No. 1 and 2, Human Physiology,	Principal.
	do 3, Grammar,	Mr. T. H. Bowen.
	do 4, Higher Arithmetic,	Mr. Webb.
	Junior, No. 1, Reading,	Miss Hance.
	Junior, No. 2, Mental Arithmetic,	Miss Ostrom.
From 11.5 to 11.15 minutes,	Change of classes and singing.	
From 11.15 to 12,	Senior, No. 1, Mental Philosophy,	Mr. Eaton.
	do 2, do	Mr. S. T. Bowen.
	Middle No. 1, Higher Arithmetic,	Prof. Perkins.
	do 2, Reading,	Miss Hance.
	do 3 and 4,	Principal.
	Junior, No. 1, Mental Arithmetic,	Miss Ostrom.
	do 2, Elementary Arithmetic,	Mr. Webb.
From 12 to 12.20 minutes,	Recess.	
From 12.20 to 1.5 minutes,	Senior No. 1 and 2, Lectures in Rhetoric,	Principal.
	Middle, No. 1, Reading,	Miss Hance.
	do 2, Algebra,	Mr. Eaton.
	do 3, Drawing,	Miss Ostrom.
	do 4, Algebra,	Prof. Perkins.
	Junior, No. 1, Elementary Arithmetic,	Mr. Webb.
	do 2, Grammar,	Mr. S. T. Bowen.
From 1.5 to 1.10 minutes,	Change of classes.	
From 1.10 to 1.55 minutes,	Senior, No. 1 and 2, Chemistry,	Mr. Clark.
	Middle, No. 1, Algebra,	Mr. Eaton.
	do 2, Grammar,	S. T. Bowen.
	do 3, Higher Arithmetic,	Mr. Webb.

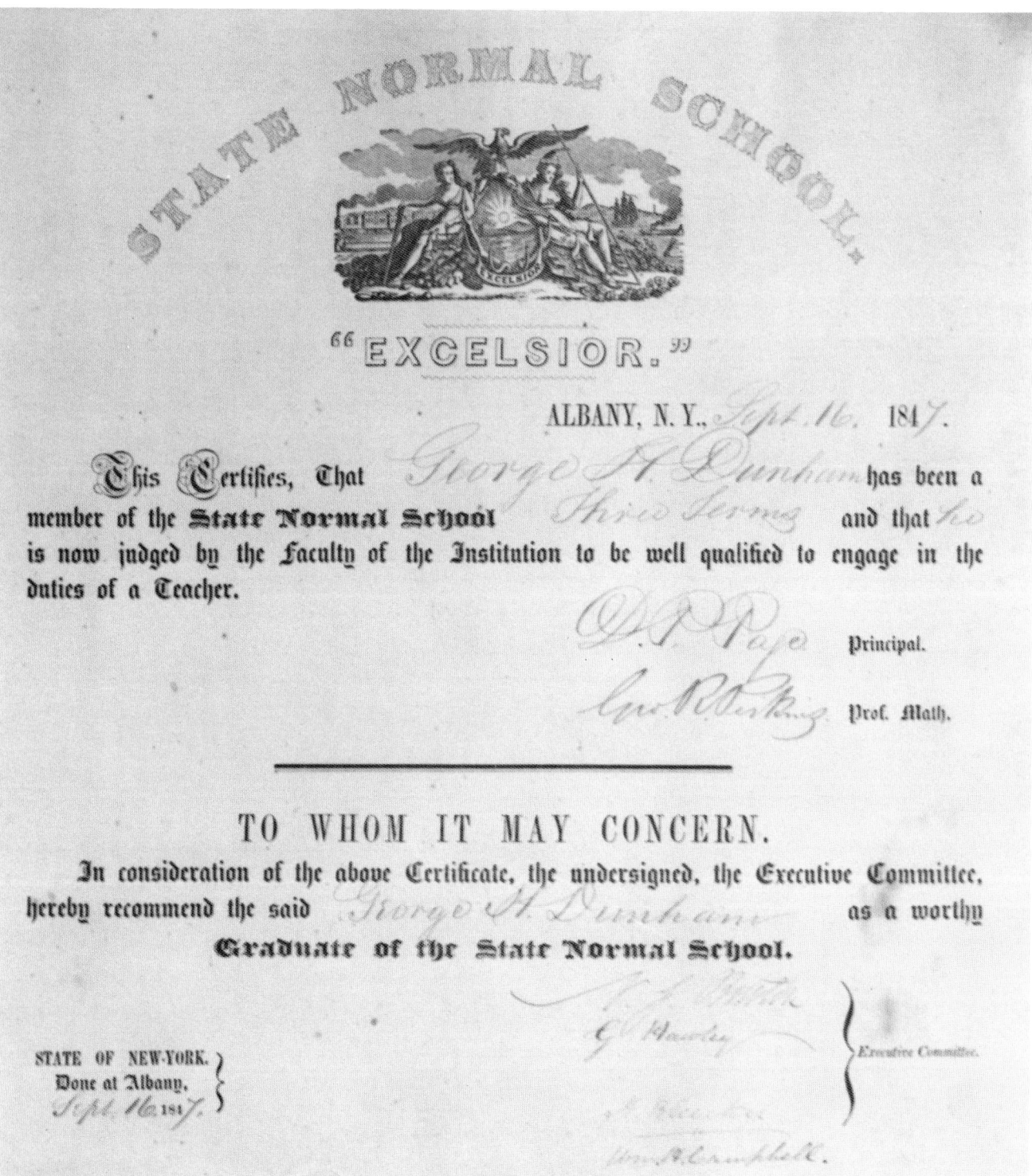

The oldest extant Normal School diploma dating from 1847. George H. Dunham taught for eight years and also served as school commissioner of his town for six years. (Gift of Alice Hastings Murphy, MLS, '40.)

held between 9:30 am and 1:30 pm with instruction in vocal music and drawing in the late afternoon.

The curriculum was organized into a two-year program offered in four terms. Students entered the program at various places, depending on their preparation. Many dropped out after a term or two to begin or continue teaching. The subject matter focused on "the common branches" of knowledge taught in the common schools. William Phelps, a student in the first class, recalled later that some students thought they had advanced beyond such elementary knowledge until their teachers with searching questions and criticisms persuaded them they had much to learn. Instruction in pedagogy and subject matter were closely tied; an early description of the classwork noted that students were thoroughly drilled in the subject matter taught in the common schools and were concurrently instructed in "the best modes of communicating a knowledge of these branches . . ." Students soon realized that they would learn "how" as well as "what" to teach. Classroom instruction was supplemented with lectures by leading academic and educational figures. One term in 1845 included appearances by physicist Joseph Henry and educator Henry Barnard. The educational program culminated in student teaching in a practice (or model) school, established in 1845.

Page's widely used textbook, *Theory and Practice of Teaching*, made up of lectures he gave his classes at Albany over a two-year period, tells us something of what went on in the school. Page offered a realistic but resolutely high-minded portrait of the good common school teacher. He began with motivation. Teachers, he asserted, had to be moved by lofty ideals since they could hardly expect to be paid adequately. Their ultimate reward was the knowledge that they had done an important and difficult job well.

Similarly, teachers had to be mindful of their own and their charges' character development. All needed good habits: punctuality, order, courtesy and neatness. But the teachers also had to be concerned for the bodily health, moral training and non-sectarian but forthrightly "religious training" of their charges.

Phoebe Ann Barnard, '47, was typical of many 19th-Century female graduates. She taught a total of fourteen years before the Civil War, and then during that conflict she served for nine months as a nurse in the U.S. Hospital in Frederick, Maryland. She married in 1866, had one daughter, and lived as a widow after 1882.

David Perkins Page

Historical coincidence has given rise to many significant innovations. The coincidence of the birth of normal schools and the birth of a man who would strongly influence the course of their development and teacher education benefited every future generation of teachers and students. David Perkins Page, "the ideal type of a noble man and perfect teacher," in the words of one of his first students, possessed the innate ability and personal courage to structure an institution of learning which continues to prosper and grow a century and a half later.

Pragmatic and utilitarian, Page knew that battles had to be won not only in the classroom but in the community. For the short span of his tenure as the school's first Principal, Page refused to lose contact with the classroom. He continued to teach classes and deliver a formal address to the students each semester. Additionally, Page developed tools from which teachers could learn and with which they could impart learning. His *Theory and Practice of Teaching* was published in the mid 19th Century and continued in use well into the 20th Century. One of the earliest teaching aids, Page's "Normal Chart of the Elementary Sounds of the English Language" was used as late as 1885.

On semester breaks from the Normal School, Page instructed at teachers' institutes across the state—the chief form of in-service education for common school teachers in the 19th Century. Such service marked a commitment by the School to carry the gospel of teacher education into the whole community. With dignity and drive, Page lobbied for and won the support of state leaders and rank and file teachers for the new Albany institution. Always searching for Normal School candidates, Page even combined extensive recruitment with his statewide instruction. (His September 1–October 11, 1845, itinerary is shown in map below.)

The "sainted Page," as he was called by his students, used his love for teaching to forge an enduring foundation for the Albany Normal School.

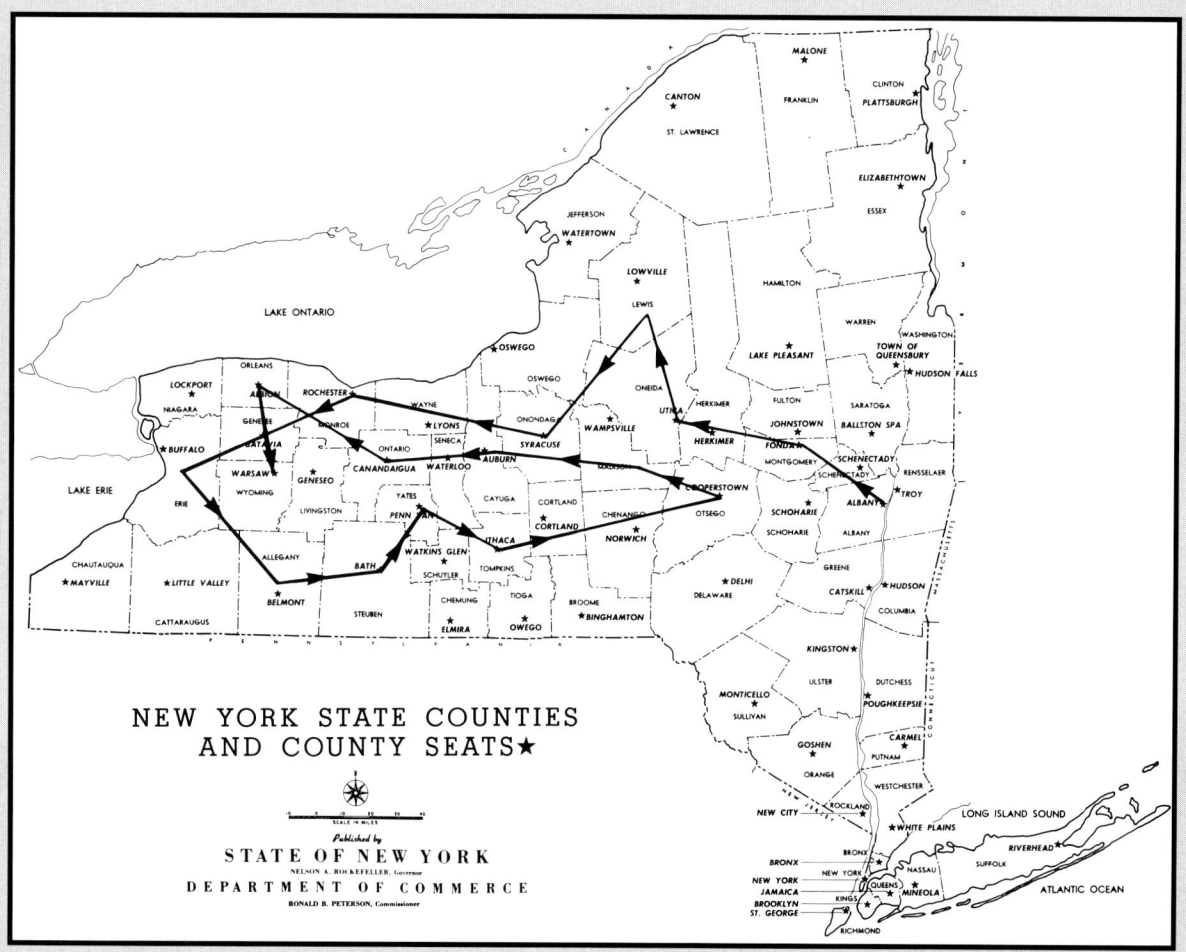

Still, the common school teacher was centrally concerned with "the intellectual growth" of the child. Page emphasized that children should study "subjects" rather than books and had much to say about proper methods and motivation, warning equally against stupefying lectures and "leading questions." He was skeptical of reward systems but also wrote at length about proper and improper discipline. Finally, he emphasized the importance of good relations between teachers and their communities. Years later, Jacob Chace, '46, summed up Page's approach by observing that he "sought to combine Christian teaching with intellectual development, and to impress his pupils with the same sense of responsibility in the pursuit of their chosen profession."

The Albany Normal School developed quickly in its first four years. By the Spring of 1845 nearly 200 students were on hand. Soon, enrollments reportedly outnumbered the students in the three Massachusetts normal schools combined. Indeed the pressure of numbers was so great that in 1845 the Executive Committee put a cap on enrollment at 256 students. There was obviously a strong demand for the only wholly tuition-free institution of post-primary education in the state.

Other faculty joined Page. Two full-time teachers as well as part-time instructors in vocal music and art were quickly added. The instructional staff was filled out with advanced students who drilled younger students in common branch subjects; the old "Lancastrian" system merged imperceptibly into the modern use of graduate students as instructors.

By 1848 the Albany State Normal School was a success, and surely David Page was responsible for much of it. He had developed a national reputation through his enormously popular *Theory and Practice of Teaching* and was an indefatigable missionary for common school education and improved teacher education. The Normal School was now carrying the gospel of teacher education into the whole community.

By 1848 the Albany State Normal School seemed well-placed to seek permanent funding from the State Legislature.

CHAPTER II
The Normal School
1848 to 1890

1848 marked an important turning point in the history of the Normal School. On the morning of New Year's Day 1848, David Page died after a week's illness. His students were grief-sticken. One wrote her mother that "I can hardly write. I feel almost as though I could bid good bye to Albany, and leave the Normal school forever. The school will go on as usual but our beloved principal will not be there. Many will be the tears shed on this occasion for his friends are not a few." The student was correct, for the school did go on. A few months after Page's death the Legislature made the Normal School a permanent part of New York's educational system.

The Normal School experiment had not been universally supported. Among the skeptics were "teachers of the old style" who resented the new educational ideas being promulgated at Albany. Indeed, Page had to dramatically ward off a hostile resolution at the 1846 Rochester meeting

(Opposite) A group of women students in a boarding house on Elm Street, one of the "suitable homes" identified by the School for its students in 1886. Women were members of the student body from the School's founding. All students lived in boarding houses until 1918. (Alumni Memorabilia Collection.)

The faculty circa 1850: George R. Perkins, Principal from 1848 to 1852, is in the center of the front row. Among the faculty pictured are believed to be Truman Bowen, '46; Darwin Eaton, '46; Elizabeth Hance, '45; Louisa Ostrom, '47, William Phelps, '45; Sumner Webb, '45.

of the newly organized New York State Teachers Association. The academies, too, disliked the Normal School's competition for limited state teacher education funds. But support for the Normal School experiment grew. Its location in Albany proved important, as potential opponents such as Governor Silas Wright and other legislators were won over by visits to the institution. National educational leaders like Mann wrote warmly of the Albany experiment. Support was bolstered by evidence of the School's success. Enrollments were good, and students quickly entered the ranks of common school teachers to demonstrate the benefits of teacher training at Albany. The Executive Committee conscientiously reported on the School's success to the Legislature. The reports also demonstrated that the affairs of the School were conducted with prudence; the financial statements showed annual expenditures of between $12,000 and $14,000 with state funding supplemented by the tuition income from the model school. The Legislature's action in 1848 was no surprise.

The permanence of the Normal School was also marked by the construction of its second building. In 1849 a $28,500 structure rose on the corner of Lodge and Howard Streets. The new building, 126 feet on Lodge and eighty-eight feet on Howard, had a basement and four stories. It was fairly advanced by the standards of the day; three large furnaces in the basement plus four strategically located stoves provided heat, and an eighty-hogshead "filtering cistern" supplied water. The Executive Committee viewed the corner lot as "a great advantage," for it afforded "separate entrances for the sexes . . ." Almost from the beginning the new building proved troublesome, however. In January of 1852 during midyear exercises the gathered throng on the top floor assembly room panicked when movement occurred in the floor. Fortunately no one was injured. The incident provoked a legislative investigation.

But the floor was strengthened, the stairs were repaired, and the Executive Committee seized the opportunity to introduce water and gas throughout the building. Further modifications were made in 1865 when the work of the Normal School was concentrated on the third and fourth floors, separated from the model school on the lower floors.

David Page's death meant new leadership for the Normal School. His first four successors served a total of nineteen years; all had distinguished careers after they left Albany. The next two Presidents served for twenty-two years, devoting the culminating years of their careers to Albany. Each Principal/President made his contribution;

The construction of the building at Lodge and Howard streets in 1849 symbolized the permanent status the School achieved that year. The building with separate entrances for men and women served as the home of the Normal School until 1885.

Four Principals/Presidents of the 19th-Century Normal School: Samuel B. Woolworth, 1852 to 1856 (top); David H. Cochran, 1856 to 1864 (bottom); Oliver Arey, 1864 to 1867 (opposite page top); and Joseph Alden, 1867 to 1882 (opposite page bottom), the first person to hold the title of President.

together they maintained a remarkable degree of continuity in the history of the institution.

Page's immediate successor was his cousin, George Perkins, who had actually been the first faculty person hired in 1844. Perkins had the misfortune to preside over the panic that occurred during midyear exercises in January of 1852. The subsequent legislative investigation uncovered evidence that several faculty were critical of Perkins for a variety of reasons: frequent absences, using school time for his own private purposes, adopting some of his own books as texts contrary to the wishes of his associates, and occupying a state-supplied residence. The Executive Committee, however, praised Perkins when he resigned in the Fall of 1852 to serve as a mathematician in the on-going consolidation of a number of railroads into the New York Central. He also later served as a member of the Board of Regents.

The next Principal, Samuel Woolworth, served from 1852 to February 1856, when he resigned to become Secretary of the Board of Regents. David Cochran had been professor of natural sciences at the Normal School for a year and a half before being chosen Principal. The first head of the school with a Ph.D., he resigned in 1864 to become president of Brooklyn Polytechnic and Collegiate Institute. Cochran's successor, Oliver Arey, was notable chiefly because he came into serious conflict with the faculty over issues that remain obscure. He left in January of 1867 to assume the principalship of the state normal school in Whitewater, Wisconsin.

The Executive Committee had difficulty in finding a successor to Arey; the post was offered to and rejected by at least three different men. But the Rev. Joseph Alden accepted the position in 1867 and stayed until his retirement in 1882. He was the first head of the Normal School to carry the title of "President," a change not made at other New York normal schools until a century later. Alden was well-qualified for the position in terms of both education and experience. He had an undergraduate degree from Union College and a D.D. from Princeton, and before coming to Albany had taught at Williams College and had served for a decade as president of Jefferson College in Pennsylvania.

Edward P. Waterbury, '49, who became President in 1882, was the first head of the institution who was an Albany graduate, having received his training under Page and Perkins. He had taught English at the Albany Academy for more than a decade and had served concurrently for eighteen months as a member of the School's Executive Committee. His death in 1889 was to mark the end of the Normal School era.

The various Principals and Presidents presided over a Normal School of modest size. In 1861, for example, there were 208 students enrolled; a decade later the average daily attendance was 275. Between 1850 and 1885, the School annually graduated sixty-five to seventy students, largely because of the limitations of the Lodge Street building, but the numbers of graduates surged upward in the 1880s and 1890s. Since many students enrolled for only a term or two, enrollments were always higher than suggested by the number of graduates.

The mission of the institution was clear: training teachers for common schools. Almost from the beginning, students were required to sign a pledge that it was their "intention to devote ourselves to the business of teaching district schools, and that our sole purpose in resorting to this Normal School is the better to prepare ourselves for that important duty." It was a commitment, explicitly or implicitly, that incoming students were to make for more than a century. An Assembly committee in 1852 suggested that students who did not teach should pay a tuition charge of $15 per term as "literary" students. No requirement was ever imposed, although Principal Perkins reported that one student desiring release from the pledge had indeed paid tuition.

The curriculum and educational practices established by David Page were little altered over the years. The School continued to operate with two terms each year. The curriculum, organized into a two-year program offered in four terms, changed little, and the faculty tried at all times to integrate the instruction in subject matter and teaching methods. Daily gymnastic exercises were introduced in 1858 out of a concern for the health and vigor of the students and because of the growing attention to the subject in schools. Proper facilities were lacking, however; as the Executive Committee noted, "Great inconvenience . . . is experienced from want of proper room and apparatus." President Alden in the late 1860s introduced more philosophy and government into the curriculum, but the course of instruction showed more continuity than change. All students received a good deal of actual teaching experience in the

William Jones, '68, was professor of mathematics from 1869 to 1890, and later became the first principal of the model high school operated by the Normal College in 1890.

Experimental School and the Primary School. The former, often referred to as the "model" or "practice" school, was a standard common school of the period. The latter, a kind of kindergarten begun in 1862, enrolled children between ages five and seven. The children attending the schools paid tuition; hence the schools were at least self-sustaining and at times profitable. The student-teachers were rotated through the various levels, had daily conferences with the superintendent, and wrote a lengthy report on the conditions of the class, methods, and other topics.

The level of subject-matter instruction remains controversial. An early description of the School noted that "The course of instruction thus far has been strictly elementary . . ." Indeed, the Executive Committee in 1860 defended the curriculum on pragmatic and democratic grounds. "To extend or elevate the course beyond what it now is, would be to put its completion beyond the time and means of most of those who now graduate; and more, it would simply educate the few who complete it beyond even the reach of the higher schools, on account of the limited demand for such teachers, and the insufficient compensation offered them."

Still, there is evidence that the instruction rose far above common school levels. There was much emphasis on writing, with each student expected to write six compositions each term. Male seniors got some field exercises with surveying and engineering instruments. A student from the 1850s later recalled that science Professor James Salisbury had on one occasion displayed a complete skeleton of a turtle in its shell from which he had dissected the flesh the night before. On another occasion, Salisbury showed the class a quantity of arsenic he had extracted from the stomach of a woman upon whom he had been called to perform an autopsy.

Would-be graduates were required to pass comprehensive final examinations. In the early years these examinations were public occasions that generated sizable audiences from the community. Questions used on examinations were reprinted in the 1860s, and one is impressed with the level of knowledge that was expected in some areas, notably mathematics.

Page's philosophy of education had emphasized the importance of morality and character development. His successors agreed with him and sought to infuse both instruction and extra-curricular life with moral training which often had religious overtones. Students often sang "a song of praise" during their opening exercises. In the 1880s there were two weekly prayer meetings, one for men and one for women. Mrs. Edward Cameron, '90, later recalled that President Waterbury thought that students studying to be teachers should strictly adhere to religious tenets and encouraged them to play and sing hymns (to which they occasionally waltzed!). While students were not required to attend church services, most reportedly did.

After the School's first year, instruction was carried on by a faculty that numbered between ten and twenty, some graduates of the institution. There was some degree of subject specialization, but everyone taught more than one subject. In the 1850s a large percentage were men, but during and after the Civil War women appeared in larger numbers, often dominating at least the lower ranks of the faculty. By the 1880s, women outnumbered men by two to one. Increasing numbers of men held advanced degrees; only one woman held such a degree since women had very few opportunities to acquire them.

In 1883, male professors were paid about $1,800 per year, women about half that amount. Still, when Alden retired in 1882 the women faculty commended him for the "pronounced and liberal views he entertains and practically exemplifies toward the advancement of woman [sic] in the teacher's profession." They

Katherine Stoneman

Kate Stoneman, Class of 1866, might be considered a woman before her time. However, she was very much a woman who impacted on her own era. Her graduation from the State Normal School began a career that spanned forty years of teaching, brought firsts to the legal profession, and strengthened the fight for women's suffrage. Shortly after graduation Stoneman returned to her alma mater to teach geography, drawing, and penmanship. However it was not long before her interests began to widen. She entered the women's suffrage movement and actively lobbied the State Legislature to advance the rights of women.

In 1882, after being named executrix for a large estate, Stoneman became interested in the law and worked as a clerk in the office of a local attorney. While continuing to teach, she studied law at night, on weekends, and during the summer. In 1886, Stoneman passed her law exams on the first attempt but was denied admission to the bar because of her sex. Undaunted, Stoneman used her lobbying skills to support the passage of legislation which allowed women to practice law in New York State. She established a law office in 1867, while continuing to teach at the Normal School, and she was listed as a lawyer in the *Albany City Directory* until 1922. Stoneman completed her formal legal education ten years later when she was the first woman to be admitted to the Albany Law School as a "special student," earning her J.D. in 1898. Subsequent law school catalogs announced that women were now eligible for admission on a regular basis. Stoneman had once again opened opportunities for women!

Stoneman was secretary of the Women's Suffrage Society of Albany and served as a poll watcher in the 1918 election, the first in which women could vote. Kate Stoneman's influence echoes today in New York's legal profession and legacy of the women's rights she helped to forge. Recognizing this, Governor Cuomo declared May 22, 1986, Katherine Stoneman Day in honor of the one hundredth anniversary of her admission to the bar.

Civil War

During the Civil War, students from State Normal School endured their toughest course ever: history-in-the-making as soldiers. Nearly one out of five men (106 of 583) who graduated before 1863 served in the conflict. Eighteen of them died.

The best known group was formed in 1862, when students and alumni became the core of a company called the Forty-fourth New York Volunteers, which participated in seventeen battles in the war. The company was put together by two professors: Rodney Kimball and Albert N. Husted, '55, both of the mathematics department. The faculty of the school outfitted each officer with a revolver, while graduates and friends contributed money to buy a rubber blanket for each Normal School member. For three weeks the men had drilling and guard duty at a nearby barracks before heading off to war.

Captain Kimball commanded the company at the Battle of Fredericksburg and left the regiment in April 1863 after being wounded. He returned to the State Normal School and taught until 1869. Lieutenant Husted was slightly wounded at the Battle of Chancellorsville and promoted to captain before the company was mustered out of service in 1864. He went on to teach at the Normal School and College until 1912, regularly addressing history classes on his war experiences.

Records also indicate that four State Normal School students served in the Confederate army, one of whom died in battle. One alumna, Phoebe Barnard, Class of 1847, left her Washington County teaching job to serve as a nurse in the war, stationed at the U.S. General Hospital in Frederick, Maryland. There she witnessed many of battle's realities. "My poor boys are trembling in their shoes about these times, for orders have come for all able-bodied men to be sent to the front," she wrote her sister on Jan. 12, 1865. "My heart aches for them—O cruel, cruel war!"

Albany students in the Civil War: (below, left to right) Thompson Barrich, '61, J. Oscar Blakely, '62, and Andress B. Hull, '62, led "colored troops" in the war. (Unidentified autograph book, 1860-61; autograph album of Helen I. Sherwood, '63.)

Faculty members Albert N. Husted, '55 (top right), and Rodney G. Kimball (right) led the Normal School company in the Civil War. They fought at the battles of Fredericksburg, Chancellorsville, Gettysburg, and Cold Harbor.

particularly appreciated his views about women's "right to a recompense, paid for the work done and not to the sex of the worker . . ."

Alumni later recalled their teachers with both respect and affection. Faculty photographs and signatures regularly appear in autograph books kept by students in the 1850s and 1860s. Both warmth and respect show through the often sentimental or humorous alumni(ae) reminiscences of faculty such as Albert N. Husted and Kate Stoneman.

From its beginning the Normal School drew its students from throughout the state. Each county was entitled to twice as many pupils as it had representatives in the Assembly, and the students were appointed initially by the State Superintendent of Public Instruction on recommendation of the school commissioners. When school commissioners failed to make recommendations, the classes were filled with "volunteers." In any one year perhaps three-quarters of the counties sent students to Albany, but a disproportionately large number in fact came from Albany and Rensselaer counties. Of the first 4,000 graduates only fourteen came from outside New York State.

The Normal School sought young people who would become good teachers, and with admirable egalitarianism Samuel Young told school commissioners in 1844 that "The general intellectual & scientific requirements, the purity of moral character, the amenity of disposition, & the capacity to communicate instruction should be the only passports. Neither sect, nor creed, nor party, nor poverty, nor riches, nor connexions [sic] should have the least influence on the selection."

Still, not all who applied were accepted. The Executive Committee in 1862 decried deficiencies in "the elementary branches, reading, writing, spelling, geography, and composition" and moved toward the development of admissions standards. Females were to be not less than sixteen years old, males not less than eighteen. Prospective students had to "furnish satisfactory evidence of good moral character," usually by a letter from the district school commissioner or the student's pastor. Finally, there was an entrance examination in "spelling, reading, writing, geography, arithmetic and English grammar." Between 5 and 20 percent of the applicants failed the examination, surprisingly high for a relatively select group, many with teaching experience. After 1882, applicants could submit a certificate attesting that they had passed the Regents' examinations in the appropriate subjects.

Female students were welcomed from the beginning. Governor William H. Seward saw women as "the natural guardians of the young," and lauded them for their "enduring patience . . . higher purity . . . and elevated moral feelings." The Executive Committee agreed; female teachers, they observed, were needed to "secure for our youth . . . those refining and chastening influences which can only be exerted by the woman, and without which no education, and no manly character can attain its most beautiful proportions." But earlier the Committee had also astutely observed that the rising percentage of female applicants could be attributed to the more "inviting and rapid avenues to enterprise and wealth which opens [sic] to young men . . ." The Civil War accelerated female enrollments; by the early 1860s there were perhaps twice as many young women as men at the School. Nearly 70

Caroline G. Parker and Nicholson Henry Parker, two of the Native American students who attended Albany from 1851 to 1853 as part of an experimental program funded by the Legislature "for the support and education of . . . Indian youths." Caroline Parker taught and Nicholson Parker acted as interpreter for the Iroquois Nation. (Reproduced from Arthur C. Parker, *The Life of General Ely S. Parker*, Buffalo, N.Y.: Buffalo Historical Society, 1919.)

percent of the graduates during the School's first half-century were women. It was all part of the larger feminization of American common school education that occurred in the late 19th Century.

By late 20th Century standards the students admitted were remarkably homogeneous. Nearly all were white. There were almost no identifiable African-Americans. One Japanese student, Senzaburo Kodzu of Tokyo, was admitted in 1875 on recommendation of David Murray, the American superintendent of education in Japan, and graduated in the Class of 1877. In the 1850s the School undertook an experiment in educating Native Americans. For several years the Legislature made an appropriation "for the support and education of ten Indian youths." Some twenty-six Native Americans attended at various times, but the only graduate was Harriet E. Twoguns of the Cattaraugus Reservation, who was awarded her degree in 1865. She taught Southern blacks for several years before marrying.

Still, in terms of age and experience the student body was often very heterogeneous. Martha Fearey Gay, '58, recalled that in her class "were a widow and her son, both practiced teachers, and a widower over forty, while the youths were men who worked the farm in the summer." Most students attended for only a term or two before resuming their teaching in district schools. The average age of the students was always somewhat higher than the minima. Perhaps only 30 to 40 percent of those admitted actually graduated.

In the 1840s the simple task of traveling to Albany posed problems. William Phelps recalled later that his 1844 journey from Auburn to Albany involved "two days of traveling over [a] rickety flat car railroad" with an overnight stay in Syracuse. D. E. Whitmore, '46, recalled riding a canal boat drawn by two weary horses from Utica to Schenectady and then taking a railroad operating on wooden rails to Albany. For many students, coming to Albany must have been a lonely and frightening experience. Willis Graves, '79, recalled his first day at the School: ". . . alone in backroom, third floor, Dove street, facing the east we stand in the evening, looking out upon the gas-lit city. The wind from the frozen north dashes the snow against the pane. We have no light in the room, preferring to drown our lonesomeness in the feeble rays which steal in from the moon . . . Tomorrow we are to enter the Albany Normal School . . ."

(Top) Senzaburo Kodzu, '77, a Japanese student, was the only known international student to attend the Albany Normal School. He returned to Japan where he published widely on western music and became a leader in the normal school movement.

(Bottom) Edward B. Horton, '86, (in a 1944 photo), was typical of Normal School graduates in his long teaching and administrative career in public education.

Programs from the Philomathean Society for women and the Gentleman's Literary Societies, both founded in the early 1870s. Such "literary societies" were the principal form of student organization in the late 19th Century.

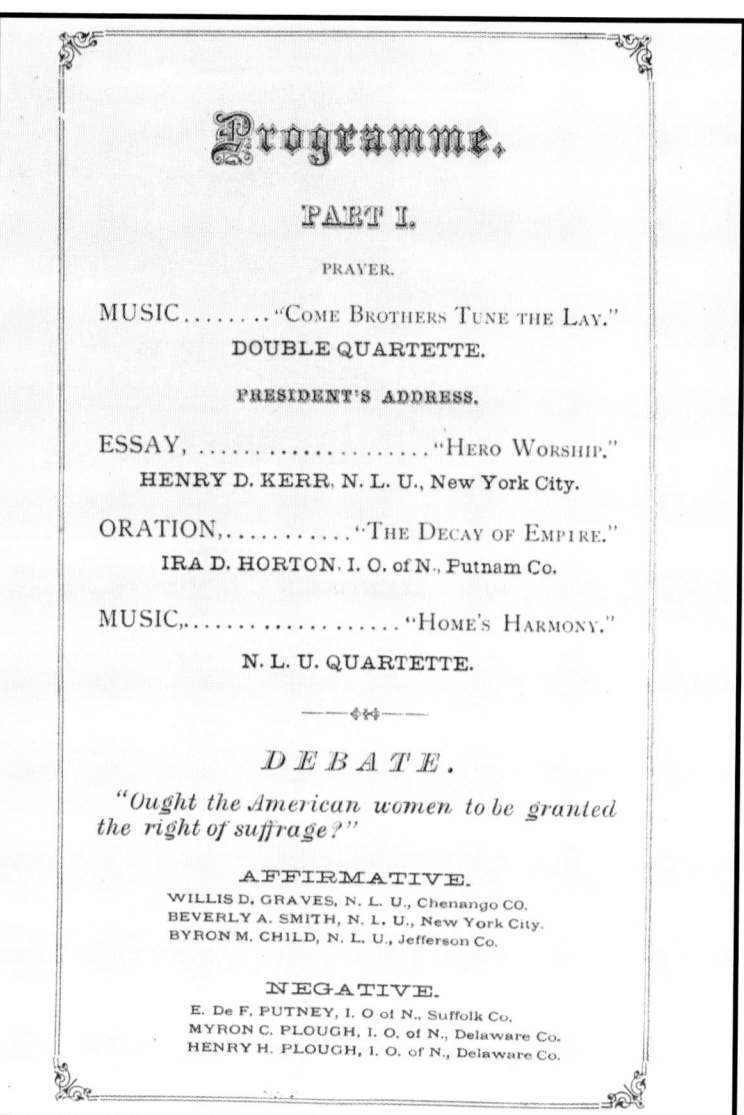

Most of the students were of modest means, and the free tuition and texts were certainly important considerations in their coming to Albany, but they still had to provide travel and living costs. One alumna later recalled that most lived on the scantiest means. For a number of years the School subsidized both travel and living costs; in 1845 such payments represented about 23 percent of the School's budget. But such subsidies were financially too burdensome and were soon abandoned.

There were, of course, no dormitories. New students were urged to report to the Normal School building "where they will be directed to boarding houses approved by the faculty," and an early student recalled that "careful attention was bestowed upon the location of the strangers in suitable homes during their residence in the city." Costs were regularly reported in the School's annual "circular." In the 1850s the price of board "in respectable families" varied from $1.75 to $2.50 per week "exclusive of washing," but the price rose inexorably to $3.50 and $4.00 per week during the Civil War and later. Some, particularly male students, reduced costs by boarding themselves in a room that cost as little as $1.00 per week in the 1880s; it was a kind of 19th Century version of apartment living. Students from nearby communities were able to reduce their costs by living at home, doubtless a factor in the relatively large number of students from Albany and Rensselaer counties.

The Normal School stood *in loco parentis* (in the place of parents) to its students and supervised their lives in various ways. Students were segregated by sex and supervised in the classrooms. Men and women were not allowed to board in the same families, and "gentlemen of the school" were not permitted to call upon "ladies of the school" after 6:00 p.m. The School's circular of 1851 assured its readers that "Particular care is taken to be assured of the respectability of the families who propose to take boarders, before they are recommended to the pupils." The School asked householders to keep no boarders or roomers other than Normal students, to schedule meals in such a way that students could keep to a schedule that occupied their time twenty-four hours a day, and to report immediately any student misconduct or violation of the rules. "Failure to comply with these requests will be regarded as sufficient ground for removing students," the School warned.

Students were expected to maintain standards of behavior becoming a future teacher, and the School disciplined students when necessary. Principal Perkins reported in 1852 that six students had been expelled for offenses ranging from noisy and indecorous conduct to theft and passing a counterfeit coin. But such examples of formal discipline were few. Student conduct was more probably regulated by the expectations of the communities in which they were to teach and by the pervasive religiosity of the day.

We know little of "student culture" in the 19th Century. There was obviously some social life, for a good many students found a spouse within the student body. Some students kept autograph books, particularly

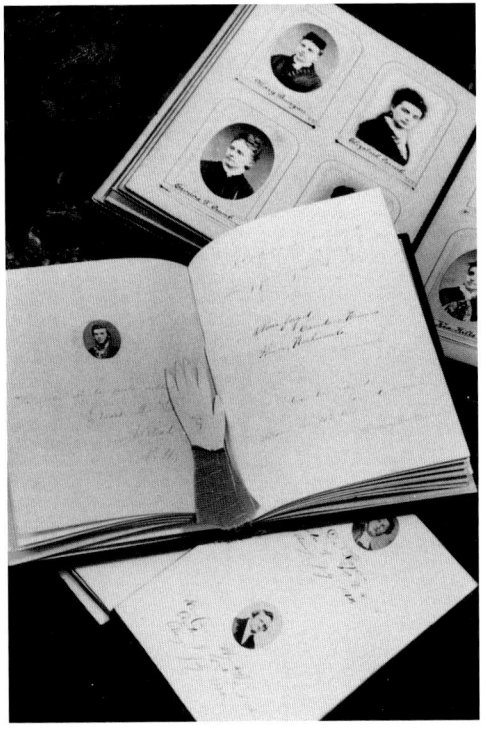

Autograph books and photograph albums were the 19th Century equivalent of yearbooks. Top to bottom: unidentified autograph book 1860-61; photo album of Mima Williams Diefendorf, '78; Friendship Tablet of Isabella G. Rawson, '57; George R. Burton autograph book, 1860. (Photo by Mark Schmidt.)

in the 1860s and 1870s. The printed volumes contained the sentimental etchings and poetry characteristic of Victorian American culture. Some included photographs of the signatories, both faculty and students, and occasionally a student noted in his or her book the later careers of classmates. Mina Williams, '74, observed of a Normal School friend that she had "met many who can truly say that they have been made better for your having lived . . ."

Student societies made their appearance in the 1870s. One alumnus recalled that in that decade the Normal Literary Union and the Independent Order of Normals were strong rival societies while the Philomathean Society was flourishing among the women. By the early 1890s the Independent Order of Normals and the Philomatheans had been joined by Phi Delta and Delta Omega and a surge of Greek life was about to begin.

Mordaunt Green in his 1848 valedictory address correctly asserted that the School had absorbed the entire energies and attention of the students who "became, as it were, a Normal community." But that student community was very different from student cultures in 19th Century American four-year colleges. Normal School students in both their origins and aspirations were far removed from the socially elite students attending liberal arts colleges. They shared their educational experience for two years rather than four; many attended the school for even briefer periods. They focused their energies on a highly structured professional curriculum far different from 19th Century liberal arts colleges.

The end of the Normal School era was marked by two events: the occupation of a new building in 1885 and the celebration of the institution's Semi-Centennial in 1894. The pressures of enrollment and the deficiencies of the old building necessitated a new home for

A letter from women faculty praising President Alden for paying women "for the work done and not to the sex of the worker." Women faculty included: Mary McClellan, '68, teacher of English grammar and history (opposite page, left); Mary F. Hyde, '69, teacher of arithmetic, geometry and rhetoric (opposite page, right). (Letter from Office of the President's Records.)

the School. A delegation from the Senate Finance Committee concluded in 1883 that the Lodge Street building was not worth remodeling and should instead be sold. In the same year the Legislature appropriated $143,000 for a new building, a structure which ended up costing nearly $200,000.

The new Willett Street building was the largest and most carefully planned facility the Normal School had yet had. It included space for chemistry and physics laboratories, an assembly hall that could seat over 600, and living quarters for the President. In subsequent years an adjoining building was purchased and modified, an electrical system was installed, and other smaller modifications were made. Equally important, the building stood opposite Albany's Washington Park; for the first time students had open spaces which they could use as a "campus."

The symbolic center of the new structure was a large stained glass "Alumni Memorial Window" installed at the end of 1892. It measured over thirty-two by fourteen feet, making it the largest such window in the United States at the time.

Albert N. Husted

Shortly after Albert Husted graduated from the Normal School in 1855, he was appointed to be an instructor in mathematics. By 1869, he was appointed professor of mathematics, and he held that position until his death at age seventy-nine. All was not math in the interim, however: Husted was appointed Acting Principal in 1889, and he also fought in the Civil War from 1862 to 1864.

Husted and Rodney Kimball, another college professor, recruited a company of men who were part of the Forty-Fourth New York Volunteers Company E [see page 32 sidebar]. Husted barely escaped capture in the Battles of Fredericksburg, Gettysburg, and fifteen other locales in the war. Once his life was saved by a diary and testament in his pocket that blocked a bullet.

On campus, Husted gave a pep talk each year to first-year male students. A former student recalls him saying, "If any of you have any doubt as to whether your cuffs or collars are fit to wear another day there is no doubt about it." Addressing teachers, Husted was once quoted in the *Echo* as saying that teachers should be "living epistles of the forces they would see illustrated in their pupils." Husted, who frequently twisted his mustache when he talked, was known for his sense of humor, friendship with students, and his role as a strict disciplinarian and vigorous teacher.

An association of graduates of the Normal School had been organized in 1849, and biennial "jubilees" had been held between 1851 and 1872 except during the Civil War years. President Waterbury revived the organization with a reunion in 1883 attended by 600 graduates; the gathering planned the window and began raising money. In the end, 1,418 alumni(ae) contributed sums ranging from 50 cents to $50 each to fund the project. It was a touching and impressive memorial both to the loyalty of the alumni(ae) and to the ideals of the Normal School.

The Semi-Centennial Jubilee of 1894 was a gala series of events attended by over a thousand people. The banquet filled the two largest dining rooms in the city. Some 610 out of 3,300 living alumni were present. *The Historical Sketch of the State Normal College at Albany . . . and a History of Its Graduates for Fifty Years . . .* , published in connection with the Jubilee, emphasized the achievements of the School's graduates and spoke to the success of the Normal School experiment begun a half century earlier.

By the late 19th Century the Albany State Normal School had clearly fulfilled its mission of training teachers for the common schools. A succession of State Superintendents praised the institution and its graduates; Andrew Sloan Draper summed it up in 1891 when he asserted that "it cannot be doubted that [Albany's graduates] make the best teachers to be found in the public schools." In the 1880s President Waterbury began collecting information about Albany's graduates. *The Historical Sketch* published in 1895 contained over 300 pages of biographical information on those who graduated between 1845 and 1895. The volume demonstrated decisively that the overwhelming majority of graduates had taught, many had very long teaching careers and many had held distinguished positions in American education.

The Normal School could look back on its first half-

The Class of 1888 in front of the new building on Willett Street. Below: The Willett Street building of the Normal School, occupied in 1885. The famous Alumni Window is located at the extreme left. The main entrance is in the middle of the Willett Street side. The building included a residence for the President.

century years with pride. But the winds of change were blowing through American education and were to alter the institution in significant ways in the next two decades.

(Above) Edward P. Waterbury, President from 1882 to 1889.

(Right) Jenny Wornham Wickham, '86, taught for eight years before marrying R. Woodley Wickham, a Normal School graduate, moving to Poughkeepsie, and raising her two children. She died in 1966 at age ninety-eight. Women's teaching careers were generally ended by marriage until the mid 20th Century.

(Opposite) The chapel/assembly hall in the Willett Street building with the Alumni Memorial Window in the rear. The stained glass window was the largest in the country in 1890. The first recorded Alumni fundraising drive paid the $5,000 cost.

CHAPTER III
From Normal School to College for Teachers
1890 to 1915

When the Normal School was founded in 1844 it had been a pioneer. That was no longer true by 1890. Albany had lost its dominance if not its preeminence in training common school teachers. Seven new normal schools had been established in New York between 1866 and 1871, and by 1883 Albany enrolled only one-sixth of the students in the eight institutions. The academies and teachers' institutes were also training common school teachers. At the same time the new public high schools were expanding dramatically and posed a new challenge to teacher education.

Change at Albany was inevitable. The agent of that change was William J. Milne, who succeeded Waterbury as President in 1889. The symbol of change was a new name, the New York State Normal College, adopted in 1890. The substance of change was a new mission: to develop the curricula, faculty, and students to prepare secondary school teachers.

(Opposite) Student culture began to emerge in the late 1800s. The 1904 editorial board of *The Echo*, a monthly newspaper/literary magazine, begun in 1892, included Elizabeth Shaver, '04, (second row, third from the right), who later joined the College staff as a history supervisor. Above: the cover from the October 1907 issue.

On Waterbury's death in August of 1889 the Executive Committee quickly mounted a search for his successor. The key figure in the Executive Committee during these years was Andrew Sloan Draper, a lawyer who had served as a Committee member since 1883 and as its chair since his election in 1886 as State Superintendent of Public Instruction. Draper chose William J. Milne, professor of moral philosophy and didactics and principal of the Geneseo Normal School since its opening in 1871. Milne promptly accepted, assuming office in October 1889. Although Milne had been Draper's chief competitor for the position of State Superintendent, the two came to respect each other and worked closely together to reshape the school in the next quarter century.

Anna Pierce, '84, (kneeling front row right) began her long career at Albany in the primary department of the model school. Aurelia Hyde, '95, first grade primary department teacher, is on the left.

The first step was the name change. The shift from "School" to "College" marked a change in both status and function. Albany had become one of the first normal schools in the nation to make the transition to collegiate status. The initial programmatic changes were, however, very uncollegiate. True, standards of admission and the minimum age of students were raised to a level more in keeping with the school's collegiate status, and the Normal College hoped to enroll graduates of liberal arts institutions. But the course of studies shifted from the traditional liberal arts toward "purely professional" studies. After 1892 only courses in "foundations of education" and in methods of teaching were offered. Students in the new programs would qualify as high school teachers and would have the proper credentials for teaching future teachers in normal schools and secondary training classes.

The transition was not easy. The Normal College introduced new "English" and "Classical" curricula, varying somewhat in content and length. Both granted a teaching license and either a diploma or a degree (Bachelor or Master of Pedagogy). The College added a cluster of programs to attract

(Top) William J. Milne, President from 1889.

(Bottom) Andrew Draper. (Photograph by Gary Gold, '70, of Edward P. Buyck painting hanging in the State Education Building.)

Milne and Draper

William J. Milne and Andrew Sloan Draper were chiefly responsible for converting the Albany Normal School of 1889 into the New York State College for Teachers of 1914. The two had been the chief candidates for the position of State Superintendent of Public Instruction in 1886. Draper won the appointment, but three years later he was influential in choosing Milne, longtime principal of the Geneseo Normal School, as President at Albany. Returning from the presidency of the University of Illinois in 1904, Draper served as New York's first Commissioner of Education.

The two educational leaders transformed the Normal College of 1905 into a four-year liberal arts college for teachers, the first of its kind in the country, and provided the College with its classical Western Avenue campus. Both died within a year of each other, Draper in 1913 and Milne in 1914.

The Willett Street building in ruins after a fire on January 9, 1906. Charles Wurthman, the janitor, saved the statue of Minerva, but otherwise all records and facilities of the College were lost. The fire led to construction of the first buildings on a new campus between Western and Washington avenues.

particular groups of students: a kindergarten program, a one-year self-designed program for college graduates, and special courses to upgrade practicing teachers.

At the heart of the new enterprise was the conviction that "subject matter" and "professional methods" could be separated and that the Normal College could effectively focus on the latter. Many other American educators, however, believed that subject-matter knowledge was all-important, that "professional methods" were mostly irrelevant, and that the graduate of any good liberal arts college could teach effectively. The controversy between the advocates of subject matter and of methods heated up in the 1890s, and partisans on both sides pushed their ideas to extremes.

On this subject Milne was a partisan. One of his students later quoted Milne as telling one of his classes in the philosophy of education that "you high school teachers need not know much chemistry; if you only know the methods of teaching chemistry, you will get along creditably."

The results of the new curricula were disappointing. The change in direction produced some painful adjustments in the faculty, particularly among the female-dominated lower ranks. Enrollments fell, although the percentage of graduates and the average age of students rose. For the most part the Normal College attracted few graduates of liberal arts colleges. A 1906 analysis by Second Assistant Commissioner Dr. Edward J. Goodwin concluded that two-thirds of the Normal College's graduates failed to gain secondary school posts because they did not "possess a sufficient knowledge of the subjects taught." No more damning comment on the 1890 curricula could have been offered.

Changes were needed, and once again Draper provided the leadership. He had become New York's first Commissioner of Education in 1904 and was once again head of the Normal College's Executive Committee. He and Goodwin concluded that what New York's secondary schools needed were teachers who were college graduates with sound professional educations and well-qualified superintendents and teachers of training classes, training schools, and normal schools. Draper and Goodwin, working closely with Milne, in December of 1905 designed a new plan for the Albany school that would set its course for more than half a century.

The Draper-Goodwin plan included four elements. First, the school abandoned programs to train elementary school teachers and concentrated on preparing teachers for the burgeoning secondary schools. Second, the Normal College was converted into a genuine four-year institution with an admissions policy equivalent to those of "other eastern colleges of good standing." Third, to train these superior students the

For three years after the fire, the College occupied temporary space in various facilities, including Trinity Methodist Church on Lark and Lancaster Streets. In the center of the graduating Class of 1907 is a group of faculty including President Milne. (Center next to woman with flowered bonnet.)

College established a four-year course "in the liberal arts and pedagogics" in which students pursued subjects essential to a liberal education as well as professional courses fundamental to the training of teachers. Finally, in recognition of the change in direction, the College was authorized to confer B.A. and B.S. degrees to graduates of four-year programs and a Pd.B. degree to college graduates who completed a year of post-graduate study. (The Pd.B was changed to an M.A. in Education degree in 1914.)

The new plan was officially adopted in December of 1905. Just a few weeks later, on January 8, 1906, the Willett Street building burned. Ice-covered streets prevented the fire department from reaching the building until it was too late. Milne's residence and the structure housing the primary school were saved, but with these exceptions the building was a total loss.

Many thought the fire a blessing in disguise. Everyone mourned the

The Normal School and College had always included science in its curricula. Professor Wetmore and students are shown in his natural science laboratory in the Willett Street building.

Because drawing was considered an essential skill for teachers, students worked in the "drawing room" on the new campus in 1911. (From the yearbook, *Our Book*, 1911.)

loss of the beloved Alumni Memorial stained glass window. But otherwise the building had long been an object of discontent. Attitudes were perhaps summed up by Draper when he observed that when he saw the fire burning "I was as officially affected as was proper, but my personal grief was not of the kind which is altogether uncontrollable."

The College community rallied to the crisis. For three years the College made do with various expedients, supplementing usable space in the old structure with rooms borrowed from the Albany Academy for Girls, two local churches, and the Albany Orphan Asylum. The student editors of the *Echo* observed that the disaster had brought the college community together and had generated a kind of school spirit never seen before.

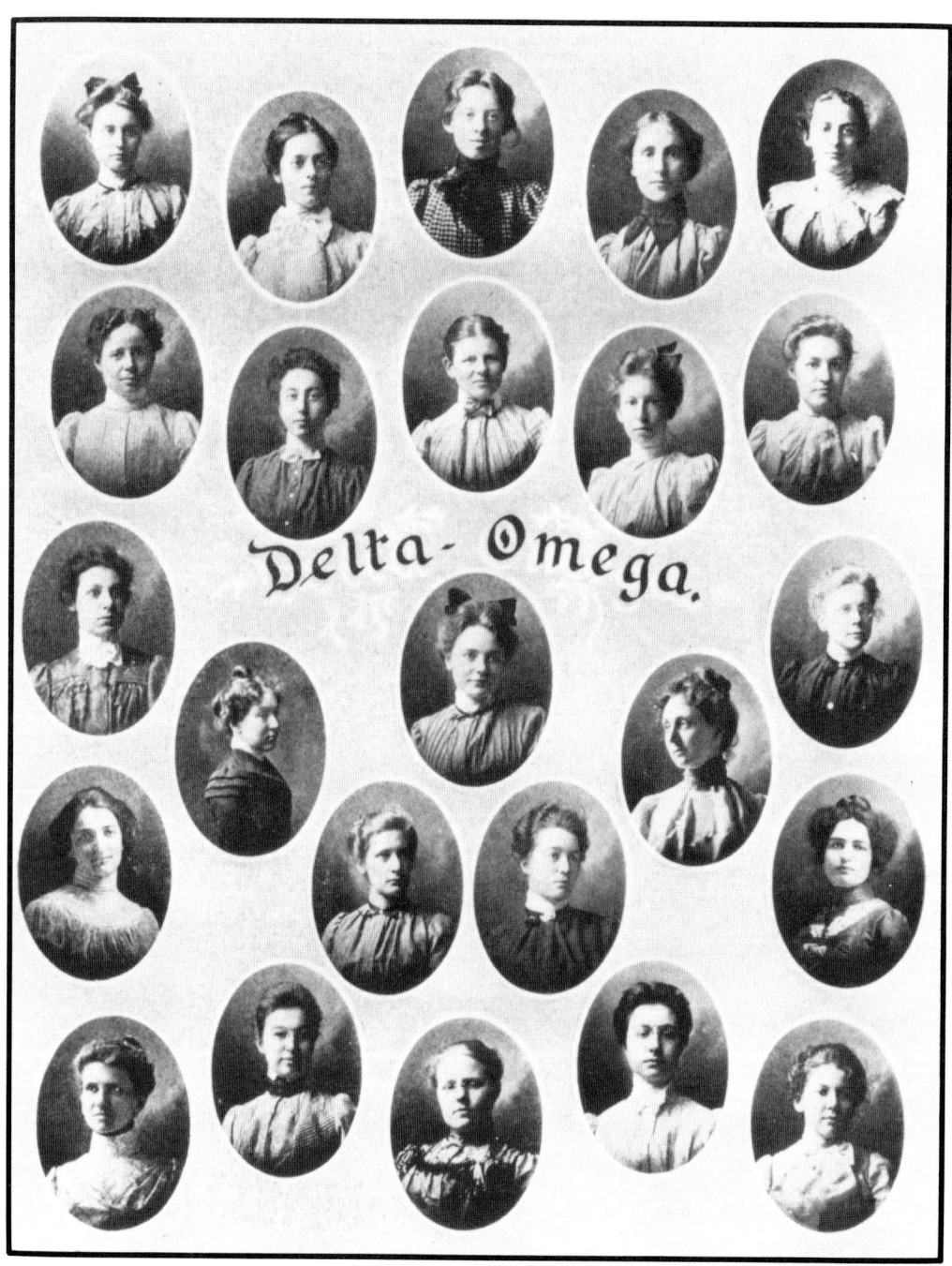

Greek life in 1900: (above) Delta Omega was the first sorority founded in 1890, and Phi Delta, (opposite page, top) the first fraternity at the College founded in 1892. Phi Delta was a successor to the Gentlemen's Literary Societies. Of the fraternities and sororities founded at the turn of the century, only Psi Gamma (opposite page, bottom) exists to this day. (Photos from *The Neon*, 1900.)

The state hastened to provide new facilities. The first issue to be resolved was location. When the Willett Street structures were built, the College had moved west with the growing city. Between 1850 and 1900 Albany's population almost doubled, approaching 100,000, and the residential areas had steadily moved along Central Avenue and the borders of Washington Park. Two faculty members tried to persuade Milne to locate the new buildings on what is today the corner of New Scotland Avenue and Academy Road. While the site would have provided

53

William B. Aspinwall, '00, was professor of pedagogical literature, principal of the Model High School and Assistant to the President. He was a member of the faculty until 1913. M. Harriet Bishop taught elementary methods from 1893 until 1912. She left for the State Normal School in Worcester, Massachusetts, after Albany concentrated exclusively on preparing secondary school teachers.

considerable room for expansion, Milne rejected it on the grounds that it was too remote. New Scotland Avenue was still a mud road, and the site at that location was too far from the trolley lines used by students living in boarding houses. Instead, College authorities chose a four-and-a-half acre site between Western and Washington avenues. The state acquired the property from the Albany Orphan Asylum, giving in exchange the Willett Street property and $75,000.

The same legislative act authorizing the property exchange appropriated $350,000 for new buildings. Not for the last time the design of a new campus engendered controversy when the Executive Committee objected to the esthetics of the state architect's original plans. In the end the State Architect designed the interiors and an independent architect, Albert R. Ross, looked after the exterior. Once construction began, work proceeded quickly and was completed ahead of schedule. Thus in the Fall of 1909, nearly sixty-five years after the Normal School began its first classes in its State Street building, another ceremony, attended by numerous dignitaries and addressed by Gov. Charles E. Hughes and Commissioner Draper, marked the opening of the new facility.

The new campus (today the Downtown Campus) consisted initially of three buildings connected by one-story peristyles. The central administration building contained offices and classrooms. It was flanked on one side by a science building and on the other by the auditorium and gym. (They remained unnamed until 1929.) The Executive Committee's insistence that a second architect design the exterior paid off. Ross's conception produced handsome structures in a Georgian style clearly inspired by Jefferson's design for the University of Virginia.

It was a fine new facility for the College, but rising enrollments after 1909 quickly made it inadequate. Complaints focused on the gymnasium, by 1913 too small to accommodate men and women from both the College and the model school, and the library, undersized and containing too few books. The psychological laboratory remained unequipped, and the industrial arts department's apparently unslakable thirst for equipment further complicated problems.

When the new campus was occupied in the Fall of 1909 the last students under the old program had graduated, and the Normal College proceeded to put in place the new curriculum called for by the 1906 plan. That curriculum involved a mix of 70 to 80 percent academic work and 20 to 30 percent professional studies, separated into different courses. Students flocked into academic courses such as English, languages, history, chemistry and mathematics. Departments were created in 1909, and what we think of as traditional academic patterns began to emerge. The integration of academic and professional work increasingly depended on the teaching practices of individual  instructors and on practice teaching. To meet the special needs of rapidly growing secondary schools the College soon added "vocational" programs in physical education (1909), industrial and domestic science (1910), and business (1913).

It was not an easy time for the faculty. Some were dismissed because they lacked the qualifications to teach in the new programs, others shifted to new subjects, and new people were recruited. Faculty lists around 1909 show names from both the late 19th Century past (A. N. Husted and Mary McClelland, e.g.) and the 20th Century future (Anna Pierce, Harry Birchenough, Adam Walker, John Sayles, and Adna Wood Risley, e.g.). By 1914 there were forty-four faculty members. Five had the Ph.D., nine the M.A., eleven the Pd.B., and seven a bachelor's degree. Ten (23 percent), mostly older faculty or instructors in the domestic and industrial "sciences," had no degrees; by contrast a 1904 study showed that 60 percent of the faculty in New York's normal schools lacked a degree of any kind. The distribution of faculty reflected the new curricula. Twenty-one taught traditional academic subjects, nine taught professional subjects, and fourteen served in other areas such as domestic science or physical education. After 1910, student/faculty

(Top) The varsity baseball team in 1900. Athletics were an important part of the new student culture, but lack of facilities and funds hampered their early development. (This earliest athletics photo is reproduced from *The Neon*, 1900.)

(Bottom) Most Normal College students continued to live in boarding houses. This 1901 photo shows a group of students in the backyard of their boarding house at 290 Lark Street. (From Alumni Memorabilia Collection.)

The three new buildings occupied beginning in 1909. From left to right: science, administration, and auditorium. The buildings were named Husted, Draper, and Hawley after the completion of Richardson, Page, and Milne in 1929.

(Opposite) After the construction of the new campus, athletics surged. An athletic association for both men and women was formed in 1909 and divided into men's and women's associations two years later. Pictured here are the men's basketball team and the women's inter-class championship team in 1911. (Photos from *Our Book*, 1911.)

ratios stabilized in the range of twelve to fifteen to one. Faculty salaries were roughly comparable to those of teachers in urban public schools: high enough to attract good young people but not high enough to guarantee that experienced people would not leave for better paying posts in other colleges or in public schools. Indeed, the economic fortunes of the faculty were tied to those of secondary school teachers until the College's conversion to a university in the early 1960s.

The size of the College changed little from the 1880s, but program changes, not to mention the fire, produced sharp fluctuations in the number of students enrolled and graduated. After each of the major curricular changes in 1890 and 1906, enrollments dropped; as students scurried to complete old programs, the number of graduates briefly jumped, only to tumble sharply for two or three years. Enrollments between 1896 and 1906 fluctuated between 314 and 414, dropped to a low of 187 in 1909, and then began a steady advance to 590 in 1913.

The student body was overwhelmingly female; between 1890 and 1914, only 10 to 15 percent of the enrolled students and 2 to 23 percent of the graduates were men. Admissions standards rose after 1906, and most of those seeking admission qualified by submitting state Regents credentials. Almost all of Albany's students were of modest means, although the costs of attending even a tuition-free institution guaranteed that there were few students from truly poor families.

The College was still without dormitories, and students continued to live in local boardinghouses. The College's 1894 *Circular* assured

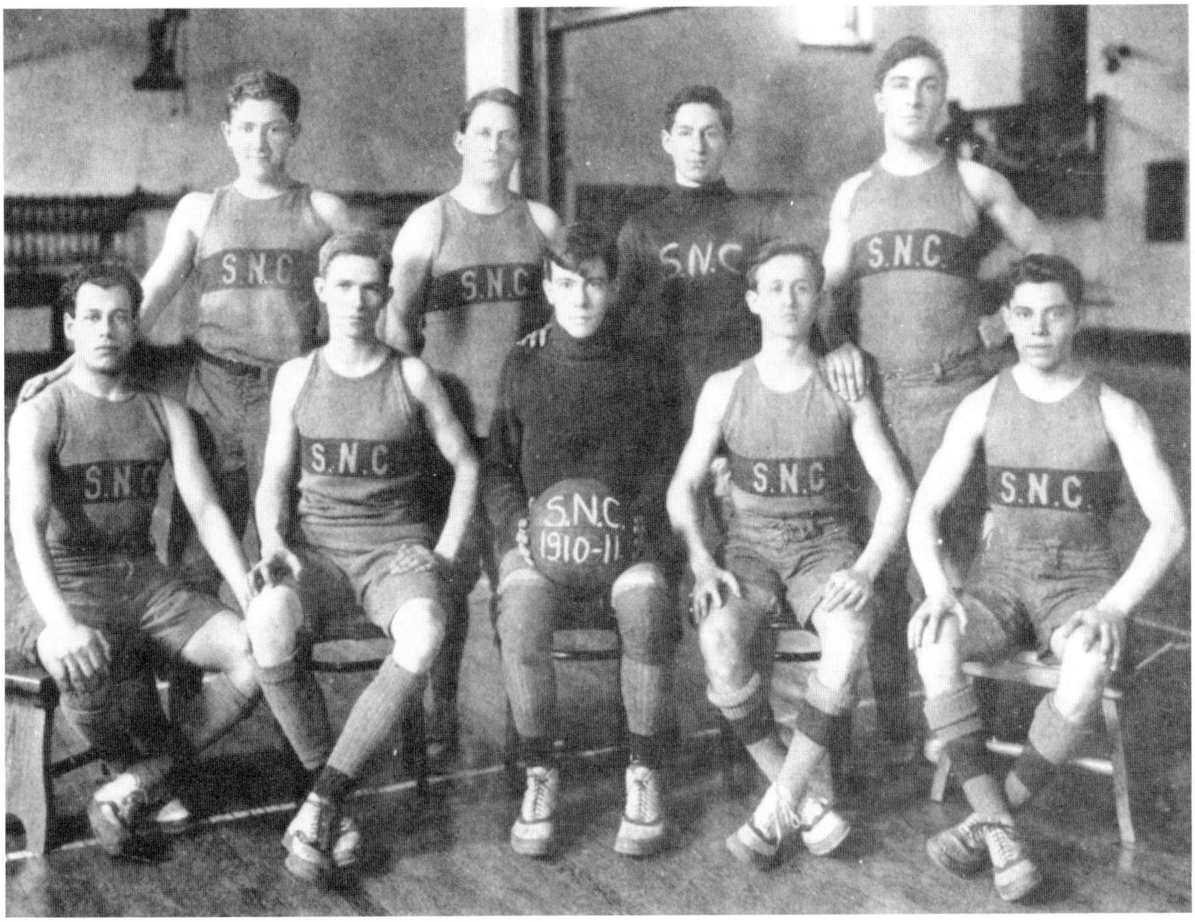
S.N.C.
S.N.C
S.N.C
S.N.C.
S.N.C
S.N.C.
S.N.C
S.N.C.
S.N.C.
1910-11

'11
'11
'11
'11
S.N.C
'11

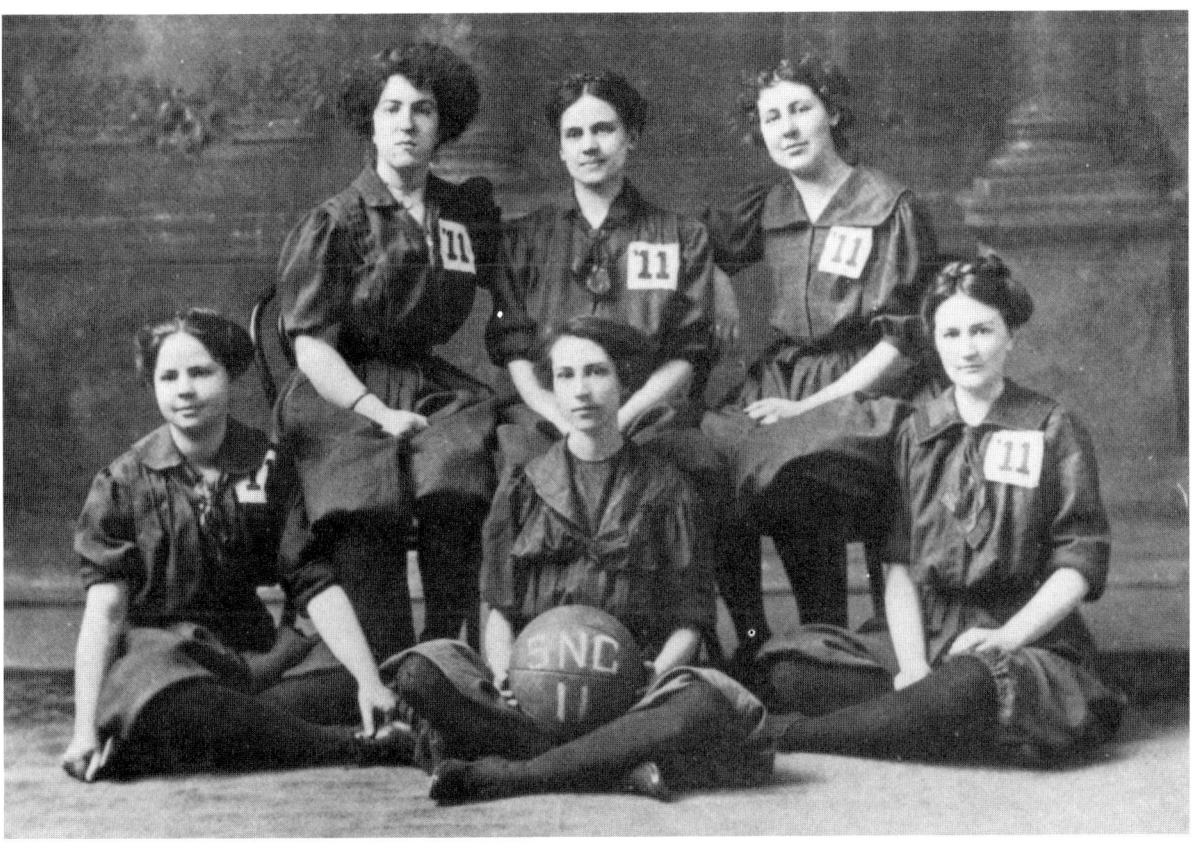

parents that "All boarding places are visited by some member of the Faculty, who inspects the house and its surroundings, and examines into the sanitary conditions of the premises." The long-standing tradition of *in loco parentis* was partially formalized in 1914 when Anna Pierce became the first Dean of Women.

Between 1890 and 1914 a self-conscious "student culture" began to emerge. The *Echo*, a monthly student newspaper/magazine, first appeared in 1892, and its pages reflected growing interest in student life. Student E. T. Van Deusen, writing in 1897, astutely observed that "More than most other forms of social living, the college is a world within itself; with its own characteristic public sentiment, its politics, its prejudices, and its body of traditional notions, maxims and usages."

Student cultures had emerged at American colleges in the 19th Century in reaction to faculty domination of student life, both in and out of the classroom. Students often fought the faculty, sometimes violently; riots were not uncommon. Since the students usually lost the struggles for power, they turned to the development of distinctive student cultures which gave them both an identity and a refuge from a perceived faculty tyranny. Albany students were often aware of what was happening at prestigious Eastern colleges and universities and may have imitated them. But at Albany, faculty-student relations remained amicable, probably because both groups felt themselves engaged in the common task of professional training.

Students supported an active arts program: The cast of the 1911 production of Sheridan's *The Rivals*. David Allison (standing, fifth from the left) played Sir Anthony Absolute. (*Our Book*, 1911; *Pedagogue*, 1914.)

At the heart of student culture was the notion of school spirit: "a force which tends to unify the students and cause them to magnify the institution and its traditions; perhaps college loyalty is the best synonym," wrote one student in 1898. "The New York State Normal College," he assured college mates, "is rich in history and in present causes for college loyalty."

These were years in which Albany traditions emerged. Students composed college songs and fiercely debated the issue of College colors (purple and gold won out). Each class of students was formally organized. The older literary societies were supplanted in the 1890s by Greek fraternities and sororities; by 1898 there were four sororities and one fraternity, and they had already formalized rushing regulations.

(Above) Aurelia Hyde, '95, was a first grade primary department teacher from 1895 to 1907. She married William Aspinwall, assistant to President Milne and later president of the State Normal School, Worcester, Massachusetts.

(Top) Bertha Brimmer, '00, was active early in religious education. When in the 1920s her children attended the Milne School, she became very active in College affairs, becoming executive secretary for the Alumni Hall Residency Fund and serving into the 1950s as the executive for the Alumni Association.

(Bottom) Anna Boocheever de Beer, '12, became a major force in New York and Albany civic affairs and was very active in alumni(ae) affairs for more than four decades.

Commencements were important celebratory occasions. By the 1890s they had become elaborate five-day affairs which began with orations, debates, dramatic performances, and music, culminated in the formal commencement ceremony, and concluded with a class banquet and reception. Baccalaureate services were a regular feature, and an outside commencement speaker appeared for the first time in 1897. In 1901 the graduating class debated and voted on whether or not to wear caps and gowns. The opponents of academic garb won on that occasion, but within three years the decision was reversed. Social activities were an important part of student life. Receptions, sponsored by both individuals and campus groups, were a popular form of socializing. They often included musical performances, recitations and readings, and the singing of college songs. Students often went some distance in search of social activity: the *Echo* reported bicycle and boat trips to Troy and elsewhere and railroad excursions to nearby places. Washington Park, of course, provided opportunities for smaller and often more intimate entertainments.

Conventional social activities often merged into more general cultural ones. Students found advantages to their Albany location. They could visit the state capitol, attend the YMCA lecture series, and hear oratorios performed by St. Peter's choristers or organ recitals at the First Reformed Church. In 1909 the staff of the *Echo* hired the Odd Fellows Hall and sponsored a performance of *The Merchant of Venice* by a group of itinerant actors who advertised that they performed plays "in the same manner as the plays were given in Shakespeare's time." Happily the performance not only elevated the cultural tone of the community but also made money.

Between 1890 and 1914, religious activities played a visible and significant role in the College's student culture. In 1893 the *Echo* observed that "Nothing is so needed in student bodies generally as strong religious life" and wanted "to see the college prayer meeting more generally attended." For several years the *Echo* published Christmas and Easter issues. Student religious organizations appeared. There was an active YWCA on campus and a "Newman Study Society" was organized in 1908. Student religious life not only upheld the traditional connections between religion, morality, and teaching but also reflected the notable increase in piety and religious concerns at many American colleges around the turn of the century.

The heart of student culture in schools like Yale and Harvard in these years was intercollegiate athletics. How did Albany compare? Not well, thought the editor of the *Echo* in 1893. "The State Normal College . . . lacks absolutely the distinctive characteristic of the American college . . . We have no base-ball team, no foot-ball team, no crew." Attempts were made to remedy that situation. A baseball team was fielded from 1896 to 1901, but it led a troubled existence, lacking a practice field and facing financial difficulties. It was not easy to find suitable opponents either; players complained of unsportsmanlike conduct on the part of a Castleton team and argued that the Oneonta team had far more professionals than normal school players.

One long-standing problem was the lack of a gymnasium, but after the new campus was occupied in the Fall of 1909 there was a notable surge of athletic activities. An athletic association for both men and women was formed in 1909 and divided into men's and women's associations two years later. Intercollegiate basketball (1909) and baseball (1912) teams were formed, and the College sponsored an indoor track meet in 1912. But the development of intercollegiate athletics continued to be hampered by inadequate facilities, by uncertain financial support, and no doubt by the relatively small number of male students at the College.

Just as this period began with a name change, so it ended with another. The College had long been embarrassed by the term "Normal," which suggested it was still a two-year institution, hardly different from New York's other normal schools. Hence in April of 1914 the institution became known officially as the New York State College for Teachers. The new title clearly recognized the four-year collegiate character of the school and symbolized the momentous changes that had taken place in the previous twenty-four years.

Almost concurrently the architects of those changes passed from the scene. Andrew Draper died in 1913 and President Milne passed away in September of the following year, shortly after the symbolic name change and just after war had broken out in Europe. In the next forty-eight years, through two world wars and the Great Depression, the College was to realize the implications of the new directions it had taken at the dawn of the century.

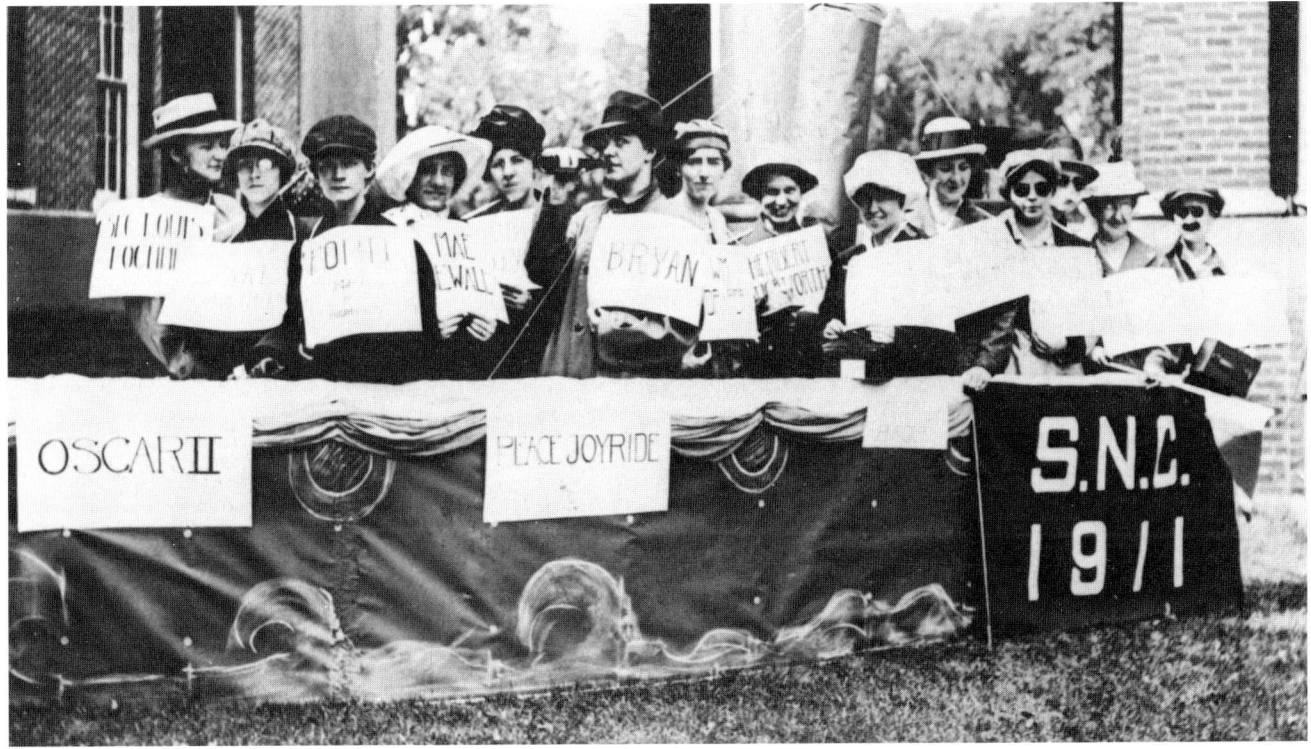

The Normal School and College alumni(ae) were a loyal group; here the Class of 1911 attends its fifth reunion in 1916. (Photo donated by Ester Woodward, '11, Alumni Memorabilia Collection.)

CHAPTER IV
The College for Teachers in Wars and Depression 1915 to 1945

*J*ust as the death of President Milne marked the end of one era, so the assumption of office by Abraham Brubacher in February of 1915 marked the beginning of another. During his twenty-four-year tenure, Brubacher presided over a College which was substantially larger than in previous decades. Its size was dictated by the market for secondary school teachers, and that in turn was affected by external conditions such as war, prosperity, and depression. After 1909, enrollments at the College rose rapidly to a pre-war peak of 1,081 in 1916. They fell after World War I to a 1921 low of 611, but then increased during the flush times of the 1920s to a peak of 1,424 in 1932. When the Great Depression began to reduce the demand for teachers, undergraduate enrollment was capped at 1,200 in 1933. College enrollments hovered around 1,300 for the rest of the decade although graduates faced greater difficulties in finding positions.

The College carried out its mission of preparing secondary school teachers while increasingly reflecting the standards and practices of smaller

(Opposite) The faculty in 1919. President Abram Brubacher is seated in the front row, center, seat on right. Front row (left to right): David Hutchinson (government), Leonard Wood Richardson (Greek and Latin), Dean Anna E. Pierce, Dean Harland Hoyt Horner, President Abram Brubacher, John Sayles (principal of Milne), Adna Wood Risley (history), Clifford Ambrose Woodward (biology). (Gift from the library of the late Dr. David Hutchinson.)

The First World War comes to the College: a Student Army Training Corps unit trained on the College campus in 1918. Chow in the mess hall was served by the Home Economics Department. After the war the department continued to serve meals, originating the school's food service.

Gertrude C. Valentine, an instructor in Greek and Latin, died in an automobile accident in France in 1919 while working for the YWCA.

American liberal arts colleges. The College sought and cherished national recognition of its new status. It was proud of being placed on the approved list of its graduates the Association of American Universities in 1921 and, a decade later, of being approved by the Association of American University Women, the first state teachers' college to be so recognized. Albany failed in its attempts to get a Phi Beta Kappa chapter, however; that organization viewed the College as a professional school rather than a liberal arts college.

Only two years after Brubacher took over the reins at Albany, the U.S. entered World War I. The College saw thirty-four graduates, 117 students, and two faculty go off to war in the armed services. Six students and one faculty member died or were killed in service (four from pneumonia, one in an aircraft accident). Three other male faculty members took leaves of absence to engage in war-related research with General Electric, the War Department, and the Emergency Shipbuilding Corporation. A number of women—students, alumnae, and one faculty—worked in canteens for the A.E.F. in France. One, Gertrude Valentine, an instructor in Greek and Latin, worked in England and France for the YWCA and lost her life there in 1919 in an automobile accident. In 1920 the College dead were remembered when alumni(ae) planted seven oaks on the campus and erected a bronze tablet in Draper Hall. Other casualties of the war were more subtle. Brubacher reported major enrollment declines in German, and he himself quietly changed his first name from "Abraham" to "Abram," doubtless in response to the pervasive anti-German sentiments of the day.

On campus a Student Army Training Corps unit operated from June to December of 1918. Twelve officers and 648 men served in the units, including over forty College students and more than sixty students from the Albany Law School. Barracks were erected on land adjacent to the College, and for a while the College cafeteria became an army mess hall. The usual military drill was supplemented by work in such subjects as auto mechanics, carpentry, pipe fitting, radio signal work, topographical drawing and "war aims."

Students at the College greeted the Armistice with the same kind of enthusiasm as Americans at large. The celebrations included a parade with "Dean Annie" Pierce riding "regally" in the front seat of an army truck and art instructor Eunice Perine "perched perilously" on the hood.

The College had always been a state-supported institution, beholden to the Legislature for funding and subject to state supervision. The nature of that supervision began to change in these decades. In the 19th Century the Executive Committee exercised a good deal of "hands on" supervision over the Normal School, sometimes overshadowing the President. Renamed the Board of Trustees in 1909 and the Board of Visitors in 1929, its powers remained unchanged. By the late 1930s, however, it fell into disuse; minutes of only two board meetings between 1940 and 1948 remain extant.

What had happened? The minutes of the board meetings during Brubacher's tenure demonstrate how he began to dominate the proceedings; the board became reactive rather than proactive. Equally important it lost much of its energy when the Commissioner of Education left it in the late 1930s. Effective supervision of Albany and New York's other teachers' colleges fell into the hands of the Department of Education's Assistant Commissioner for Teacher Education and Certification, Hermann Cooper. For three decades, beginning in the mid-1930s, Albany's presidents turned to Cooper rather than the Board of Visitors for counsel and support.

Brubacher in his annual report in 1922 observed that "It is generally accepted theory that subject matter is relatively more important than the method of presentation in high school

(Top) Edward Eldred Potter, '18, a member of the Army Air Corps, was another of the College's wartime casualties. He later gave his name to a prominent local fraternity.

(Bottom) Students engaged in Red Cross war work.

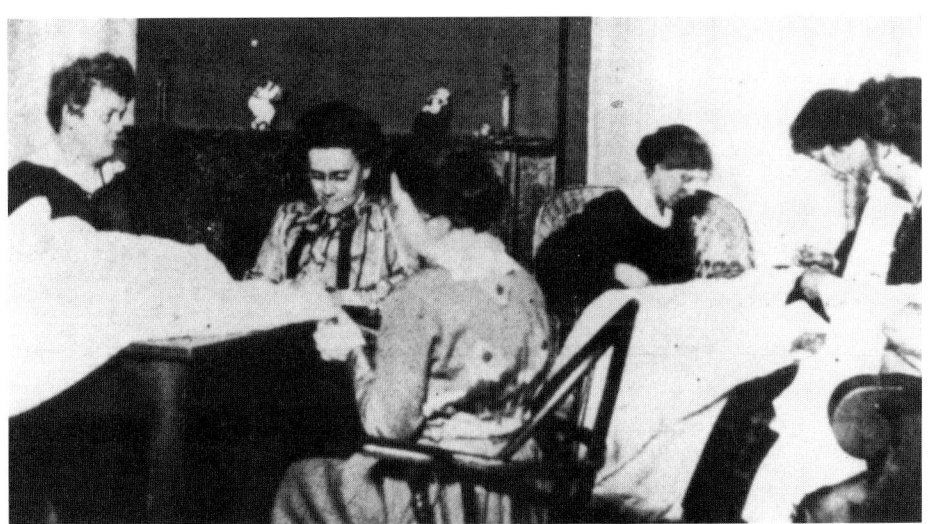

(Top) Organized student life flourished during these decades. Helping organize and lead student government was Myskania, pictured in 1918. Myskania founded the Student Association in 1921, and continued to exist as the Student Judiciary until the 1970s. (Photo from *Pedagogue*.)

(Bottom) The Class of '18 at Moving-Up Day in 1917. (Gift of Edward L. Long, '17, Alumni Memorabilia Collection.)

teaching . . ." That principle underlay Albany's academic programs until the 1960s. Academic work—the major, minor and general education requirements—made up 85 percent of undergraduate requirements; professional courses accounted for the remaining 15 percent. That distribution differentiated Albany from the normal schools of the day, where the relationship between academic and professional work was more like 50/50.

Program changes in the 1920s and 1930s reflected shifting faculty interests and external influences, particularly the changing demand for secondary school teachers. In the 1920s, for example, the College became involved in immigrant education. Philosophy disappeared from the curriculum in 1935 when the College chose not to replace a retiring faculty member. Some of the special programs developed shortly before World War I also disappeared; industrial arts with its costly equipment was dropped in 1920, and home economics met a similar fate in 1930-31. By contrast the undergraduate program in commerce, begun in 1913, flourished as secondary schools began offering such courses. Commerce enrollments at the College began to expand in the mid 1920s, and by the late 1930s one-fifth of Albany's students were enrolled in the program. Even in the depressed job market of the 1930s, 90 percent of Albany's commerce graduates found positions. Such curricular changes, however, left unchanged the relative importance of academic work and professional studies.

The model school grew with increased College enrollments. It received a new building in 1929 and was named in honor of President Milne. Under the leadership of John Sayles, the Milne School developed a full six-year secondary school program, annually admitted a class of seventy students, and trained some 300 student teachers each year. For about four decades the Milne School was an important educational element in the Capital District and generated several thousand loyal alumni(ae).

Albany had begun offering graduate work early in the century, but it became a significant factor at the College only in the 1930s; between 1930 and 1939 the College granted 719 master's degrees. Graduate students came for different reasons. Some were administrators seeking certification. Others were secondary school teachers looking for the higher salaries that came with additional course work. Still others were Albany graduates hoping to enhance their ability to find a teaching position. By 1937,

Most students continued to live in boarding houses. A group of women have a "Freshman Party at '25" according to the scrapbook notes of Dorothy Graninger, '16. She recorded that she "played 500, had 'Salmon Wiggle' and fudge." A group of men students, including Jay Ellis and Joe Sproule on the left and Neil Quackenbush on the right, are seated on the steps of their boarding house about 1917. (Gift of Edward Long, '17.) (Photos from Alumni Memorabilia Collection.)

Students in industrial arts in 1915. Begun in 1910, the program, with its costly equipment, was dropped in 1920. Physical education and athletics in 1915 were hampered by the limited facilities in the basement of the auditorium/gymnasium building, now Hawley.

Brubacher and the faculty systematically began to prepare for the day in 1943 when the State Education Department would require a "fifth year" of study for permanent certification.

The development of a program in librarianship also reflected changing demand. A Department of Librarianship was established in 1921 to offer an undergraduate program. It became a school in 1926, and within a few years began offering a master's degree. It was one of the first such departments to specialize in training secondary school librarians and by the early 1940s had become the College's first exclusively graduate program.

Extension and summer programs were added to serve new clienteles. The Normal School in the 19th Century had sent its principal and many of its students to the teachers' institutes common in those years. But extension programs in the modern sense began at the College in 1911 and expanded steadily in the next three decades, reaching enrollments of 500 to 600 per year in the 1930s. The largest group of students was elementary school teachers without baccalaureate degrees, but graduate enrollments also increased until they represented about 40 percent of the total by the late 1930s. The College's first summer session was held in 1917 and by the 1930s annually enrolled 1,300 to 1,600 students, 85 percent of them graduate students. Summer sessions and extension courses were expected to be financially self-sustaining. Tuition was charged and faculty members were paid out of the proceeds. For students it meant the first erosion of the notion that an education at the New York State College for Teachers was tuition-free. For faculty it meant a source of supplemental income, although at the uncertain cost of time for intellectual growth and scholarship.

Larger enrollments meant a larger faculty. Its size increased by fits and starts from forty-five in 1915 to 105 in 1940. Brubacher's long tenure as President meant that by his death in 1939 he had appointed ninety-two of the 103 faculty. His appointments were conventionally academic; the percentage of faculty holding earned doctorates rose from about 10 percent in 1915 to about 35 percent in 1939. Some were hired with the doctorate, others earned theirs while teaching. Both the pursuit of the doctorate and scholarly research were encouraged by a liberal policy of leave without pay as well as sabbaticals, introduced in 1922.

Brubacher fought hard, although not always successfully, for better salaries. The state in 1916 introduced a system of ranks and salary increments that governed faculty pay until the 1960s. In 1916 the salary schedule called for a minimum of $1,200 for instructors and a maximum of $4,000 for full professors; nine years later the comparable figures were $2,000 and $5,000. The sharp deflation of the 1930s meant rising real income for faculty members even though all those earning more than $2,000 were forced to take a 10 percent pay cut. The system was inflexible, however; the percentage of faculty in each rank was fixed by law. The result was a high rate of turnover in the lower ranks as ambitious young faculty, faced by the prospect of slow promotion and salary increases, went elsewhere.

Still, there was no lack of continuity in the faculty. A considerable number devoted most of their professional lives to the College. Some, although by no means a majority, were held to the College by alumni(ae) ties, but clearly a good many found the College an attractive place to teach. Many of Brubacher's appointments in the 1930s stayed to form the core of the faculty in the next two decades, and three—Edith Wallace, Ralph Beaver, and Luther Andrews—played leadership roles in the transition to university status in the 1960s.

During these years the College also entered the mainstream of American academic life in the area of academic administration. Between 1906 and 1913, William Aspinwall as Assistant to the President began to perform some of the functions of a dean. His successors, Leonard Blue (1914-1917) and Harlan Hoyt Horner (1917-1923) were the first officially to be bestowed the title. Mathematician

(Top) Leonard Anderson Blue, first Dean of the College, in 1916. (*Pedagogue*, 1916.)

(Bottom) Edna Merrit, '18, left rear, was one of many Albany graduates who became missionaries. She is pictured here in 1936 with the junior high graduating class at Sienyu in Fukien, China. (*Alumni Quarterly*, Fall, 1936.)

History Professor Adna Wood Risley in class circa 1922. Professor Risley is said to have owned the first automobile in Albany. (Gift of Dr. Edith O. Wallace, '17.)

William Henry Metzler, earlier dean of the graduate school and of the college of liberal arts at Syracuse, served from 1923 to his retirement in 1933. Milton Nelson, a 1924 graduate of Albany with a Cornell Ph.D., returned to Albany as an assistant professor of education and became dean in 1933, serving until his retirement in 1950. The dean and the President were the most influential figures in the academic life of the College, but they were also assisted by nine or ten faculty committees with responsibilities in areas such as appointments, curriculum, scheduling, examinations, and student activities.

Surging enrollments in the 1920s made the chronic problem of physical facilities ever more urgent, but progress was slow. Only in 1922 did the state enlarge the campus by paying $70,000 for an additional two acres of land between the science building and Albany High School. It was another seven years before three additional buildings—Richardson Hall, Page Hall, and the new Milne School—were completed. The $868,000 project was characterized by a combination of disagreements with the architect, construction delays, and financial problems. A 1936 addition to the Milne School rounded out the expansion of physical facilities during this period.

The new facilities eased but did not eliminate the space problem. The 1929 construction permitted the College to convert the former auditorium and gymnasium into Hawley Library, which opened in 1933. Inadequate though it was, it was far better than anything the College had enjoyed before, and the library looked even better when in 1934-35 Works Progress Administration artists decorated it with a set of murals. The basement of Page Hall contained the first real gymnasium the College had ever had, but it provided only for an undersized basketball court (the size of the space unobstructed by pillars had been a source of fierce conflict with the architect), and it had to be shared with the Milne students.

By 1937 expansion of the library and provision of a health and recreational center were at the top of Brubacher's list of priorities, but the underlying problem of additional construction was land; the campus was hemmed in by the city. The state declined to purchase the aging buildings of Albany High School adjoining the campus both to the east and the west. Brubacher looked longingly to the south side of

Western Avenue but to no avail; the Depression made further construction impossible.

During these years the College continued to have a statewide student body (virtually every county was represented each year) although as many as a third of the students came from the five-county area around Albany. Both the number of applications and admission standards fluctuated. Qualifications other than high school graduation virtually disappeared during World War I, and the attrition rate for first-year students zoomed to 36 percent in 1915-16. Brubacher was very dissatisfied.

(Top) Richardson, Page, and Milne (center left) were built in 1929 following financial problems and construction delays.

(Bottom) In the 1920s the school was still small enough (611 students in 1921) for all-college events to fit into the gymnasium in the basement of Hawley. Pictured are the Classes of 1920 and 1922 at a Halloween party. (Photo by Marshall Studio, Alumni Memorabilia Collection.)

71

Athletics in the 1920s: (above) women's horseback riding; (opposite page) a short-lived intercollegiate football program in 1922; and the 1929 tennis team. Tennis at the college dates from 1898. (Photos from *Pedagogue*, 1923 and 1929.)

A college training teachers, he observed, "must insist upon educational virility." To achieve that, the College steadily raised the minimum high school average needed for admission. To deal with the attrition problem, the College in 1917 began a system of freshmen faculty advisers and a form of freshmen orientation. During the 1930s, when demand for admission was very high, admission standards rose further. Nearly half of the entering class in the Fall of 1933 had high school averages of 90 percent or higher, and no one had an average of less than 85 percent. During the 1930s the College attracted nearly 10 percent of all the Regents' Scholarship winners in the state.

Beyond academics, the College continued to be concerned about the physical health and psychological qualifications of incoming students. World War I created concerns about the health of the American population. The College used federal funds in 1919 to establish a Department of Hygiene, which offered courses required of all students, conducted physical exams of every matriculated student (grading the students on an "A" to "D" scale!), and prescribed corrective gymnastic training. In the Fall of 1921, students had assessed themselves an annual "infirmary" fee, which provided room and routine nursing care in Albany hospitals for short-term illnesses. By the 1930s, incoming students had to bring a personal health record from their physicians.

In addition, students were subjected to I.Q. testing and were evaluated on a "Trait Index" designed to weed out candidates unsuitable for teaching. In his final report in 1939, Brubacher noted that the College consciously evaluated students on the basis of "scholastic achievement, emotional stability, character, forcefulness, purposefulness, resourcefulness, voice, speech, health . . . The strength of the selective effort," he observed, "lies in the fact that weak personalities are excluded or, having been admitted, are identified and eliminated." By whatever criteria, the College by the 1930s had become and was to remain one of the most highly selective public undergraduate institutions in the nation.

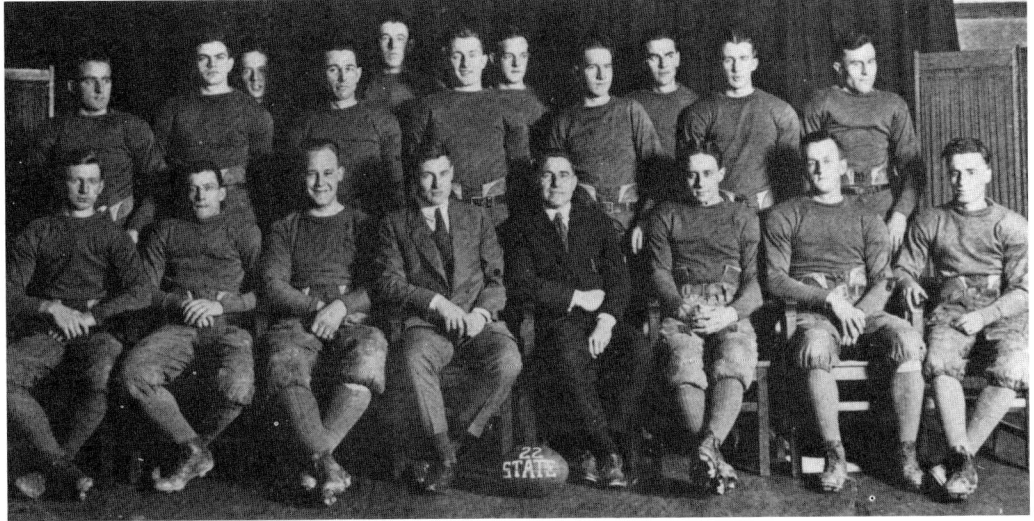

The College continued to give attention to the moral and physical welfare of and to stand *in loco parentis* to its would-be teachers. That relationship had been formalized with Anna Pierce's appointment as Dean of Women in 1914. The Dean of Women, she asserted in her 1928 book, *Deans and Advisors of Women and Girls*, should be responsible for "The strengthening of the student's moral fiber and imparting to her the knowledge of essentials in life . . ." In Dean Pierce's view, achieving those goals involved among other things attention to a female student's religious life, her manner of dress and personal appearance, and her social activities. No activities "called questionable by any large portion of the parents

The first dormitory for women, Syddum Hall in its second location in Englewood Place, was founded by Marion Syddum Van Liew, head of the home economics department in 1918.

. . . of the students should be planned or encouraged."

Dean Pierce was concerned with providing female students with housing of a kind that would foster the virtues she thought so important. The College from its founding had insisted that students live only in College-approved homes and boarding houses, but by World War I they were both in short supply and difficult to supervise. Brubacher reported that in 1919-20 nearly half of the students lived in approved boarding houses. A 1933 study showed that about a third of both men and women lived in private homes while another third of the women lived in group or sorority houses.

Between 1917 and 1921 the President annually appealed, unsuccessfully, through the Board of Trustees to the Legislature for funds to establish dormitories for at least 700 women students. By the early 1920s it became clear that the dormitories could be provided only through private effort and financing. Hence Brubacher supported the formation of a committee headed by Dean Pierce and John Sayles, then Director of Training, to initiate a drive for funds to construct dormitories. Alumni(ae) and local benefactors gave their support, and by the early 1930s the Alumni Association's committee (eventually chartered as the State College Benevolent Association) had raised $293,000 in pledges. Property between Partridge and Ontario streets was acquired and, in the Fall of 1935, Residence Hall Number 1 (renamed Pierce Hall in 1941) opened to provide accommodations for 162 women. Under Sayles' leadership, the Benevolent Association proceeded to build a dormitory, this one for men, which opened in 1941 as Sayles Hall. Students seemed pleased by the new accommodations. The dormitories provided not only good living conditions but also opportunities for special interest housing: in 1942 "La Maison Francaise," consisting of thirteen French majors and a French-speaking chaperone, was housed in a section of Pierce Hall.

The enterprise of the alumni(ae) and the College had significant reverberations. It doubtless influenced the organization in 1944 of the State Dormitory Authority, which first provided state funding for college and university dormitories in New York. And for another two decades the Alumni Association operated smaller houses for groups of Albany students.

The student culture which had sprung up around the turn of the century flowered during these decades. For the four decades after World War I that culture was characterized by two things: an astonishingly high level of extra-curricular activity and a phenomenal degree of organization. Albany students often seemed to spend more time out of the classroom than in it, and they often seemed incapable of doing anything without formal organization. Still, the extra-curricular activity generally received faculty and administrative support, for both faculty and students were bound together by the common goal of preparing first-rate secondary school teachers. Extra-curricular activities played an important role in achieving that goal.

The student body became highly organized. Milne in 1914 had rejected a student overture for permission to organize, but a year later Brubacher proved more receptive. He appointed a faculty committee headed by English Professor Harry Hastings which reported in April of 1917. The committee recommended the appointment of an all-senior student council and chose eleven seniors on the basis of scholarship and leadership to begin student government. The group of students, whatever their scholarly qualifications, quickly demonstrated an abundance

(Top) Women dancing in the parlor of Newman Hall, a group home sponsored by the Roman Catholics. Newman Hall was founded in 1922 with the purchase of the large red brick mansion at 741 Madison Avenue—its location until 1956. (Gift of Helen Krizka Wright, '42, Alumni Memorabilia Collection.)

(Bottom) Sororities and fraternities quickly followed suit and bought their own houses. This is Chi Sigma Theta House on State Street.

(Top) Religious groups played a significant role in student life. The Menorah Society was founded in 1923.

(Bottom) In the early 1920s faculty and alumni(ae), led by Anna Pierce and John Sayles, mounted a drive to raise money to build dormitories. Here students urge contributions. The fund-raising drive came to fruition with the opening of Pierce Hall in 1935. (Alumni Memorabilia Collection.)

of leadership. They called themselves "Myskania" (the meaning of the term was known only to members), decided that half of the ten members should be chosen by the faculty and half by the outgoing members, and selected their successors.

By 1921 Myskania had established the Student Association, had written its constitution, which provided for student officers, and had become both the creator and guardian of student traditions. Early Myskanias established weekly assemblies, organized class rivalry, came to the support of the infant student newspaper begun in 1916, and enlarged the activities of Moving-Up Day, initially begun in 1913. Selection to Myskania soon became the highest honor extended to students for their leadership and extra-class activities.

College traditions became firmly established in this era. Frosh were inducted into the College with the rituals of freshman week, advanced with the activities of Moving-Up Day, left the institution with Commencement, and moved into the ranks of the alumni(ae) with Torch Night (begun in 1930 or 1931), where they sang the *alma mater*, "College of the Empire State," chosen in 1916 in an alumni(ae)-sponsored contest. Student leaders promoted College "spirit" so successfully that it sometimes got out of hand. Freshman hazing was limited to one week in the Fall of 1929, and in 1934 Myskania had to suspend part of sophomore-freshman "rivalry" when student enthusiasm spilled over into vandalism. In 1944 Pierce's successor, Dean Ellen Stokes, was forced to clamp down on "unorganized rivalry" which had involved "scalping" the president of the freshman class and inter-dorm raids resulting in jam-smeared hair, clothes marked with lipstick, and pails of water thrown in rooms and corridors.

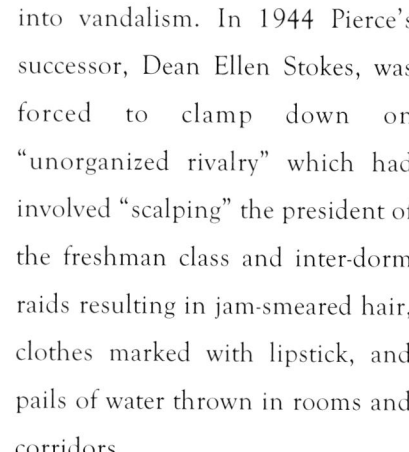

Students soon discovered that student government, like all governments, was only as strong as its financial resources. The Student

Anna Eloise Pierce

Beginning her career as a fifteen-year-old schoolmistress in a one-room log cabin, Anna Eloise Pierce, '84, arrived at the Normal College in 1883 as a student, later became a secretary to the president, then a substitute and finally a full-time teacher. As her duties grew over forty-nine years, so did her role as mother figure to female students. When the school became the New York State College for Teachers, Pierce was in place as the first Dean of Women.

Pierce held a formal tea for first-year female students and also conducted a series of lectures as a required course on etiquette, proper classroom conduct, dress, and proper relations with young men. In her annual published "greetings" to each new class of females, she said she would always be ready to do whatever a loving mother would do, and urged them to talk to her whenever they were "in doubt about anything, or are lonely and want sympathy . . . I am in my office every morning and the latchstring is always out."

The dean, author of the pioneer book *Deans and Advisors of Women and Girls*, made herself available because she felt students could not achieve their best if they were afraid or worried. The "all important thing," she said, "is to have at your command all of your powers of body, mind and heart."

An advocate of dorms as a place for quality conditions, social support, and unified college spirit, Pierce was remembered when a dorm was built on the downtown campus in 1935, two years after she retired, and later named after her. The *State College News*, commenting on the unveiling of her official portrait in 1927, noted the accurate representation of "her capable hands which have grasped each task with courage and sincerity."

DEAN PIERCE'S IDEA OF SIGMA NU KAPPA HOUSE

(Top) Anna Pierce, (Portrait by David Lithgow, photo by Mark Schmidt.)

(Bottom) *The Pretzel*, a publication of Psi Gamma sorority, pokes good-natured fun at Dean Pierce.

(Top) The Class of 1931 in their freshman year. (From the Class of '31 scrapbook, Alumni Memorabilia Collection.)

(Bottom) "A Day at Ken Miller's farm, during which the Potter Club may or may not have been born." Art Jones, Larry Newcomb, Al Basch, Andy Heitz, Sam Dransky, Ken Miller, Gren Rand, Bernie Kerbel, Babe Kaplan, Russ Ludlum, and Walt Driscoll. (From the Class of '31 scrapbook, Alumni Memorabilia Collection.)

Board of Finance (supervised by a faculty member) appeared in 1920 to oversee the expenditure of an annual student tax of $5.00, first imposed in 1917. The size of the assessment and its collection inevitably became matters of controversy. Since the tax was voluntary, many students refused to pay it, particularly in the hard times of the 1930s. Peer pressures were applied; at various times the names of students who had not paid the tax appeared in the *State College News*. Ultimately, the students sought the assistance of the administration; in 1937, seniors had to pay the tax before the College would recommend them for a teaching position.

Helen Krizka, '42, thought a half century later that "This fee surely was a bargain!" Perhaps it was, for the students used the funds, which ran as high as $12,000 in the 1930s and 1940s, to support a wide variety of activities. Some funding went to student publications. The most important was the *State College News*, which began publication in 1916 and has had a continuous existence to the present. The College yearbook, *The Pedagogue*, begun in 1913, conscientiously recorded College life. While the older literary societies had mostly disappeared by the beginning of this period, magazines such as the *State Lion* and the *State College Quarterly* attested to continuing student interest in creative writing, ranging from humor to more serious literary enterprises.

Student organizations and activities proliferated. Some were academic honoraries. The College, having been rejected by Phi Beta Kappa earlier, in 1930 established Signum Laudis, a general academic honorary. Herodotus, a history honorary affiliated with the national Pi Gamma Mu, was formed in 1927. Kappa Phi Kappa, a professional education fraternity, appeared in 1927, and Pi Omega Pi, a national honor fraternity for business education teachers, was begun in 1943. An almost endless array of clubs serving special student academic interests sprang up.

Religious groups, so prominent in the first decade of the century, clearly played a lesser role in the life of the College than they had earlier. Still, they maintained a significant presence. The YWCA, so significant in the earlier period, was transformed into the Student Christian Movement and sponsored a wide variety of programs and speakers including Professor Croasdale's annual talks on marriage. Canterbury Club and the Lutheran Club served other Protestants. The Newman Club was joined in 1916 by Chi Sigma Theta, a Roman Catholic sorority; in 1941 the Albany Catholic Diocese was operating Thomas More House, which provided housing for students from State

(Below) Arvid Burke, '28, served for years as director of studies for the New York State Teachers' Association and completed his career as a faculty member from 1960 to 1971 in Albany's School of Education.

(Above) Gladys Newell, '30, was a dedicated social studies teacher for 40 years and served as president of the New York State Teachers' Association in 1966.

(Right) Paul Bulger, '36, became a distinguished educator, serving as an Assistant Commissioner of Education in New York and as president of the State University College at Buffalo.

Members of the Class of '33 at their first reunion June 16, 1934. Alumni(ae) were fiercely loyal during these years. (From the Class of '33 scrapbook maintained by Alvina Rich Lewis, Alumni Memorabilia Collection.)

College, Albany Pharmacy, Albany Law School, and Christian Brothers Academy. Jewish students, long represented by Menorah, transformed themselves into Hillel in 1942.

Several student organizations appealed to College-wide interests. Debate Council, organized in 1927, debated not only Hamilton, Rutgers, Cornell and Syracuse but also a visiting team from Scottish universities. The long-standing student interest in music was mobilized with the formation of the Music Association, which sponsored both student musical performances and campus appearances by professional groups.

Agnes Futterer, '16, helped organize the Dramatic and Art Association, governed by an elected council of six students, in 1919. D&A Council sponsored speakers and performances by outside theater groups but more importantly forged links between classroom instruction and student initiative in theater. Albany was only the third American college to offer formal classes in drama, and most theater productions at the College were products of Futterer's Elementary and Advanced Dramatics classes. Productions of *Lady Windermere's Fan* and *The Electra* in the 1920s and *Death Takes a Holiday* and *Hedda Gabler* in the 1930s were characteristic examples of quality College theater during those decades. Futterer and the D&A Councils established a tradition of superior theater at Albany. Theater alumni(ae) were a remarkably loyal group, and some went on to distinguished teaching and professional careers in theater.

Albany students shared the common collegiate enthusiasm for athletics in these years. Intramural sports flourished, but intercollegiate athletics fared less well. The men's basketball team begun in 1909 continued, but attempts to field teams in football, baseball, swimming, and hockey were soon aborted. Part of the problem was inadequate facilities. The

Agnes Futterer

Today's theater students, when they are relaxing between classes and productions, can often be found sitting around the Agnes Futterer Memorial Lounge in the Performing Arts Center. If they haven't already heard of Futterer, for whom the lounge was named, they can see her likeness above them on the wall in a rich portrait of a graceful and dynamic woman.

A 1916 graduate of the College, Futterer studied at the American Academy of Dramatic Arts at Columbia University for advanced training before she began teaching at Albany in 1917. For forty-one years she taught classes, directed performances, gave solo recitals, and traveled throughout New England for readings of twenty-seven plays she had memorized.

Described by students as "formidable" and both "inspirational" and "inspired," nicknamed "The Dutchess," "The Queen," or just "Aggie," she even had a reputation as a mischievous matchmaker. Tall, with reddish brown hair, magnificent posture and grace of movement, she always included in her attire a string of beads to match her dresses—muted tones in the winter, bright colors for spring.

But "Aggie" was more than style. She developed courses like Elementary and Advanced Dramatics, Modern Drama, and Playwriting that made Albany only the third college in the nation to offer such an extensive drama program. Later she taught classes in oral interpretation of literature. Her students included future movie and television star Harold Gould '47 and Broadway's *The Sound of Music* director, Vincent Donehue.

In 1955 a group of 300 students established the Theater Alumni Association, which later commissioned the Futterer portrait and also set up the Agnes Futterer Award, given annually to a senior who has made the most significant contribution to theater.

This influential and highly involved teacher continued to do readings and to take classes at the college after her retirement, and she also enjoyed gardening. She died in 1973, and the lounge was dedicated to her the following year.

gymnasia available were at best inadequate, there were no swimming pools or hockey rinks, and even the available playing fields produced chronic criticism from Albany's athletes. The state provided no funds for intercollegiate athletics apart from the salaries of physical education instructors, and intercollegiate sports at Albany's level produced little revenue. The Student Association budget for athletics (only $3,365 in 1934-35) was simply inadequate. Still, the interest was there. The annual alumni banquet in 1932 produced a resolution urging that College teams "play more difficult and better known opponents" for the "advantageous publicity" that would accrue to the College.

Social activities played an important role in student culture. Formal and informal dances, teas, receptions, dinners, outings, and parties abounded. There was great interest in the annual choice of a Campus Queen, and in 1931 the *State College News* was keeping track of the hair color of the winners: six blondes, three brunettes, and one redhead between 1922 and 1931.

The Greek societies played a vital role in this social life. Five sororities founded between 1890 and 1909 were still active during these decades, and at least six more appeared. The growth in the number of men produced at least five new fraternities between 1913 and 1938 to join the one founded in 1907. The Greeks in turn organized themselves into an Intersorority Council (1920) and an Interfraternity Council (1937), in part to oversee rushing and hazing. Most, although not all, had group houses.

(Above) K. Leroy Irvis, '38, became Democratic leader and speaker of the Pennsylvania House of Representatives. He received an honorary degree from Albany in 1986 for his achievements. African-American students attended Albany from the late 1850s onward.

(Right) Dorothy Griffin Griffin, '34, became a businesswoman and president of the Varflex Corporation in Rome, New York.

The administration occasionally had qualms about all of this extra-curricular activity. In 1925 Brubacher observed that there were too many dances and too much movie-going among the students; the College needed to awaken the serious interests of students. An alumna recalled that when she enthusiastically described to her family the parties and receptions extended frosh in her first year in the Fall of 1938, her father sternly reminded her that "you are in college to study, not to socialize."

Yet Brubacher and other administrators remained generally supportive of these experiences as an essential part of the process of "socializing" students to their future status as secondary school teachers. An editorial in the *State College News* in 1930 drove home the point. Commenting on the discourteous behavior of students who accepted invitations from faculty for social gatherings and did not attend, the writer asserted that "such flagrant violations of ordinary courtesy are more becoming to grammar school children than to prospective teachers who are expected to transfer culture and knowledge to others."

The campaign to properly "socialize" College students was continuous. Formal orientation programs such as "freshman camp," introduced for men in 1930 and for women the following year, were supplemented by advice from Dean Pierce and teas and receptions hosted by faculty. Rules of conduct for women in group houses and the appropriateness of smoking on campus were debated, and students were condemned for discourteous behavior at theater productions or lectures. As Brubacher had pointed out in his book, the public expected a secondary school teacher to be a certain kind of person as well as to know what and how to teach.

The focus on training teachers and the high level of extra-curricular activities suggest that the College community during these decades tended to look inward. Indeed, there is relatively little evidence of concern for events in the larger world, and such evidence as there is

Members of the Class of '35 clowning around for the camera.

Abram Brubacher

Abram Brubacher was named president of the College in 1915, and he used his strong work and educational credentials to bolster the level of excellence of both students and faculty for twenty-four years. When he began his long tenure, his professional roles already included teacher, high school principal in Gloversville and Schenectady, and superintendent of schools in Schenectady from 1908 to 1914. His educational achievements included a Ph.D. in Greek from Yale University.

Brubacher was also a well-published author, and his 1927 book, *Teaching: Profession and Practice*, deals with every aspect of a teacher's life from good grooming to professional training "to their broader social and political roles."

His writing was inspirational in tone, and his aspirations for the college were no less vaunted. In looking to improve standards, he focused on both teachers and students. Concerned about the high failure rate of the freshman class, he steadily raised the minimum high school average needed for admittance. He also emphasized graduate programs, and during his tenure the number of master's degrees awarded rose dramatically. Brubacher's hiring of more faculty enabled more courses to be offered: from 1915 to 1940 the number nearly doubled, to 260. He promoted scholarly research, hired many more holders of Ph.D.s, introduced sabbatical leaves, and expanded the campus by three new academic halls and one dormitory, all part of his fervid quest to raise the College to a more prestigious rank among post-secondary institutions. His efforts were dramatically successful.

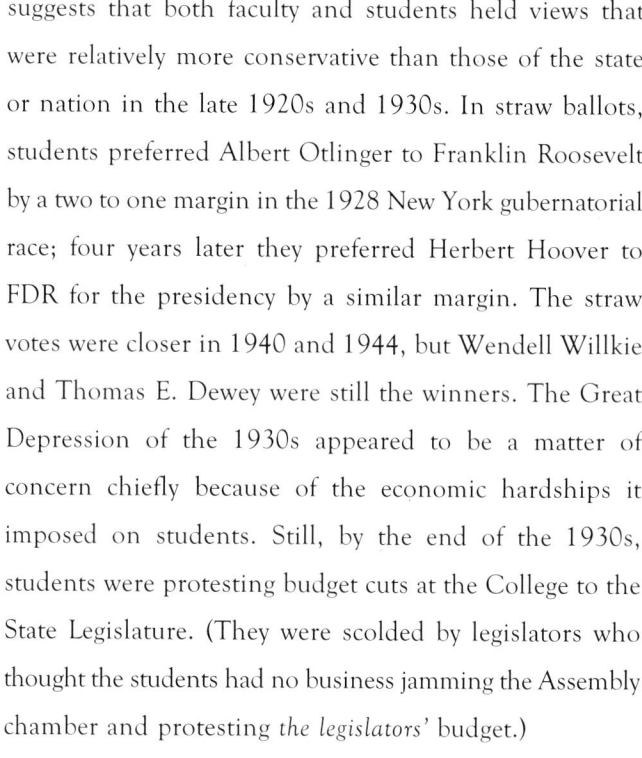

suggests that both faculty and students held views that were relatively more conservative than those of the state or nation in the late 1920s and 1930s. In straw ballots, students preferred Albert Otlinger to Franklin Roosevelt by a two to one margin in the 1928 New York gubernatorial race; four years later they preferred Herbert Hoover to FDR for the presidency by a similar margin. The straw votes were closer in 1940 and 1944, but Wendell Willkie and Thomas E. Dewey were still the winners. The Great Depression of the 1930s appeared to be a matter of concern chiefly because of the economic hardships it imposed on students. Still, by the end of the 1930s, students were protesting budget cuts at the College to the State Legislature. (They were scolded by legislators who thought the students had no business jamming the Assembly chamber and protesting *the legislators'* budget.)

The Fall of 1939 marked important changes at the College. President Abram Brubacher died in August of that year, leaving behind an important and much admired legacy, for he was the individual most responsible for the transformation of the State College for Teachers into a genuine collegiate institution. His successor was John Sayles, a 1902 alumnus, who had served on the Albany faculty since 1905. President for eight years until forced to resign for reasons of ill-health, Sayles was deeply committed to and thoroughly familiar with the College and its mission; he pursued a straight course through difficult times.

Just a few days after Brubacher's death, Germany invaded Poland. World War II affected the College in many ways. Enrollment fell by more than a third, from 1,379 in 1939 to 865 in 1943. Military service denuded the College of males; they had constituted about a third of the student body in the late 1930s but only a twelfth in 1944 and 1945. The faculty shrank from 105 in 1939 to

   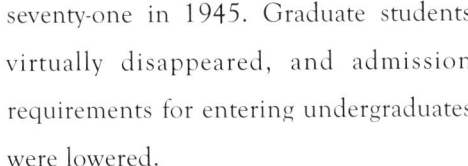 

seventy-one in 1945. Graduate students virtually disappeared, and admission requirements for entering undergraduates were lowered.

There are no accurate figures for the number of alumni and faculty in service in World War II. Between fifteen and twenty faculty were involved in the armed forces or such supporting agencies as the American Red Cross; more than 625 students and alumni(ae) similarly served. Available records suggest that at the end of the conflict seventeen had given their lives and one was still listed as missing; several had been prisoners-of-war.

(Clockwise from top left) Dean Milton Nelson; faculty members Ruth Hutchins (art); Harry Birchenough (math); Mattie Green (physician); Robert Frederick (education).

Characteristically, the campus organized itself enthusiastically for the war effort. The War Activities Council sought to coordinate student war work on campus; by the Fall of 1942 some 60 percent of the students reportedly had signed up. Activities ranged from sewing and a salvage campaign to air raid precautions and blood donations. More than seventy female students reportedly worked as nurses' aides in area hospitals. A "Memorial Presentation" in 1944 included the bestowing of a $2,500 War Bond. The WAC made a serious attempt to keep in contact with students and alumni serving in the armed forces. The *State*

A "field trip" in the Pine Bush with Dr. Gertrude Douglas of the biology department (1919 to 48). Jean Cady, '41, is in the center with the sample case. (Gift of Jean Cady Sroka, Alumni Memorabilia Collection.)

College News ran a weekly column entitled "Jargon in G.I." devoted to keeping in touch with College G.I.s, and faculty members Donnal Smith and Louis Jones put together a newsletter for servicemen. Other aspects of campus life changed. A conference on campus in the Summer of 1942 suggested that education had to be adapted to the changing technologies of the "air age." Both fraternities and sororities toned down their initiation rituals; the former virtually disappeared from the campus. Night activities on campus were limited. By 1943, intercollegiate athletics had disappeared to be replaced by intramural sports and other physical training designed to keep men "physically fit in preparation for joining the various armed services of Uncle Sam."

In the midst of the conflict the College observed its Centennial. On May 5 and 6, 1944, members of the College community gathered to hear speeches by appropriate dignitaries: Commissioner of Education George Stoddard, author John Erskine, Hermann Cooper, and Dean Charles F. Russell of Teachers College, Columbia. Looking backward, the College sponsored the publication of a history: *College of the Empire State: A Centennial History of the New York State College for Teachers at Albany* by William Marshall French and Florence Smith French. Looking forward, attendees at the celebration watched the first showing of a film, "Tomorrow's Teachers," shot in color and produced by faculty and students. The Centennial observance was a satisfying if subdued recognition of the achievements of the institution over a century.

Two issues of the *State College News* reported stories that in different ways reflected the College response to the war years. The second issue of the paper after Pearl Harbor featured an article on the program for student war service; on the next page an article advised female students how to get ready for a prom—what gown to wear, the proper *coiffure*, how to wear flowers, *etc*. Almost four years later the paper carried an article reporting that Jack Smith '43 (and later long-time professor of physics at the College and University), had witnessed the explosion of the first atomic bomb in New Mexico. The College had struggled through World War II into the nuclear age.

John Sayles succeeded Brubacher as Acting President in 1939, and President in 1941. (*Pedagogue*, 1944.)

In 1944 the College was one of nine campuses nationwide to participate in a nationally funded study of intergroup relations, leading to a student-run conference on the topic. Led by Shirley Passow, '46, a few students decided to continue the spirit of the study and conference by forming the Inter-Group Council to promote understanding among all races and nationalities in the community. The charter members were, first row left-to-right, Kathryn Hagerty, professor of education Mary E. Conklin, and Marian Carter, '46; and back row, professor of social studies Watt Stewart, Celina Axlerod, '47, founder and president Passow, Edna M. Marsh, '45, and Louis Jones, professor of English.

World War II took faculty, students and alumni(ae) into the armed forces. Political scientist Robert Rienow (left) served in the Army and later served for many years as an officer in the New York National Guard. Thurston T. Paul, '35, (above) in his service uniform. Lt. Zollie Privett, '48, (opposite, upper left) in the cockpit of his Tenth Air Force fighter plane. Two alumnae serving in the WAVES (opposite, right). The woman on the left is Marjorie Bishop, '42. Jack Smith, '43, (opposite, lower left) later a long-time physics professor at Albany, was present at the explosion of the first atomic bomb in New Mexico in 1945. (Privett photo from Louis C. Jones Papers; Bishop photo from Class of '42 scrapbook, Alumni Memorabilia Collection.)

By May 1946 all State College servicemen had been discharged. To celebrate the end of the war Kappa Beta held a reunion dinner in downtown Albany. Attendees ranged from "founding fathers" to members still enrolled. From top left: Steve Greenwald,'40, Maurice J. Levin, '43, '47, Irwin Swire, '46, Harry Kensky, '43, Art Flax, '43,'49, Professor Stewart, Sol Greenberg, '43, Herman Kleine, '41, George Stangler, '40, Harry Passow, '42, '47, Dick Ribner, '39, Earl Dorwaldt (faculty advisor), Gadlin Bodner, '41, Ralph Clausen (faculty advisor), Bernard Bernhardt, Moe Sweetgall, '38, Paul Wagner, '47, '48, Herbert Frankel, '40, Jack Shapiro, '41, Dan Preston, '41,'46, Baird Poskanzer, '42, Abe Savitsky, '42, '49, Bernard Arbit, '43, Allen Woodell, '42, unidentified, Morris Gerber, '42, '48, Louis Greenspan, '41, Henry Brauner, '42, Percy Forman, '38, (first president), William Miller, '47, '48 Al Stiller, '42, David Slavin, '43, Ira Freedman, '43, '48, Ainard Gelbond, '42, Bernard Palmer,'42, Haskell Rosenberg, '40, Arnold Ellerin, '41, and George Pearson, '41. (Gift of Ira Freedman, '43.)

The College observed its centennial in 1944. At the podium is President John Sayles. Left to right on the rostrum: Author John Erskine; Regent Leland Thompson; U.S. Commissioner of Education George Stoddard; Chair of the College Board of Visitors, Judge Newton B. VanDerzee.

CHAPTER V
The Apogee of Teacher Education
1945 to 1962

The end of World War II transformed the College. Students on military leave were allowed to reenter almost as soon as they were mustered out, and many additional veterans were quickly admitted. The three-year surge of returning veterans meant that the percentage of male students on campus rose from eight percent in 1945 to 29 percent in 1947.

The expanded enrollment caused a serious housing shortage. The College made a plea to the community, and Albany householders provided rooms for rent to at least 118 students. The Salvation Army even provided temporary dorm space for thirty-five men in 1946. The Alumni Association operated two group houses for men, Sayles Annex and Vanderzee Hall. The latter provided the male students with housing that would have seemed luxurious (gilded bath fixtures, for example) except for the number of students assigned per room. Married students, an entirely new category of undergraduates, had to fend for themselves.

Campus life was transformed by the return of men. Handholding

(Opposite) The 72,000-volume Hawley Library was small and crowded, but efforts throughout the 1950s to win funding for new buildings were unsuccessful. (*Pedagogue*, 1940.)

and public displays of affection called for promulgation of new rules of etiquette. Single women complained that married males did not always wear wedding rings, complicating their task of identifying suitable social partners. Sororities had flourished throughout the war, but now fraternities revived. Men were now on hand to play the male roles in the plays presented by Agnes Futterer's Advanced Dramatics class and to make possible a resurgence of intercollegiate athletics.

Most veterans had their college costs paid for them under the G.I. Bill, and the lack of tuition charges made the College a desirable choice for those who had to stretch allowances farthest. Some GIs may have seen the College more as an opportunity to get an inexpensive liberal education than as professional preparation for high school teaching. But the curriculum was not altered for them; all took the required professional sequence in addition to the liberal arts course. The returning GIs were well-motivated and able students, considered by the faculty who taught them as among the ablest and most stimulating students they had ever had.

The immediate post-World War II years brought new leadership to the College. John Sayles, President since 1939, fell ill in 1947 and hastened his planned retirement. Dean Milton Nelson stepped into the breech and served as Acting President for two years while the Regents searched for a replacement.

The new President who arrived in the summer of 1949 was thirty-eight-year-old Evan Revere Collins. Educated at Dartmouth and Harvard, he came to Albany after three years as dean of the College of Education at Ohio University. He believed in the mission of the College and was also an exceptionally attractive person: charming, patrician, combining an Ivy League air with personal warmth and accessibility.

Collins was a strong administrator, observing that every

The return of men to the College after the war caused a serious housing shortage. Below is Vanderzee Hall which was operated by the Alumni Association. Opposite, men play pool in Vanderzee Hall. It was luxuriously appointed but very crowded.

administrator was at heart autocratic, making the final decisions and "reserving the right to make his own mistakes." When Milton Nelson retired in 1952, Collins chose as dean Oscar Lanford, a chemistry professor from the Albany faculty who for nine years provided vigorous academic leadership and a strong sense of academic standards. At the same time, Collins picked Edgar Flinton to become Director of Graduate Studies to oversee a growth area in the 1950s. Mathematician Ellen Stokes, who had earlier succeeded Anna Pierce as Dean of Women, was joined by David Hartley as the school's first Dean of Men. The administrative structure in the 1950s remained modest, with decision-making centralized in Collins' office. The relatively small size of the College and the limited secretarial assistance encouraged informal administration and held down the paperwork.

Monthly general faculty meetings were most often informational, but there were sometimes lively debates over curriculum or student academic standing. Meetings just prior to graduation to pass on the qualification of graduates often produced vigorous discussion of particular cases, and faculty sometimes made last-minute accommodations to permit individuals to graduate. Three councils carried on much of the day-to-day business of the College. The Academic Council, made up of administrators and department heads, oversaw academic matters. The Student Personnel Council, composed of personnel staff with some faculty members, dealt with student life issues. The elected Faculty Council was concerned with a variety of faculty welfare issues.

Enrollment increased from the 1,555 full-time students when Collins arrived in 1949 to just over 4,000, including about 1,100 part-time students, in 1962. The College's budget rose four-fold in the same period. Still, such enrollment and budget increases were not so great as to require Albany to abandon the atmosphere and practices of a small college.

Rising enrollments accentuated long-standing space problems. The most immediate issue was student housing. The system of residence halls begun in the late 1930s was expanded in the 1950s through the State Dormitory Authority. Brubacher Hall was dedicated in 1951, and what is now Alumni Quadrangle was completed with Alden Hall in 1958 and Waterbury Hall in the following year. Yet the demand was such that the College several times used lotteries to allocate the precious rooms.

Residence halls were supplemented by smaller group houses; the number fluctuated, but the College directory in the Fall of 1960 listed seven such houses for women. In the same year eight sororities and three fraternities provided living quarters for their members. Others occupied rented rooms in the surrounding community. The housing problem was so persistent that in 1958 the College appointed as its

Evan Revere Collins, President from 1949 to 1969, led Albany for two decades as it became, first, a premier teacher education institution and later a research university. President Collins and his wife, Virginia, created a close sense of community among students and staff. (Bottom photo by Karsh, Ottawa.)

first full-time housing coordinator R. Keith Munsey, later Albany's first track coach.

Academic space was also inadequate. A sizable addition to Draper Hall, occupied in 1951, and an annex to Richardson Hall in 1956 only temporarily eased the shortage. Physical education facilities were hopelessly inadequate. The small gym in the basement of Page Hall with its undersized basketball court had to be shared with Milne students. The 72,000-volume Hawley Library was small and crowded, and library hours were a persistent issue of student concern. Throughout the decade the College eagerly sought new buildings but to no avail; the problems were to grow worse before they got better.

The faculty at the end of World War II was a good one; in 1945-46, thirty-three out of forty-six professors and assistant professors (there was no associate professorial rank) had the doctorate. While the College often looked to its own graduates when seeking new faculty, in 1947-48 only one out of four faculty in the two higher ranks had an Albany degree. Some had served the College for many years; thirteen faculty active in 1945-46 had been appointed before 1920. By 1960 the faculty had grown to 190 full-time people; over half held earned doctorates from thirty-eight different institutions.

Albany recruited able faculty members in the 1950s because it was an attractive place to teach in the depressed academic markets of the time. By the late 1940s, tenure was awarded after a relatively brief three years of probation. Albany salary schedules were competitive, roughly similar to those at California state colleges at the time. And faculty benefited from good health and retirement plans, the former relatively new in the 1950s.

On the other hand the rigidly structured ranks and salary grades made faculty advancement slow. Teaching effectiveness seems to have been the primary criterion for salary increases. Teaching loads were substantial. At the

Oscar Lanford

Whoever has the impression that chemists spend most of their time in labs should take a look at the life of Oscar Lanford. Starting at State Normal College as a chemistry professor, Lanford then became chair of the department, and was later tapped to be Dean of the College, a position he held from 1952 to 1961 during the school's transition to university status.

Lanford, who earned a Bachelor's degree from Virginia Military Institute and a Ph.D. in chemistry from Columbia, turned his exploratory nature toward new ideas for growth in education while he was dean. He coordinated the development of several doctoral programs and helped to create the Atmospheric Sciences Research Center atop Whiteface Mountain in the Adirondacks, where cloud sampling is still done today. He also served from 1942 to 1944 as consultant to the Manhattan Project, and was director of a research effort on nuclear energy sponsored by the Atomic Energy Commission.

A genial, soft-spoken Southerner who enjoyed gardening, riding and photography, Lanford went on to become president of the college of education at Fredonia. He held that post for a decade and then became vice chancellor for campus development at SUNY Central and manager of the State Construction Fund. His son William is now a professor in the Department of Physics at Albany. Lanford expressed his feelings about knowledge in the 1959 *Student Handbook*:

"Education is a wonderful thing, but it is well to remember that nothing which is really worth knowing can be taught."

end of the decade more than a quarter of the faculty taught fifteen or more hours per week, and almost half had four or five preparations. Under such circumstances faculty research was difficult, and the 1961 Middle States accreditation team noted that limited travel funds and state regulation of their use hampered faculty development. While the College prided itself on its faculty's research and publications, outside observers noted that many of the publications were "not research types of writing."

The mission of the College remained unchanged: preparing young people to become secondary school teachers. Most planning during the decade assumed that the mission would not change. Entering students were asked to commit themselves to becoming teachers; few publicly demurred. If newer faculty were oriented more toward their discipline than toward teacher education, all were encouraged to think of themselves as engaged in the common task of training teachers.

Programmatic changes in the 1950s reflected both traditional liberal arts commitments and changes in the teaching profession. Liberal arts work still made up 85 percent of an undergraduate's work. Psychology and philosophy were added to the offerings in the 1950s in response to student demand, not for professional reasons. Yet some of the liberal arts were shaped by professional goals. For instance, students majored in social studies rather than history or sociology because secondary school curricula were organized around the former. The professional sequence culminating in the student-teaching experience made up the remaining 15 percent of the coursework. Enrollment increases meant that the Milne School could not handle all of the student-teachers, and in 1947 some began going off campus for their teaching component. In 1950 the state began requiring thirty credits of graduate work beyond the baccalaureate degree for permanent certification of teachers, and Albany's graduate enrollments rose sharply. Most graduate students were employed teachers, seeking master's degrees on a part-time basis to win higher salaries and protect their certification.

At Albany during the 1950s most classes remained small, and students received a good deal of individual attention. There were occasional complaints about the quality of instruction. A *State College News* columnist argued in 1951 that Albany professors should be

Academic leaders for the decade included Edgar Flinton, Director of Graduate Studies; and Ellen Stokes, Dean of Women. (Dean Stokes photo from *Pedagogue*, 1944.)

At right, Governor Thomas E. Dewey visited the campus in 1950 to inspect the construction of Brubacher Hall, the first dormitory built with State funds, and the new Draper Annex fronting Washington Avenue. The original dormitories, including Pierce Hall, bottom photo, which had been built by alumni(ae) in the 1930s and 1940s, were not bought by the State until the 1960s. All new dormitories after 1950, beginning with Brubacher, were built by the State Dormitory Authority. Below, the beginning of Brubacher construction, which was completed in 1951. (From the scrapbook of Ruth Boynton, '50.)

"graded" as student-teachers in Milne were. But such public grumbling was rare. Course examinations were rigorous (they were reduced from three to two hours only in 1956), and grading practices suggested there were few easy "A's." Most graduates became successful teachers, but a 1963 national study of the undergraduate origins of doctoral students

also showed that Albany ranked Number 1 among institutions of its type and size between 1920 and 1962 in sending graduates on to successful doctoral study.

A profile of the student body in 1960 characterized it as largely lower middle class and ethnically heavily second and third generation Americans. Women made up between 53 percent and 62 percent of the undergraduates. Students came in roughly equal numbers from rural and urban backgrounds, and three-quarters were first generation college students. For many, becoming secondary school teachers was a means of moving up the social scale. Many came to Albany because of the low costs; most worked summers to earn a third of their annual living costs.

Admissions were relatively selective. The class of 620 that entered in the Fall of 1959 had been chosen from 2,160 active applicants. The vast majority came from the upper quarter of their graduating classes, and entering freshman classes included substantial numbers of students who had won various kinds of high school honors. Pre-admission testing began in 1954, and test scores of

Life in the dormitories: (top) women in the late 1940s in a room in Sayles Hall, (below) and men cleaning up the cafeteria at Sayles Hall. Originally built for men, Sayles was used as a women's dorm from 1941 through the Spring of 1951.

incoming students slowly rose. Faculty remember these student generations as earnest, hard-working, and somewhat conventional, typical of America in the 1950s.

The student culture of the 1950s showed strong similarity to that of the 1930s. While students and editors periodically complained about student apathy in the pages of the *State College News*, there was still a high rate of participation in student life. Student Association conducted its affairs through weekly assemblies, although by the late 1950s the growing size of the student body made that kind of "town meeting" democracy increasingly difficult. Annual elections of student officers were the highlights of the school year.

The entering class began its integration into the student body with a freshman camp, usually held at a nearby lake. Upperclass students served as student guides for the frosh, leading them through the various school-opening activities, culminating in the annual reception by the President. The process continued with Rivalry, a year-long series of competitions between freshmen and sophomores that included elaborate musical and/or dramatic productions.

Moving-Up Day was an elaborate affair by the late 1940s. Shortly before graduation each year the entire student body gathered in Page Hall. Student election results were announced and the winners were "tapped" by outgoing student officers. The frosh symbolically "moved up" to sophomore status by coming down from the balcony and taking seats on the main floor. Students exited by class and watched outgoing seniors plant ivy, and the day concluded with a variety of social activities.

Rising enrollments and

The drawing room in Pierce Hall circa 1947. Pierce's elegant formal areas were deliberately designed to elevate the sensibilities of the women students.

The dining room in Sayles Hall. Originally built for men, the design was meant to suggest an English country manor, a proper atmosphere to train young gentlemen.

increases in the student tax meant larger budgets for Student Association. A $23,700 expenditure budget in 1946-47 rose to nearly $60,000 in 1959-60. Periodic surpluses enabled Student Association in 1956 to buy 700 acres of Adirondack land that became Camp Dippikill. A Faculty-Student Association was organized in 1950 (although it would be long without student representation on its board) and used revenues from various service operations on campus to finance group housing.

Typically, publications and intercollegiate athletics each absorbed a quarter to a third of the Student Association budget. The weekly *State College News* and the College yearbook, the *Pedagogue*, continued to thrive. Intramural athletics for both men and women involved large numbers of students. The principal intercollegiate sport was basketball, and during the 1950s Richard "Doc" Sauers began coaching his teams to a series of non-losing seasons, still unbroken in 1994. Both wrestling and baseball became intercollegiate sports at Albany during the decade, but another of the periodic attempts to introduce intercollegiate football in 1951-52 fell victim to inadequate finances and facilities.

Publications and athletics took the majority of student funds, but enough remained to support an impressive array of cultural organizations and activities. The local academic honorary, Signum Laudis, was highly visible. Faculty members organized a Philosophy Club that met regularly in the friendly environs of the Boulevard Cafeteria; its success played a role in the creation of a philosophy department in 1952. Touring lecturers such as Andre Siegfried or performing artists such as the Bach Aria Group and Margaret Webster's Shakespeare group stopped at the Albany campus regularly. The music department and Music Council put on productions of Gilbert & Sullivan operettas in the early 1950s. Agnes Futterer's Advanced Dramatics class continued to present high quality performances. Student Harold Gould, '47, went from playing Sheridan Whiteside in *The Man Who Came to Dinner* at Albany to a distinguished acting career in stage, screen and television. English faculty member Paul Bruce Pettit established a highly successful arena-style summer theater in the Page Hall gym in the early 1950s.

Traditional social activities continued to be an important part of undergraduate life. The *State College News* during 1956 reported on twenty dances, six class banquets, twenty-three College-sponsored social events, six trips, thirty-seven sorority-sponsored events, sixteen fraternity-sponsored events, seven films, and eleven social events sponsored by religious groups. Major occasions included State Fair, the Junior Class weekend, Moving-Up Day, Campus Chest, and Rivalry.

Student dress of the 1950s became more informal. A 1958 survey of attire preferences showed that only eight percent of the men wore suits, 80 percent were without sports coats, and 67 percent preferred khaki slacks. The women were a bit more conservative; although they preferred skirts to dresses by a four-to-one margin, half said that among dresses they preferred the full-skirted variety and 80 percent favored high necklines in any event. No one mentioned slacks or shorts.

Student culture continued to value female beauty and grace. The College community glowed with pride when Miriam Sanderson, a junior English major, became Miss New York State in 1958, but two years later, students also selected a campus "king," voting as they contributed to the annual fund-raising venture, State Fair.

Students were attracted to fraternities and sororities largely because of the social life they

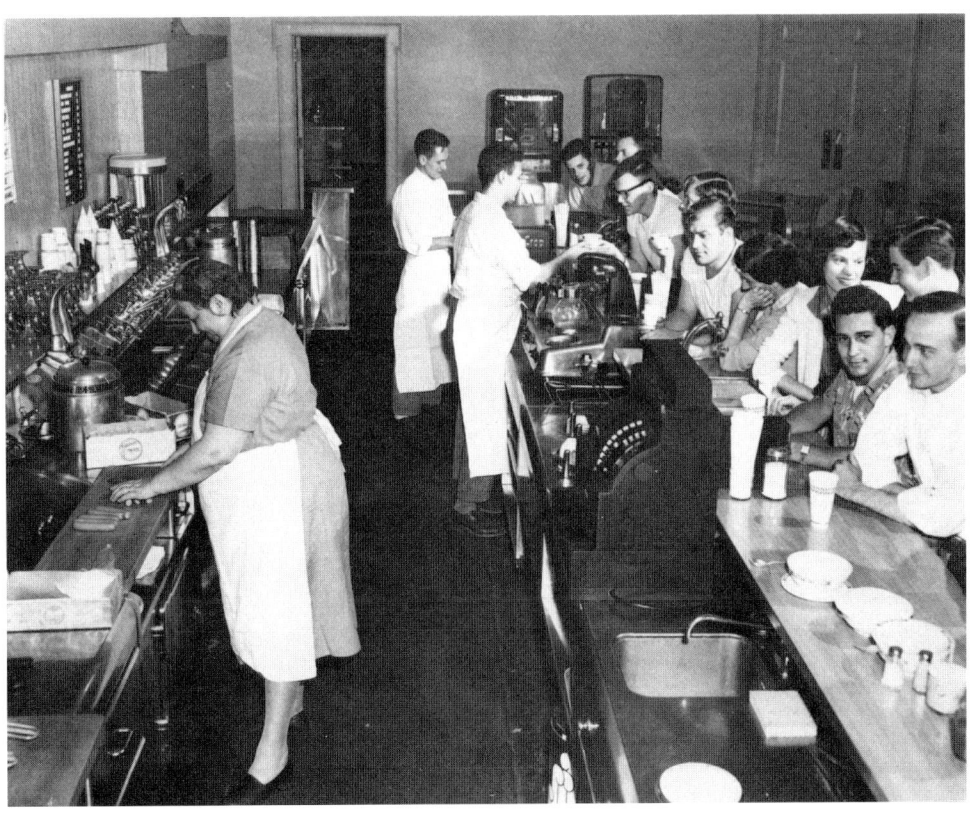

A favorite activity in the 1950s and early 1960s was a visit to the Brubacher Snack Bar.

The faculty of the 1950s: (top) Ralph Tibbets, MA, '42, (education); (bottom) Vivian Hopkins (English and comparative literature); (opposite page, top) Paul Pettit (English and comparative literature); (opposite page, bottom) Josiah Phinney (economics).

offered. Some, notably the Edward Eldred Potter Club, were local, but many in the late 1940s had national affiliations. The Greeks came under fire during this period. A survey of the attitudes of freshman women in 1945 showed that nearly two-thirds did not want to join a sorority because of their "lack of democracy." One sorority, Beta Zeta, quickly amended its constitution to remove religious qualifications for membership. Seven years later the sixty-one members of the local chapter of Kappa Delta Rho resigned from the fraternity because of racial and religious discrimination in the national organization and then promptly reorganized as a local fraternity, Alpha Pi Alpha.

A decisive resolution of the issue came in 1953 when the State University of New York (SUNY) Board of Trustees ruled that no organizations on SUNY campuses could bar students because of race, creed, color, religion, national origin or other artificial criteria, and additionally barred fraternities or sororities with national affiliation from SUNY campuses. The ban held despite legal challenges. Although national fraternities and sororities disappeared, local groups continued to flourish.

Albany students often seemed politically conservative on state and national issues. Republican candidates for New York governor or U.S. President won every College mock election conducted during the 1950s. At times, students seemed politically oblivious, as illustrated by an incident during the Presidential election campaign of 1952. In October of that year, out-going President Harry Truman stumped upstate New York in support of Democrat Adlai Stevenson. At Truman's Albany rally, George Warnock, son of an RPI math professor and a student at Albany, appeared wearing an Eisenhower-Nixon button and carrying an "I Like Ike" banner. He was quickly arrested by Albany police on a charge of disorderly conduct. Warnock's hearing was twice postponed, and the case never came to trial; Warnock himself died tragically a year later in a Troy car accident. The revealing part of the incident was that there was nary a mention of the student or his arrest in the *State College News*.

Yet students often took relatively liberal positions on issues concerning student life. One observer wrote that "State has gone democratic (small 'd') with a vengeance in 1945. Since the beginning of the year all assembly programs have contained at least one motion for change of an undemocratic rule or group or organization." Myskania, because of its self-perpetuating character, became one of the targets. On March 25, 1946, Myskania dissolved itself and burned its constitution and records; however, some of the members of the dissolved body joined with other student leaders to recreate Myskania, with members chosen more democratically, and it continued to thrive throughout the 1950s.

Students also felt strongly about academic freedom. In 1946 a student came to the defense of sociology professor Ted Standing when Standing was charged with exposing students to "crass materialism" and "sniping at religious beliefs." Albany's would-be teachers were also concerned about the 1949 Feinberg law which sought to eliminate alleged "subversive" teachers from New York schools.

By World War II, students were showing concern for issues of discrimination. In 1944 the College participated in a nationally funded study of intergroup relations. One feature of the study was a student-run Conference in November 1944, titled "Inter-Group Relations," attended by students from various colleges and featuring a talk by Eleanor Roosevelt. In the following year, students organized the Inter-Group Council on campus "to offer opportunities for culture, contact and understanding among members of every race and nationality in the community." These anti-discriminatory attitudes showed up in other areas of campus life as well. In 1946 the College community watched an Advanced Dramatics class performance of five scenes from *Romeo and Juliet* with a white Romeo (Arthur Collins, '48) and an African-American Juliet (Mary Cheatum '49). The overwhelmingly white student body twice elected African-Americans as president of Student Association during these years—John Jennings, '49, in 1948-49 and Clyde Payne, '57, in 1956-57.

In 1962 the College received national recognition in a lengthy article in the *Saturday Review*. Author David Boroff summed up his conclusions by observing that "Albany State has a distinguished history. As liberal arts college go, it is a good one. As teachers' colleges go, it is superb." The accolades were well-deserved. But they arrived just as the institution was facing its greatest challenge: transforming a "superb" teachers' college into a public research university. The process was getting under way at the very time Boroff summed up the achievements of the College for Teachers.

Naoshi Koriyama, '54, returned to Japan where he became a professor of English at Toyo University. He is a noted poet in his homeland, writing predominantly in English. His works have been published in the United States, Canada, and Australia and translated into Italian. In his books of poetry, he acknowledged Vivian Hopkins' influence in suggesting that he write in English. He was one of the first international students at Albany since the 19th Century. (*Alumni Quarterly*, January 1958.)

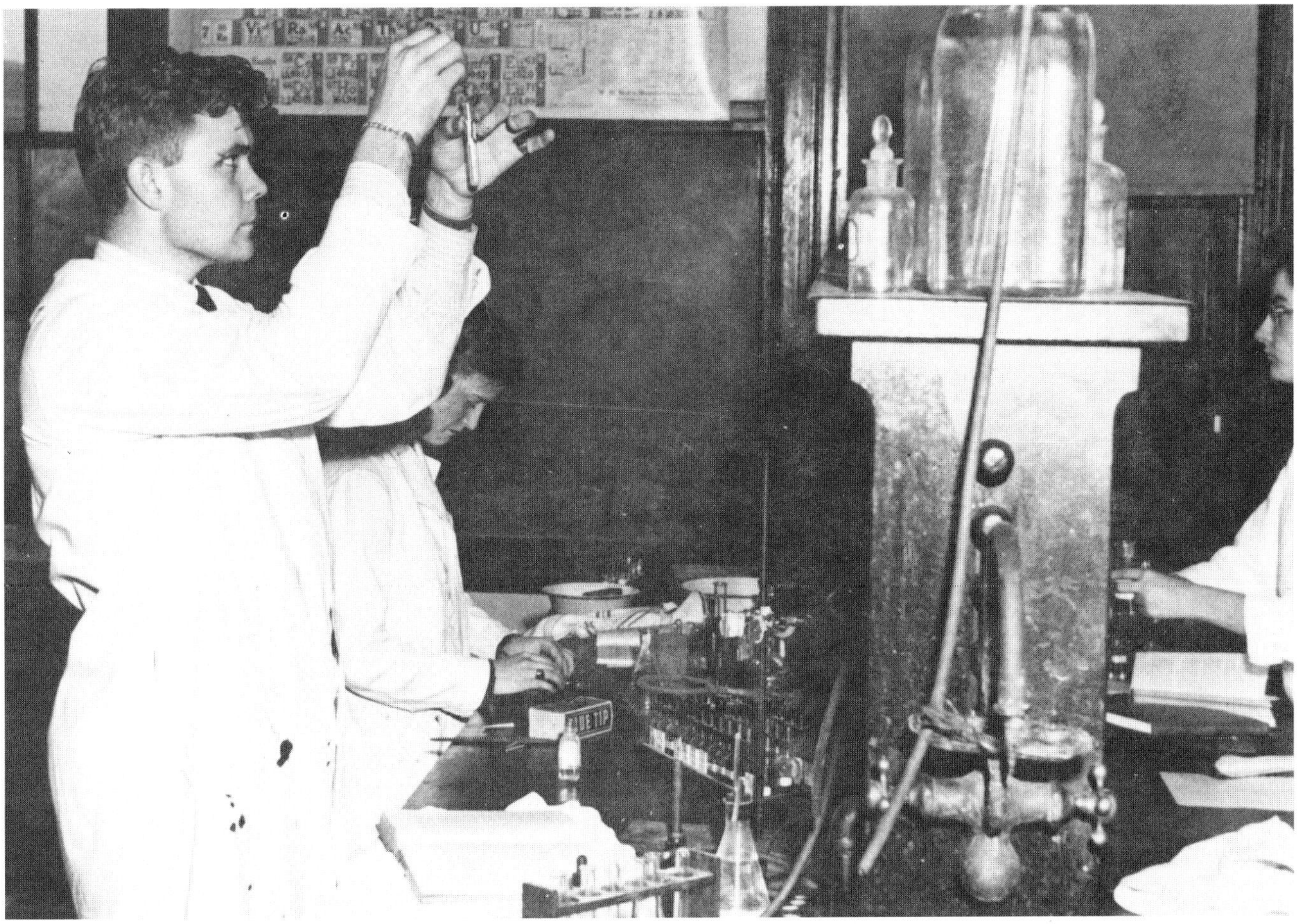

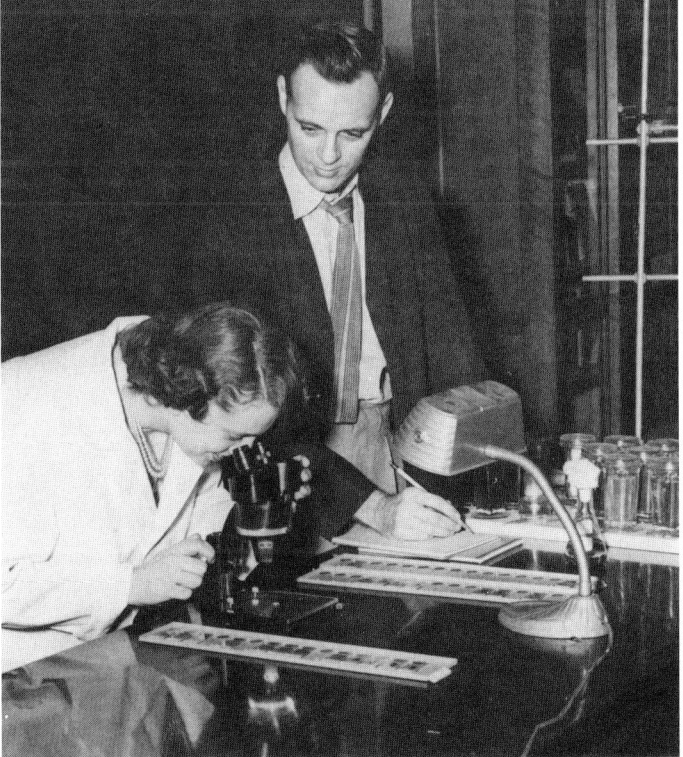

The academic program was rigorous and Albany was the top college in the nation among institutions of its type and size in sending graduates on to obtain doctoral degrees from 1920 to 1962. Here are biology and chemistry laboratories from the late '40s to early '50s.

"Freshman Camp" circa 1950, below, where upperclass students served as guides for new students, usually at a nearby lake or in the Helderbergs. "Rivalry," at right, begun in the 1920s by Myskania to build school spirit, lasted through the mid '60s. Initially continued all year between the freshman and sophomore classes, it later took place during the first weeks of school.

108

Intramural sports for both men and women thrived in the 1950s. Women's sports were supervised by the Women's Athletic Association. Pictured are a 1946 women's gym class in the Page Gym and a 1948 softball game.

The Boulevard Cafe was the meeting place of the Philosophy Club, whose success, in part, led to the creation of a philosophy department in 1952. (*Pedagogue*, 1940)

Social activities, such as dances, continued to be an important part of undergraduate life in the 1950s. Pictured is a December 1947 "Christmas Formal" sponsored by the Inter-Sorority and Inter-Fraternity Councils.

Agnes Futterer continued to teach dramatics and stage productions in the 1950s. Above she fences with student Arthur Lennig, '55, who later became a faculty member in the Art Department. At left, her most famous student, Harold Gould, '47, who went on to a successful stage and television career.

Founded in the early 1940s, Hillel offered Jewish students a forum for cultural programs. This 1948 photo is of Marvin Wayne, '49, and Rabbi Moseson, the group's advisor.

Dorothy De Cicco, '52 (Gamma Kappa Phi), Joan Reilly, '53 (Chi Sigma Theta), John Stevenson, '51 (Sigma Lambda) and David Wetherby, '51 (Potter Club), follow student tradition and "meet at Minnie" in Draper Hall.

(Opposite) Queen Audrey Koch, '50, and her court in 1949. The tradition of selecting a campus queen—and occasionally a king—continued through the 1970s.

113

From the *Alumni Quarterly*, July 1956: "One of the most cherished traditions at Albany is the Torchlight Ceremony. It originated in 1930 when the torch was first passed to Louis Wolner (left), president of the graduating class. Leonard E. Friedlander, '39 (center), president of the Alumni Association, passed the torch this year to Sigmund Smith (right), president of the Class of 1956."

John Jennings, '49 (center), the first African-American student elected president of the Student Association (1948-49), presents Donald Ely, '51, leader of the victorious Green Gremlins, with the Campus Day Cup as Harold "Sparky" Vaughn, '50, leader of the Yellow Jackets, looks on.

(Left) Joseph Persico, '52, became a speech writer for Nelson Rockefeller and published several books including a biography of Edward R. Murrow and a study of controversial FBI Director William Casey.

(Above) Clarence Rappleyea, '57, became a successful lawyer and politician, serving as Republican Minority Leader of the New York State Assembly.

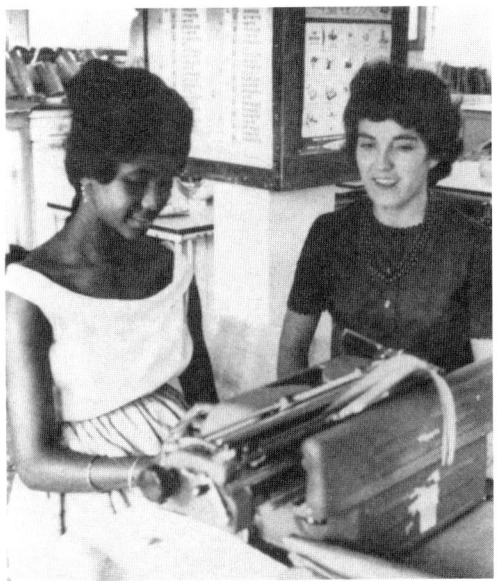

(Left) Betty Duda, '59, was one of many Albany graduates to become a Peace Corps volunteer. She taught secretarial skills in Jamaica, and prior to joining the Peace Corps taught business subjects in Morrisville and Hamilton, New York.

(Left) Harvey Milk, '51, was a student on the G.I. Bill and later became a gay rights activist and a city supervisor in San Francisco until his assassination in 1978. (*Pedagogue*)

Edith O. Wallace

One of the University's cornerstone buildings on the Uptown Campus is the Edith O. Wallace Humanities Building, named after the first chairperson to administer the Division of Humanities, a woman whose dedication to the students of the College and University made an indelible mark both in and outside the classroom.

A member of the University faculty for forty-seven years, Edith Wallace, '17, was first appointed in 1918. In 1928 she was made chair of the Department of Ancient Languages, and three years later assistant professor of Latin, eventually rising to the rank of full professor. Wallace also created a course in humanities, that later developed into a Department of Comparative and World Literature.

Outside of the classroom, Wallace was a charter member of both Myskania and the Student Council. She served as chair of the curriculum committee and both the college and federal loan program committees. A 1913 graduate of the Milne School, she was a president of the Alumni Association. When she had time left over from her University duties, she relaxed with photography and weaving.

Before devoting herself to the education of thousands of University students, Wallace had completed her own education with an M.A. in English literature and a Ph.D. in Greek and Latin literature from Columbia University.

David Boroff's positive *Saturday Review* article brought national prominence to the College just as it was beginning its transition to a University.

(Opposite) Between classes, the crowded portico connecting Hawley and Draper circa 1955.

CHAPTER VI
Creating a University in the 1960s

Between 1959 and 1962, Albany changed its name three times. In the Fall of 1959 it became the New York State University College of Education at Albany. Two years later the "of Education" was dropped, and in the Fall of 1962 the institution became the State University of New York at Albany. The final name symbolized a major change in mission: an institution which for more than a century had trained teachers was now commissioned to become a university.

Why this new direction? The answer is summed up in two words: "demographics" and "Rockefeller." Educational planners realized in the mid 1950s that the "baby boomers" would generate very strong demands for higher education in the 1960s. A SUNY Trustees' study released in 1956 showed that even assuming a 40 percent increase in the capacity of private institutions, SUNY would have to expand by 186 percent to meet the demand for higher education. Subsequent events showed that the study underestimated the total demand and overestimated private expansion.

(Opposite) Gov. Nelson A. Rockefeller throws a shovelful of dirt on the Albany Country Club's 16th fairway to mark the ground-breaking for the University at Albany's new campus in 1962. Left to right: Lt. Gov. Malcolm Wilson; Governor Rockefeller; SUNY President Thomas Hamilton and President Collins. (Photo by *Times Union* staff photographer Wilder.)

One of the earliest student protests at the State Capitol occurred over the imposition of tuition in 1962 when the college became a university.

It was Gov. Nelson A. Rockefeller who provided the drive and political skills to transform SUNY and with it the Albany College. The State University of New York had been established in 1948 in response to the post-World War II surge of college enrollments created by returning veterans. Governed by its own board of trustees, SUNY was initially composed of the state's teachers' colleges (including Albany) and grew modestly in the 1950s, its budget and enrollment rising about 50 percent. SUNY took over two medical schools, offered liberal arts programs at Harpur College in Binghamton, and encouraged the development of eleven community colleges during the decade.

Why was SUNY's development so slow during the 1950s? Part of the problem was politics. Governors Dewey and Harriman showed little interest in the system. The private institutions continued to protect their educational turf, and relations between Regents and Trustees were at best wary. Chancellor Samuel Gould in the early 1960s realized the extent to which SUNY had been a creature of New York State politics; the effect, he said, was "a little like looking into the eyes of a snake."

By the late 1950s, SUNY seemed without energy and direction. In 1957 a construction bond issue for SUNY was approved by the voters, but trustees and administrators seemed uncertain just what to do with the money. In the same year SUNY President William Carlson persuaded Theodore Blegen, a distinguished historian and dean of the graduate school at the University of Minnesota, to survey the system's research efforts. Blegen opened his report by asserting that the "State University is an academic animal without a head." He argued that SUNY needed a central campus devoted to a full range of academic instruction and research through the doctorate. The Trustees, who had known little about the study, quickly rebuffed the report and reiterated their established policy of decentralization. The political fiasco cost Carlson his job.

It took the political drive and skills of Governor Rockefeller to work the revolution within SUNY that occurred in the early 1960s. Rockefeller first appointed a three-man commission headed by Henry Heald, president of the Ford Foundation. The Commission confirmed the alarming numbers of students who would be seeking higher education and proposed to meet the need with a politically astute program of expanding public higher education while offering state aid to private institutions.

SUNY's 1960 Master Plan proposed expanding the community colleges, gradually converting the teacher-training institutions into liberal arts colleges, and creating graduate centers at four locations (in accord with the principle of decentralization). Such expansion required major construction. To avoid politically complex and uncertain bond issues, Rockefeller turned to the notion of a public benefit corporation to finance construction. The State University Construction Fund, authorized in 1962, borrowed money to be repaid through tuition income. The Construction Fund concentrated on academic buildings; the State Dormitory Authority took care of campus residential facilities. It was a brilliant stroke even if it did raise the politically prickly issue of tuition. Rockefeller placated the private institutions with a Scholar Incentive Program, regulated in such a way that initially all of the money went to students paying substantial tuition at private institutions.

"Rivalry" in 1962. Both Rivalry and Moving-Up Day, traditions of long-standing, disappeared between 1963 and 1966. (Alumni Memorabilia Collection.)

Albany was more acted upon than actor in this unfolding political and educational drama. At the dedication of the campus in 1909, Commissioner of Education Draper noted that Albany "is to be a pedagogical college. It is to give liberal training to men and women who will be teachers. It is not intended that it shall grow into a state university." Whatever the thoughts of individual faculty members or students, the College never wavered from that central charge.

Yet in many ways in the 1950s the College longed to grow out of its existing niche. Collins regularly pushed for the idea of the College preparing *college* teachers (which would have required doctoral work) as well as *high school* teachers, and the College worked on a proposal for the Ed.D. throughout the decade. Nor was the College unaware of the approaching demographic crisis. A 1956 meeting of Capital District institutions revealed that area private colleges planned to increase enrollments between 1955 and 1970 by about 40 percent; yet statewide enrollments between those years were expected to increase 142 percent. The implications for Albany were clear: it would surely grow. Yet projected enrollments were far below what they were to become in the 1960s, in part because the College never envisioned itself as a multi-purpose university center, and in part because even the modest expansion envisioned in the late 1950s was blocked by long-standing space problems.

Alumni Day, 1962, included a donation from the Quarter Century Club of a silver service by Henrietta Brett, '15, Jacob Epstein, '15, and Florence Linindoll Hilton, '31; and the presentation of the Agnes Futterer Award to Robert Steinhauer, '62, by Dr. Arthur Collins, '48.

The change in Albany's mission took place between 1960 and 1963. The first Ed.D. program was approved in 1960. Two years later the name change to State University of New York at Albany was accompanied by non-teaching baccalaureate programs, reorganization of the school, and plans for Ph.D. programs. Rockefeller put the final imprimatur on the change in his budget message of 1963 when he noted that "the long established academic tradition of the college [at Albany], its fine faculty, the breadth of its curriculum, its experience in graduate programs, and its strategic location in the capital district will make it possible for the college to become a source of strength in graduate education and research."

Albany was expected to become a "university center." But what kind? In October of 1965 sociologist David Riesman visited the campus to give a lecture. "What is your model?" he asked of everyone he met. "What kind of a university will you become?" He received no clear responses. In a very real sense, Albany in the

An aerial view of the Albany Country Club circa 1960. When the move to acquire the land for the University was stalled, Governor Rockefeller threatened to move the entire institution out of the city. (Photo courtesy of the Albany Country Club.)

1960s was a university in search of an identity, and an important part of that identity was to be a new campus, already under construction as Riesman asked his question.

Construction at the College between 1945 and 1962 made only a dent in long-standing space problems, and the space available on the existing campus permitted no further expansion. Several nearby possibilities were explored in the mid 1950s: the St. Mary's Park area near the residence halls, land between the academic buildings and residence halls, the old Albany High School west of Milne and the Annex east of Hawley, and finally about ten acres south of Western Avenue in the Thurlow Terrace area. The first three sites were rejected on grounds of cost. Site plans and tentative building designs were drawn up for the area across Western Avenue, but ultimately that plan too was abandoned; it would cost $1.7 million, displace an estimated eighty-four families, and remove $670,000 from the property tax rolls. Most important, it would provide space only for a campus serving 3,200 students, and by then expected enrollments at the College were moving above that figure.

The alternative was to search for a site a reasonable distance from the $7 million Alumni Quadrangle. Under the Harriman regime it appeared that 150 acres would be available on the state office campus, but the Rockefeller administration decided after a space study that it would need all that land for state offices. Hence the state turned to the adjacent Albany Country Club.

The proposal to appropriate the Albany Country Club for a new campus for the College generated a heated public controversy. Members treasured their old and handsome club and strongly resisted the move. Mayor Erastus Corning, concerned about the state abandonment of downtown Albany, was clearly opposed, although his concern was eased two years later with the proposal for a major state office plaza south of the Capitol. The state argued that if the College was to expand beyond 3,200 students, it needed much more space within distance of the existing residence halls. Which, it asked, should the state take, a country club or a large number of existing homes?

The country club stalled until September of 1960, when Rockefeller issued an ultimatum: either the club would be sold to the state or the College would be moved lock, stock, and barrel out of the city. A local newspaper headed its editorial, "L'Etat—C'Est Nelson." But there was simply no other acceptable location within the city. In January of 1961 the state filed appropriation papers. The issue remained in the courts for a couple of years before the final price was settled on; subsequent purchases enlarged the site from the 292 acres acquired from the country club to about 360 acres.

Albany Mayor Erastus Corning and Governor Rockefeller look over the model of the planned campus.

Building plans moved ahead quickly. Harrison and Abramovitz, a prominent New York architectural firm which had designed Rockefeller Center, by June of 1961 completed a comprehensive site plan for the country club property. Then a sudden change occurred: Wallace Harrison withdrew from the SUNY Albany project after taking on another state responsibility. The new architect was Edward Durrell Stone. At the time of his selection, Stone was at the peak of his power and influence and had just completed a church

Scenes from the construction: (above, left) aerial view shows completed Dutch Quad circa 1965; (left) the Main Fountain area and lecture centers under construction, 1966; (above) a section of precast concrete is hoisted onto the Education Building, 1965. (Photos of fountain and Education Building by E. M. Weil.)

in Schenectady in his mature architectural style. Stone worked quickly, and by June of 1962 Rockefeller was able to unveil in the rotunda of Albany's Capitol a model of the design for the new campus.

The plans were both striking and highly formal. Stone proposed to

Walter Tisdale, a retired U.S. Army Engineer, served as the University's liaison with the architect and successfully influenced the final design of the campus in several important ways, including location of buildings.

level the country club property. He clustered the academic buildings together, integrated by a platform (the famous academic "podium"). It was, he told reporters, foolish to scatter buildings around a site and thereby increase the need for roads and utilities on the campus. At each corner of the academic complex, Stone designed a three-story dormitory quadrangle with a high-rise building in the center. In order to create a calm, cloistered atmosphere for the University, the 10,000-student campus was to be free from automobiles, which were confined to parking areas on the perimeter of the campus. Construction used technologically advanced pre-cast concrete segments whose repetitive patterns produced some striking formal effects.

The College had almost nothing to say about the choice of architect or the basic site and architectural plans. Still, within limits, Collins and his assistant, Col. Walter Tisdale, a retired Army engineer, were regularly consulted and tried to influence things. There were some victories, some defeats. A plea to preserve the old clubhouse and swimming pool for University use fell on deaf ears. But the architect accepted some suggestions for changing the locations of certain buildings on the academic podium.

The most important campus input to the design was the allocation of academic space. Stone had provided an "envelope" containing enough space for a 10,000-student university, but it was largely up to the people at the College to allocate that space. It was not an easy job. As Collins later observed, the planning process "involved, literally scheduling an imaginary student body for an imaginary program for a plant that hadn't been developed." For example, the College had to plan space for an anthropology department when there was not yet a single anthropologist on the faculty.

Rockefeller broke ground for the new campus on August 24, 1962. Site preparation took place in the Summer of 1963. By October of that year the service buildings were half up and construction on Dutch Quad residence halls was beginning. Work on the academic complex began the following summer. Some of the statistics are mind-numbing. The contract for the first half of the academic complex was purportedly the largest single academic construction contract ever let. It was estimated that the construction used over 270,000 cubic yards of concrete and fifty miles of copper tubing. Someone reported that if the 500 architectural drawings were put side to side they would reach for a half mile.

Speed was important. Enrollments were rising fast, and the new university desperately needed additional academic space and student housing. Construction delays were inevitable, however. Earth-moving activities in the Summer of 1963 generated irritating sandstorms that seemed appropriate accompaniments to the screening of *Lawrence of Arabia* at the nearby Hellman Theater; the project manager observed that "It is the only place where I ever saw a snowstorm and a dust storm at the same time." Fires, explosions, and the collapse of cranes set back schedules. Both work stoppages and shortages of key crafts slowed the pace of construction.

Meanwhile the University "made do" with a variety of rented space near the Downtown Campus: former churches, warehouses, synagogues, stores, and the U.S. Navy Reserve Training Center were all temporarily converted to academic facilities. One new sociologist was startled to find that his office was located above a shop selling baby clothes; another faculty member, housed in a former auto supply store, reported that people periodically wandered in off the street in search of car mufflers. Students found living quarters in dorms, private housing, and even hotels and motels; often the only thing they had in common was crowding.

The great move began in October of 1964, when students, temporarily located in motels, moved into the first units of Dutch Quad. By February of 1965, 1,100 students were housed on the new campus and were shuttled by bus back to the Downtown Campus for classes. In the Fall of 1966 the first part of the academic podium was occupied; most classes were now held there, and the buses began carrying students and faculty housed near the Downtown Campus to the new facilities. Buildings were occupied as they were completed. The administration moved up in the Fall of 1967, and by early 1969 only the Mohawk Tower and a few halls in the Lecture Center area were uncompleted.

In a 1972 interview, Stone expressed great satisfaction with the results. He defended the original design and took pride in the facts that there had been no major plan changes and that the campus had been built within the budget and standards established by the state.

Not all were so satisfied. Stone's attempt to keep the automobile off

The laying of the cornerstone on Dutch Quad in 1964 included the burial of a time capsule by students.

(Top) The final graduation at the Downtown Campus in 1965.

(Bottom) The 1965 Homecoming Queen Harriet Tucker.

the campus failed because Americans seemed unwilling to walk more than fifty feet if they could drive; campus parking bedeviled Albany as it has every other American university campus. The integrated academic complex purported to shelter its users from upstate New York weather, but faculty and students, shivering as they traversed the wind-swept podium, often retreated to the service tunnel that connected the academic buildings. Classroom acoustics were poor. It was probably a mistake to put the Performing Arts Center and the library in the center of the complex; access for outsiders attending performances at the PAC was not easy, and the location of the library meant that there was no simple way to expand it when it reached its capacity in the mid 1980s.

Some of the errors could not have been foreseen. It was impossible for the faculty in 1961-62 to forecast accurately the space needs of departments and programs not yet in existence. Fortunately the original designs involved few interior load-bearing walls, facilitating rearrangements of interior space. Nor could anyone foresee the skyrocketing energy costs of the 1970s that showed how energy-inefficient the construction was.

Perhaps, most crucially, while Stone believed that his integrated design would facilitate the development of a sense of community, the opposite seems to have been true. The massiveness of the buildings, the formal design with its lack of warm colors and textures, and the absence of natural small-group informal gathering places on campus all contributed to a sense of individual isolation.

Yet the new campus remained an immense achievement. The job was completed quickly, the quality of workmanship was high, and costs were reasonable. The formal design and the massive buildings made the campus above all impressive. The contrast between red carpets and white walls, the play of the fountains, and the spectacular exterior lighting, all produced eye-catching effects. The new campus helped provide the University with an identity. It gave both faculty and students a sense of what the old New York State College for Teachers was becoming and helped define the institution that rose on the former country club golf links.

The academic complex designed for 10,000 students was stuffed a mere five years after the University began occupying it. Between the Fall of 1962 and the Fall of 1970, enrollments rose from about 4,000 to over 13,200. Undergraduates made up between 65 percent and 70 percent of the student body. Financial resources to support this astounding rate of growth were there too. The $3.5 million operating budget of 1962-63 multiplied ten times by 1970-71. Budget increases were not automatic; even in the flush years of the 1960s there were periodic threats to reduce the following year's budget. Proposals for reductions in University funding or tuition increases generated student (and sometimes faculty) protests in the 1960s.

Such extraordinarily rapid growth posed major leadership problems for the University. In the 1950s, Collins had practiced centralized decision-making and had depended on a strongly personalized leadership style. He tried to maintain those practices into the 1960s. The annual presidential reception for the entire freshman class continued, and he retained his weekly open meetings with students and faculty in the Campus Center. One of the public relations staff observed that "You can tell when there's trouble brewing by the number of coats piled up outside the door. The more coats, the bigger the problem."

Yet Collins was hardly so naive as to believe that the organizational methods he had used in the 1950s would serve for the University of the late 1960s. Beginning in 1962 the administrative structure of a conventional public university began to appear. At its heart was a College of Arts and Sciences (1962) surrounded by a cluster of professional schools: Education (1962), Library Science (1962), Business (1962), Social Welfare (1963), Criminal Justice (1963), the Graduate School of Public Affairs (1966), and Nursing (1968). University College (1964) dealt with undergraduates in their first two years. Four vice-presidencies were established: Academic Affairs and Student Affairs in 1965, Business and Research the following year.

Not all of this was accomplished without contention. Within Arts and Sciences there was a long debate about splitting the College. The

A new mascot for Albany athletics: from "Pierre the Ped-guin" to a "Great Dane," suggested by Kathy Earle, '67. She won the Mascot Nickname contest in 1965 with her suggestion of the Dane, which she argued had "size, strength, character, courage, speed and stamina." The Dane is also "amiable and dependable." (Pierre donated by Mary Young Osielski, '64; Dane banner gift of University Bookstore.)

An old tradition on a new campus: Torch Night in 1966. (Opposite) Governor Rockefeller addresses the first graduation on the new campus in 1966.

reason was simple: department chairs were eager to gain direct access to all-important new resources, usually controlled by the Vice President for Academic Affairs; they viewed the College structure as a wasteful barrier between them and the Vice President and felt disadvantaged relative to the professional school deans in the competition for funding.

Albany's absorption of the Graduate School of Public Affairs generated some problems as well. The GSPA had originally been developed by Syracuse and New York Universities to offer work in public administration to state employees in the Capital District. While it became part of the State University in 1962 and was attached to Albany in 1966, it cherished both its autonomy and its clusters of faculty in public administration, political science, and economics. Ultimately, its economists moved to the economics department in Arts and Sciences, but political scientists remained with the GSPA.

New academic structures had to be created as well. A graduate faculty and an elected Graduate Council appeared in 1961. By 1965 it became apparent that the faculty had grown too large to fulfill its responsibilities through general faculty meetings. Hence a committee was formed, by-laws were written, elections were held, and in the Fall of 1966 a newly created Faculty Senate with an elaborate array of councils overseeing almost every aspect of University life took over.

Long-time members of the University staff exercised leadership roles during these critical years. Only seven out of thirty-seven administrative officers in 1965-66 had arrived on campus after 1962. But by February of 1970 only twenty-one of the fifty-eight people occupying administrative positions had come to Albany when it was a college.

The very rapid growth and rising pressures of the 1960s made administrators feel like bronco-busters: they used all of their time and energy staying on top of things and had remarkably little control over what happened! There were endless battles over resource allocation, it was often difficult to get decisions made, and routine paper flows were often dammed. Every University leader of those years can recount horror stories of administrative confusion. There is a story that at least one faculty member received tenure because the appropriate authorities simply overlooked the need for a tenure decision. Yet no major scandals emerged, and the job of building a university got done.

In the Spring of 1969, as Collins approached his retirement, he appointed an internal Committee on the Organization of the University. The Committee laid out some principles to guide Albany into the 1970s. It was a useful moment of stock-taking, and the Committee's principles were sound, even if their assumptions of future growth were to prove false. Effective reorganization of the institution was left to another generation.

A faculty of around 115 in the early 1950s doubled to 244 by 1962-63 and then trebled to 746 by 1970. Recruiting a faculty of such a size would have been a huge task at any time, but recruitment in the 1960s was complicated by some special circumstances. Competition for qualified faculty was fierce. Every college and university in the nation was seeking faculty to meet the flood of students, and Albany was not the only former teacher-training institution trying to become a university. The academic marketplace was ill-organized in the early 1960s, and success or failure often depended on personal contacts. Albany sensibly required that every candidate be interviewed before being offered an appointment, but the University had no funds to bring people in for such interviews. Some candidates paid their own way to Albany, while others were interviewed by department chairs in airports or at professional meetings. In the early 1960s, Collins let it be known that he thought some chairs were afraid to recruit faculty more able than they were. One chairman responded flippantly that he just hadn't been able to find anyone smarter than himself!

Recruitment was helped by rising faculty salaries. In the early 1960s, Albany did not fare well compared with other public doctoral-granting universities. In 1963-64 Albany got mediocre "C" ratings in the annual AAUP faculty compensation studies. But that changed. The old system of ranks and salary grades which governed promotions and salary increases slowly broke down, and by 1969-70 Albany achieved an "A" or "AA" rating for its faculty compensation.

Albany clearly had become competitive, and it showed in the credentials of the faculty. The proportion holding the doctorate rose from roughly half in the early 1960s to more than two-thirds in 1970. The University recruited both young people and senior professors, although the most effective strategy was fiercely debated. Turnover was relatively low. In 1968-69 only 11 percent of the full-time faculty had to be replaced for all reasons: death, retirement, movement elsewhere, and failure to reappoint. But the faculty had grown so rapidly that by 1970-71, 61 percent of the full-time faculty had been on campus less than five years, and 38 percent had arrived since 1968. From 1966 to 1970, between 75 and 104 new faculty arrived on campus each fall.

Faculty recruited before 1962 were in an uncomfortable position. As Collins observed in a 1984 oral history interview, "the senior members of the faculty who had been selected and who developed according to one pattern, now were no longer the wise old heads." They lost their leadership positions and watched new faculty with research reputations get the promotions. "At the same time," Collins noted, "we were asking these old timers to hold things together and to do this planning for the future." "It was," he added, "an agonizing time for a lot of people . . . change was being forced on them faster than they could accommodate to it, or should be asked to."

He cited Ralph Beaver as an example of this process. Beaver had been a long-time chair of the mathematics department and leader of the College for Teachers faculty. Like most of those faculty, he was a superior teacher who had done no publishable research. Collins was deeply grateful when Beaver offered to step aside as chair, permitting the President to recruit seventeen people in two years and create a new mathematics department oriented toward graduate instruction and research.

Almost two-thirds of the faculty in place in 1961 were still there a decade later. Their fortunes varied: some retired, some made the transition and played productive roles in the new university, and others lingered on, feeling under-appreciated.

Students moved into the new campus beginning in 1964 with Dutch Quad, the first residence hall completed. Most classes were held uptown by 1966. (Opposite) Fraternities and sororities continued to be an active part of campus life throughout the '60s as this Sigma Tau Beta rush in 1968 illustrates. (Photo by Steve Lobel, '70.)

The hallmark of a university is graduate study through the doctorate, and the College had begun developing plans for an Ed.D. in Educational Administration in the early 1950s. By 1958, Collins was seeking an Ed.D. in student personnel services and was proposing development of a Ph.D. in humanities or social studies to prepare college teachers. But authorization was slow to come. The Ed.D. in Educational Administration was approved only in 1959-60 and began accepting students in the Fall of 1960.

The new mission given the University in 1962 meant very rapid expansion of graduate work. To oversee this development, Collins formed in the Spring of 1961 a Graduate Faculty which in turn elected a Graduate Council. The

Graduate Council (which became the Graduate Academic Council with the organization of the Faculty Senate in 1966) and the Office of Graduate Studies under the watchful eye of Dean Edgar Flinton took the responsibility for reviewing and tracking the new programs. The growth was explosive. The 1962-63 *Bulletin* showed one Ed.D. program in Educational Administration, one University Certificate program, and nineteen master's degree programs, six of them in education. The 1970-71 *Graduate Bulletin* revealed twenty-six doctoral programs, seven university certificate programs, and fifty-two master's degree programs. Roughly 200 new graduate courses were added during the 1967-68 academic year alone. Three to four new doctoral programs were introduced annually between 1962 and 1969.

The process varied greatly from field to field. Many arts and sciences departments modified a few requirements and generated new master's programs from existing teacher-education-oriented programs. Graduate degrees in the School of Education multiplied logically from the original Ed.D. and used long-established faculty. English and history Ph.D.s were based on presumed faculty strengths in the College of the 1950s, although the faculty there had to develop doctoral programs while teaching rapidly increasing numbers of undergraduates. The School of Business had to

133

The two campuses were, and still are, connected by University-operated buses.

build a completely new staff oriented toward business rather than business education. Other schools, such as social welfare, started from scratch, building a faculty and program concurrently, while criminal justice had the luxury of being able to assemble a high-quality faculty and plan its program carefully before teaching a single student.

Inevitably, the results were mixed. The number of master's degrees awarded rose rapidly from 293 in 1962-63 to 1,108 in 1970-71. The number of doctorates awarded grew much more slowly; the first two were awarded in 1962-63, there were twenty for 1968-69 and fifty-two in 1970-71. The School of Education flourished. It offered a broad range of programs to a large constituency of public school teachers and administrators, eager to enhance their skills and credentials. Education enrolled about 40 percent of the graduate students in the University and conferred the majority of the doctorates. Other schools had greater difficulty in attracting qualified students and helping them complete their degrees in a reasonable time. A few such as criminal justice achieved almost immediate distinction.

By the end of the decade a few warning signs began to appear. A 1967-68 *ad hoc* committee, charged with examining many facets of doctoral study at Albany, concluded "that a good case can be made for the thesis that this institution has proceeded too rapidly on too many fronts in developing graduate work." Three years later the visiting team from the Middle States Association expressed similar reservations. In the exuberant atmosphere of growth at the time, few took note of such cavils.

At the heart of advanced graduate study is research—faculty and graduate students working at the forefront of their disciplines to advance human knowledge. If the research achievements of the 1960s seem sparse, the institutional arrangements for future success were being put in place.

Universities encourage faculty research by providing incentives. Characteristically, Albany used both the carrot and the stick. Research slowly but surely became a central consideration in appointments, tenure decisions, promotions and salary increases, fueling endless debates about the relative importance of teaching and research.

Faculty members needed time for their scholarly pursuits. One way of getting it was to reduce teaching loads. But someone had to teach the burgeoning numbers of undergraduates. The practice of varying teaching loads was inevitable, but it also raised some serious problems of equity. At the end of the decade the student/faculty ratio in social and behavioral sciences stood at 19:1 as compared with 12.5:1 in sciences and mathematics and 13:1 in the professional schools. The first group's faculty felt discriminated against. Similarly differential teaching loads within departments produced complaints of inequity. Faculty support services often seemed inadequate. The sciences complained of shortages of laboratory equipment and supplies, and there was never enough travel money to support trips to professional meetings, much less research-related travel.

A team from Albany competed on the nationally televised G.E. College Bowl in January 1966, the first time a State University of New York institution was represented. The team lost by the narrowest margin, "by the split second of a reflex action at the final whistle," according to a reporter.

Administrators for the new University: (below) Webb Fiser, Vice President for Academic Affairs; (Opposite page, top) Clifton C. Thorne, Vice President for Student Affairs; (Opposite page, bottom) and Milton Olson, a faculty member since 1948, Dean of Business 1962 to 1966, Vice President for Business 1966 to 1973. (Olson photo by Liz Hannock.)

A research library did not exist in 1962. The library had been inadequate even for the College of the 1950s, and a new building always ranked high on the list of institutional priorities. The new campus for the first time provided adequate space, and the size of the collections began to grow at an astounding rate. The Middle States visitors in 1971 noted that research libraries in the 20th Century generally doubled in size every sixteen to twenty years; Albany's had increased seven times in the previous five years! By the Fall of 1970 the Library had grown to over 650,000 volumes, subscribed to about 7,600 periodicals, and had an annual acquisitions budget of over $850,000.

The University also began to encourage organized research activities. Late in 1960, Dean Oscar Lanford took advantage of some local opportunities to organize the Atmospheric Sciences Research Center. Approved by the Board of Trustees in February of 1961 as a unit of the State University, it was attached to and its benefits redounded chiefly to the Albany campus. In 1963 a newly organized Department of Atmospheric Science, separate from but related to the ASRC, began offering undergraduate programs in the field, and by 1970 it awarded its first Ph.D. Vincent Schaefer, the first director of research for the ASRC and later its overall director, and weather forecaster Ray Falconer became well known in the Capital District and had a knack for generating popular interest in science. During the 1960s the ASRC both produced serious scientific research and persuaded the general public that organized scientific research in a university was an important enterprise, well-deserving of public support.

The University also began the search for external research funding. The program of individual faculty research awards begun by the SUNY Research Foundation in the 1950s continued to provide significant financial encouragement to faculty. By 1971 the University was also able to report several substantial development grants from the National Science Foundation, the Ford Foundation, and the Carnegie Corporation.

Undergraduate education remained the bedrock of the growing University. Albany's long reputation for providing a quality education, the new image provided by the new campus, and the Albany location proved attractive to large numbers of students.

The evidence of test scores and rank in class suggested that incoming

Albany students were of very high academic quality. In the Fall of 1964, for example, Albany chose 1,800 from among 5,000 applicants to create an entering freshman class of 1,100. The liberal arts options made Albany more attractive to males; by the Fall of 1971 there were almost equal numbers of men and women in the undergraduate student body. The University admitted several hundred transfer students annually, partly to better populate upper division courses, partly to provide opportunities for baccalaureate study for the growing number of students in New York's community colleges.

The conversion of a teacher-education institution to a liberal arts school went smoothly, although more slowly than some had predicted. Departments quickly adjusted their teacher-education majors to create conventional liberal arts majors. Departments newly established in the 1960s gave undergraduates access to areas of knowledge not available to earlier generations. By the Fall of 1971, undergraduates could choose from fifty-eight majors, some of them interdisciplinary. They could spend a semester abroad at one of five foreign study centers operated by Albany. In 1973 the first-ever undergraduate exchange program with the Soviet Union brought eight to ten language students to the campus while a similar number of Albany undergraduates studied in Moscow. An increasing number of foreign students arrived in Albany, mostly for graduate study in the sciences and mathematics.

Albany's reputation for teacher education combined with a strong job market for teachers meant that teacher-education programs remained well-populated. In the Fall of 1964 about two-thirds of entering freshmen expressed a desire to become teachers, and four out of every ten members of the graduating class of 1969 had prepared for the field.

The undergraduate academic experience changed in many ways during the 1960s. Certainly the old College tradition of small classes, close faculty attention, and some degree of individualized attention slowly disappeared. The average undergraduate class size rose, and some very large classes appeared. By early 1970 Acting President Kuusisto told the faculty that in his weekly conferences with students, two concerns continually surfaced: academic advisement (faculty seemed both uninterested and ignorant) and too large undergraduate classes. For their part, faculty interested in undergraduate teaching expressed comparable

Faculty in the 1960s: (Top, left) Merlin Hathaway joined the staff in 1944 and oversaw the rapid expansion of physical education and intercollegiate athletics in the 1960s. (Top, right) Helen Horowitz came to Albany in 1960 in economics and became one of the most respected undergraduate teachers in the University. (Bottom, left) Mathematics professor Violet Larney began teaching at Albany in 1952 and saw the transition of mathematics from an undergraduate teaching department to a graduate and research-oriented unit. (Bottom, right) Catherine Wolkonsky, a Russian émigré scholar, had retired from Vassar College when she came to Albany and established a tradition of interest in Russian language and literature.

frustrations: crowded classrooms, poor acoustics, equipment shortages, and heavy faculty workloads.

The University had made efforts to forestall such developments. In the early 1960s the traditional freshman week orientation was abandoned in favor of summer planning conferences for incoming students. The University College, organized in 1964, sought to provide guidance for students in their first two years before they chose their majors and came under the academic supervision of the departments. Ultimately such efforts were not fully successful. Undergraduates had to take a larger share of the responsibility for their own education. They seized that opportunity in the late 1960s and wrought a major educational revolution (to be discussed in the next chapter).

Between 1844 and 1962 the Normal School and the College for Teachers, with a clear mission—to train public school teachers—had developed a tightly knit college community. For the first four years of University life, that sense of community seemed to hold. Faculty, students, and administration intently debated the future of the University in the coffee house, "The Golden Eye." Successive all-University symposia in 1964 and 1965 brought in distinguished speakers and generated large audiences from both the University and the surrounding community. Students busied themselves modifying traditions, making them more appropriate to Albany's new university status. The "Great Dane" became the new mascot. The old *State College News*, after a brief period as the *State University News*, was transformed into the *Albany Student Press*. The *Pedagogue* became the *Torch*. The Latin motto of the institution was suitably modified (with the aid of classicist Edith Wallace). The Alumni Association acquired its first full-time director and a new charter in 1964.

All of that seemed to change with the move to the new campus in the Fall of 1966. The sense of a small, closely-knit community with loyal faculty, students, and alumni began to decline as centripetal forces took hold. Some with strong ties to the University were disturbed, but in retrospect it is clear that the shift was inevitable.

It was difficult to develop traditional faculty institutional loyalties when seventy-five to one hundred new faculty appeared on campus each fall. Research-oriented faculty developed stronger ties to their disciplines than to the University. Within the University, loyalty to the department or professional school supplanted loyalty to the institution as a whole. Faculty resided all over the Capital Region; many rarely came to the campus other than to meet their academic obligations.

Graduate students, concerned with discipline-oriented or professional rather than general education, were separated from their undergraduate counterparts. Those who looked for graduate student organizations or a "graduate student ambience" on campus mostly searched in vain.

Unifying undergraduate student traditions also declined. Moving-Up Day and the traditional freshman-sophomore rivalry disappeared between 1963 and 1966. For many students tradition-

(Below) Randolph Gardner (left) came to Albany in 1947 and led the College of Education as its dean during the critical transition of the 1960s. Richard Teevan (right) arrived as chair of the psychology department in 1969. (Bottom left) The *Collegium Arcanum,* from left, M. I. Berger, '50, '52, education; Richard Kendall, '58, history; Harry Staley, English; Walter Knotts, English; Morris Eson, psychology; Kendall Birr, history; and Arthur Collins, '48, English. Paul Wheeler, sociology, was also a member of *Collegium Arcanum,* which met eight to ten times a year between 1958 and 1971 to discuss a book they had read in common. (Bottom) Samuel McGee-Russell (left) and Robert Allen (right), chair of the biology department, were character-istic of the research-oriented faculty who were recruited in the late 1960s and early 1970s.

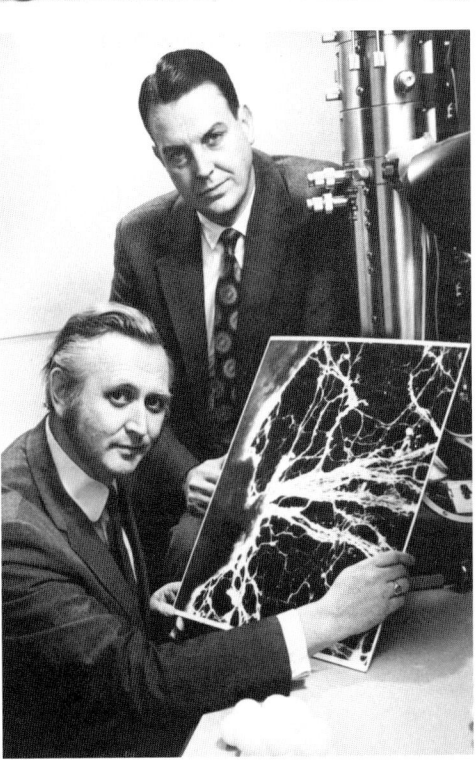

In the 1960s the University organized the Atmospheric Sciences Research Center, one of the earliest ventures into research, which has distinguished itself since as one of the world's leading centers for the study of the atmosphere. Pictured (above) on field research at Yellowstone are researchers (standing) Vincent Schaefer, Larry Proctor, Dale Hartlief, August Aver, Griffith Morgen, John Stockner, Austin Hogan; (seated) Richard Layton, Charles Robertson, Thomas Henderson, John Hirsch, Robert Smith Johnson. Schaefer and Ray Falconer (right), became well-known figures who generated a great deal of popular interest in scientific research.

building seemed irrelevant. "Traditions are important to some of the older people," a young history student said, "but we just do things we want to do, and stuff like no freshman can look Minerva in the face, or patting her nose or something, is gone."

Albany's students were socially less homogeneous than they had been in the 1950s. Although most were white and middle class, more came from the metropolitan New York area than heretofore. Student educational and vocational goals were clearly more diverse than they had been a decade earlier. Undergraduates were separated by residency: some commuted, others filled the residence halls, and still others occupied private facilities, mostly around the Downtown Campus. While the University in 1963-64 forced the Greek societies to give up their houses and move into the residence halls, they continued to flourish throughout the decade; there were nine each of fraternities and sororities in 1969, some newly organized.

After 1966 the University operated two campuses tied together by a bus service consisting of the University's "green monsters." The downtown seemed remote from the centers of University activity while the Uptown Campus remained curiously isolated. Standard urban services (shopping, entertainment and general service facilities) never developed within easy walking distance of these uptowners. A "set of wheels" became essential for those eager to live the good life during their four years at Albany.

Student government tried to oversee student activities in a growing and increasingly diverse community. An elected student Senate had already replaced the Student Assembly in 1956-57, but in preparation for the move to the new campus, the students wrote a completely new constitution in 1965. The heart of the new system was the broadly representative Central Council; while it provided for diverse inputs, it lacked strong executive leadership until early 1970s' changes provided for a directly elected Student Association president and vice-president. Myskania retained some judicial functions but became more and more of an honorary group. SA budgets rose from $52,800 in 1960-61 to more than $330,000 in 1969-70, exclusive of intercollegiate athletics.

Much of the money went for the *Albany Student Press*, *Torch*, and the new student radio station, WSUA. Student publications multiplied during the 1960s. Some, like the *Primer*, the principal literary magazine, were supported by Student Association. Others remained independent. The most interesting was *Suppression*, a weekly mimeographed journal begun in 1962 in reaction to David Boroff's assertion that Albany students were "dull." As if to demonstrate the falsity of Boroff's charge, *Suppression*'s pages were filled with provocative material, especially opinion pieces dealing both with University affairs and issues in the larger world. It showed considerable ability to irritate. In late 1962, for example, the Roman Catholic chaplain blasted the journal for alleged pornography. In the late 1960s it became increasingly

Vincent Schaefer

Vincent J. Schaefer, a self-taught chemist who invented cloud "seeding" and created the first artificially induced snow and rainfall, was perhaps the first person in history who actually did something about the weather. Grand hopes for his discovery—moderating droughts, reducing hail, quenching forest fires—were never realized, but lesser uses have proved valuable. And possibly of even more value was his founding in 1961 and later directorship of the University's Atmospheric Sciences Research Center. His deserving fame proved a magnet for attracting talent to what has become one of the leading research centers on the weather in the world. Beginning in 1962, Schaefer began broadcasting four to five-minute weather forecasts twice a day over local radio, a duty that was in later years assumed by his ASRC colleague, Ray Falconer. So popular were his readings of the latest and future conditions, delivered in layman's terms, that he would have to phone in reports even while on vacation from as far away as Canada, New Orleans, and Yellowstone National Park. His forecasts in 1964 won the Seal of Approval from the American Meteorological Society.

A self-made genius, Schaefer's only formal education was as a teen at the Davey Institute of Tree Surgery. Later, without a high school diploma, he went to work at General Electric Company in Schenectady and pestered his way into lab research. His ingenuity there caught the eye of Dr. Irving Langmuir, the Nobel laureate. In 1931 he became Schaefer's mentor, supplying the young (age twenty-two) man with science books that resulted in a home-made education. Together during World War II they developed gas mask filters, submarine detectors, and a machine to conceal military maneuvers by generating smoke.

Schaefer's invention of cloud seeding began with successful attempts to form crystals in his home ice box. Soon he was able to duplicate the feat in the atmosphere from an airplane, injecting dry ice into natural clouds.

The inventor died in Schenectady at age eighty-seven, in 1993. (Vincent Schaefer is pictured in photo on opposite page.)

radicalized. Whatever its ideology, it played a lively role in campus life until its demise in 1969.

SA expenditures for arts and entertainment burgeoned during the 1960s. The Council for Contemporary Music, Dramatics Council, Music Council, and Homecoming each received 1969-70 appropriations in the $10,000 to $25,000 range. Student support shifted from traditional high culture (classical music) to popular music and rock groups. The 1968-69 year included visits from folk singers like Judy Collins, Theodore Bickel, and Tom Paxton, pop groups like Union Gap, and above all others, the icon of late 1960s rock, Janis Joplin.

Student interest groups multiplied. SA appropriations for 1969-70 supported among others the Albany Film Making Society, Black Students' Alliance, Chess Club, Fencing Society, International Film Group, Judo Club, Outing Club, and a long array of academically oriented student groups.

Students in the 1960s paid increased attention to community affairs and social change. Student groups raised money and offered their services to a variety of charitable causes. An annual "Telethon" in 1967 raised funds for mental health; two years later it provided twenty-four hours of entertainment and had become the culminating event in a week long "Campus Chest." Interact, a student organization supported by SA funds, worked with local orphans, while Greek societies collected clothes for Albany's poor or became involved in "big brother" operations.

"The Cave" in Husted Cafeteria in 1965-66.

One of the most interesting student ventures into social change was the Ebenezer Howard project of 1971, a kind of experiment in community building. It proposed building student housing as part of a major neighborhood development project in Albany and sought to construct a completely new community in Greene County, south of Albany. The projects never came to fruition, but drawings of some of the proposed buildings serve as a reminder of the ambitious idealism that informed at least part of the student body in the late 1960s.

Rising revenues from the athletics tax combined with the facilities on the new campus brought a considerable expansion of intercollegiate athletics. Lacrosse, track, and swimming moved from club to varsity status in the late 1960s. Women's tennis, softball, field hockey, basketball, and swimming appeared as major sports. Intercollegiate football was approved in 1968, and in the Spring of 1970 Bob Ford was hired to teach physical education and to coach the team. With the opening season in 1970, Albany had belatedly gained a central element in traditional American collegiate culture.

U.N. Secretary General U Thant visited the campus in 1966 as part of a University Seminar Series on Peaceful Change.

As SA income rose, so did the claims on it, and by 1969 a crisis was at hand. The problem was two-fold: student apathy and a legal challenge to the student tax. In 1965 a faculty member of Central Council questioned an appropriation for the Religious Affairs Commission on the grounds that it violated the separation of church and state. SUNY lawyers approved the appropriations, arguing that payment of the student tax was not required for registration at the University. By 1969 about 30 percent of the undergraduates were refusing to pay the tax. The authorities finally ruled that students could make the tax compulsory if they so approved in a referendum. One was held in the Spring of 1969. Less than 22 percent voted (a valid referendum required a 20 percent turnout), but the compulsory tax was approved.

Perhaps the most important change in student life in the late 1960s was the abandonment of the principle of *in loco parentis*. The practice had long been justified at Albany by the need to inculcate students with the values and behavior acceptable in the communities in which they would teach. But most students in the 1960s were not headed for teaching careers. Many came under the influence of the "counter-culture," with its emphasis on individual freedom and self-expression, and pressed for less University supervision. Faculty had neither the will nor the energy to resist. Some had joined the counter-culture themselves, all applauded the principles of individual freedom and responsibility,

Intended for sale at १¢ but Dean Thorne required that it be a give-away sheet.

State College — Friday, Feb. 9, 1962

SUPPRESSION

No. 1

Why "suppression"?

David Boroff, in an article for the Saturday Review, classified the State College student mentality as "Tame and unimaginative...hardly intellectual...peevish about school regulations rather than critical." "suppression" is our rebuttal to Mr. Boroff. We welcome any intellectual endeavor, all intelligent criticism. All subjects will be considered: political, sociological, mathematical, etc. We are out to prove a point.

Controversy gives rise to the intellectual. Rational criticism is a means of expression. Those who would condemn "suppression" are as myopic as Mr. Boroff, are as quick to generalize. We do not seek to create controversy, but investigate situations which give rise to it and create from it. Every member of our student body and faculty may write for "suppression". The freedom we enjoy gives us, a greater sensitivity. We all are capable of reacting to our environment on an intellectual plane.

"suppression" is an optimistic endeavor. It denies "Intellectual life on campus is low-voltage". It welcomes dissent not for the sake of sensationalism but as evidence that Mr. Boroff leaned too long and hard on Minerva and consequently was stoned by obvious and superficial. "suppression" needs you and your ideas and we believe you and your ideas need "suppression". Place your contributions in the student mail under S; address all correspondance to "suppression". We are self-supporting and would appreciate any size monetary contributions.

Yesterday Dark

Whisking about sharp pointed stars, these clouds
Blow from the sea dust, dusting the ironwoods
With cloudy feathers. They are movement and shadow,
Blown to this shallow rock from the windy trades
Dusting our calm night with outwaters,
With worlds of oceans and long, thready skies.
 Sea wind whistles in the meshed fronds of dates
And coconut palms; it garnishes the coral coast
With swirly spume that luminescently lifts
Beneath the starlight; the libidinous breeze
Rustles stealthily the grasses, and makes
The long roll of the sea to roar.
 Distance is desolate with the ocean.....
The nights not close but world about,
And desire shifts nervously as the stars,
Stars puncturing electric sky, stars tumbling
In the ocean, distant, tumultuous.
 The night is sad and loud in cloud dust;
Pale ginger and the red hibiscus rise
Breeze lifted to scent the hollow ocean;
The dark leaves us behind. And it stirs
Flesh, the breeze, shocks the skin roots.
 And then, in yesterday dark, the night
Blew out of the ocean distance you,
Blew promise and you to chasten dark sense
Of the stealthy tropical clouds, and it was like
To the helmsman a Salem wind in a Clipper's rig
Beating down the gusty northeast trades.
       Thomson Littlefield - Angaur, 1945

J.D.Salinger: Public Enemy No.1

JD Salinger has been probed and prodded from more angles, from more points of view, than a microbe being studied under a Ford Foundation grant. Another consideration, therefore, of the creator of Holden Caulfield (The Catcher in the Rye), Franny and Zooey (from the novel of the same name), can do little harm, and perhaps some good.

Salinger is a paradoxical figure. At one and the same time, he is an anonym, and the most widely acclaimed author of our time. That he should be both is a tribute to his talent for, and devotion to, writing, and that the public world should insist upon trying to peep into the anonymity he has chosen to embrace is a crime against his integrity and his privacy. Furthermore, such public prying is an invasion of the tabernacle of artistic endeavor, and threatens the solitary freedom of all artists everywhere.   (over)

when i was a freshman
i used to get blind on four beers
and write profound poetry
on the backs of beer coasters in myriad bars
and incredible dreams of hot-sweatered coeds
with buttered breasts and chocolate nipples
nights i used to lie there in bed the room
rolling around me delirious
and talk in great drunken voices of truth
never to be again or since - -   Ken Taylor

Conservation

Who's this creature chopping at the tree
That's lived a century?
A thousand eyes of nature curse him
And when the tree falls
An entire forest groans.
What's that, Mother?
What's that noise?
Sleep little one--
On the window taps the rain,
A candle shivers and goes out,
In the darkness below
Is the scrapping of a dragged tree,
Mother, I shout
Tell him to put it back. - - Andrew Neiderman

 Do you dare paint murals on the side of a house when you're paid for production, not creativity, with one color paint--white, and not care. But why dare, in that you become an artist. The alternative, I don't know...I don't expect to meet him.   B. Baker

and most were otherwise occupied with pressing academic obligations.

Signs of change occurred everywhere. Dress codes faded. In 1960, faculty frowned on female students wearing shorts to class, even in the summer session. *Viewpoint '73-'74*, a volume of information and advice for students, asked the question: "What to wear?" The answer was "ANYTHING GOES! The 'basic' blue jeans or dungarees (depending on what part of the state you're from) form the foundation of the well dressed college student's wardrobe. The grubbier they are the better (wash at least six times before wearing). A patch sloppily sewn on here and there, also enhances the appearance . . . So, dress away. Be yourself—sweaters, T-shirts, slacks, shorts, sweatshirts, jeans, mini, maxi—it's up to you. Remember, ANYTHING GOES!"

Alcohol, drugs, and sex became important symbols of student liberation. In January of 1968, alcohol became legally available in the Campus Center, the Mohawk Campus and Dippikill, and fourteen months later the University Council approved a new policy that permitted alcohol in the residence halls. Albany students experimented with the drugs of the day. Drug arrests of Albany students were often reported in the local press, particularly from 1969 to 1971. Some students apparently claimed for themselves a traditional right of sanctuary on the University campus. The Student Health Service director argued that heroin use was an infectious health problem that should be dealt with in a non-punitive fashion, but the University also undertook vigorous anti-drug educational efforts.

Faculty chaperones were no longer required for student social affairs. Faculty applauded the move for they no longer felt comfortable performing an

(Opposite) *Suppression*, an alternative newspaper, arose following David Boroff's *Saturday Review* article which charged that "intellectual life on SUNYA's campus is low voltage." *Suppression's* editorial policy was that "all subjects would be considered." That stand was condemned by at least one local clergyman, but President Collins stood up for the students' right to free expression.

Rock icon Janis Joplin appeared on campus in 1968. (Photo by Ed Potskowski, *Torch*, 1969.)

Evan Revere Collins

Evan Collins, whose tenure as Albany President stands second in length only to Abram Brubacher, was a complex man who oversaw an equally complex era in the University's history.

Charming, patrician, and by his own admission an autocrat, he nonetheless granted students much more responsibility for the conduct of their lives, agreeing to the elimination of chaperones and the installation of student representatives on the University Senate, and officially approving alcoholic beverages in the dormitories.

He also shepherded the changing focus of the institution from teaching to research as it moved from College to University. He watched old friends on the faculty become out-of-date with the new roles expected of University professors. Some of the intimate, personal style he had enjoyed in the old College had to be set aside as the faculty expanded from 125 to nearly 700, and the student body from 1,500 to more than 10,000 during his tenure.

How did he manage? Considering everything, brilliantly. Equal to his charm was his acceptance of new ideas, and of listening to administrators, faculty, students and outside evaluators in order to make the policy changes necessary for a burgeoning institution. At heart was his belief that the University was a positive agent of change, a "rich resource" for understanding and solving social problems. His belief in students' integral place within that change and his willingness to discuss situations with them was no doubt a factor in the respectful treatment he received in return—at a time when hundreds of University presidents throughout America were enduring far less deference.

Still, he must at times have longed for those days in the 1950s when he and wife Ginny made informal, often unannounced welcoming visits to new faculty members (Ginny Collins becoming one of the organizing forces behind the Faculty Wives group), and the evenings when he casually joined with three faculty members to form a string quartet. When he left the University in 1969 and began another distinguished career on the faculty of education at Boston College, he must have felt he had already lived two professional lifetimes.

increasingly ambiguous function at such affairs. Regulation of students in the residence halls rapidly came apart. Women's "hours" were first expanded and then eliminated altogether; student "sign-outs" ended in the Fall of 1968. Visitation hours in the residence halls were eased, and in 1969 the University Council approved a policy that allowed each residence hall to establish its own visitation policy by a two-thirds vote of the residents. Traditional concern for student discipline was replaced by concern for protecting students who might be arrested; alcoholism became a matter for counseling rather than disciplinary action. Faculty and administrator-enforced University regulations were replaced by a mostly student-operated judicial system. The demise of *in loco parentis* was complete.

In May of 1969 the University dedicated the new campus, noted the retirement of President Collins, and observed the 125th anniversary of the founding of the Normal School. U.S. Commissioner of Education James E. Allen, the principal speaker, described the process of moving "Toward Tomorrow's University." There were special symposia on topics of the day such as pollution and pornography. A committee identified and honored 125 notable alumni(ae) of the College and University. But there were also athletic events and a chicken barbecue, and the alumni magazine reported that students spent a lot of time splashing in the fountains. The celebration reflected the many facets of the new University culture. But there hardly seemed time for calm reflection on past accomplishments, for the University was about to experience several years of turbulence.

Intercollegiate athletics during the late 1960s included such new sports as women's softball and men's soccer.

Students in the 1960s paid increasing attention to community affairs. The annual "Telethon" raised money for community organizations. (Pictured is a 1971 Telethon.)

The most significant change of the late 1960s was the disappearance of the concept of colleges serving *in loco parentis* (in place of parent). The University Council approved a policy in 1969 allowing each residence hall to establish its own visitation policies. Alcohol was permitted in residence halls the same year. (Exterior photo by Tae Moon Lee, MLS, '66.)

Alumna Judith Mysliborski, '69, like many Albany students from this era, ultimately pursued a career other than teaching. Dr. Mysliborski is a dermatologist in Albany today.

Robert Peterkin, '66, MA '76, is director of the Urban Superintendents Program and Francis Keppel Senior Lecturer on Education at Harvard University's Graduate School of Education. Formerly he was superintendent of the Milwaukee schools.

Drew Zambelli, '70, is Secretary to New York Gov. Mario M. Cuomo.

Harriet Dyer Adams, MLS '60, was former head of the University Libraries Special Collections in the 1970s. In 1993 she provided for the establishment of the Biodiversity Program at the University in memory of her father, conservationist Charles Adams.

Homecoming Parade. Sigma Tau Beta, winners of the prize for best float in the 1969 Parade. (Gift of Steve Lobel, '70.)

President Collins speaks at the formal dedication ceremonies of the new campus on May 17, 1969.

Alice Hastings Murphy, MLS '40, director of the University Libraries, addresses a gathering at the dedication of the libraries in 1968. She was the daughter of English Professor Harry Hastings and Louise Clement Hastings, a critic teacher in the Milne School.

CHAPTER VII
Weathering a Turbulent Era
1969 to 1976

Universities reflect the societies of which they are a part. The turbulence that characterized America in the late 1960s came to Albany in the 1969-70 school year.

➤ In November of 1969 students erected three "Vietnamese huts" on the podium as a political protest. One hut was burned and a student arrested before students agreed to remove the remaining structures.

➤ A couple of students presented Acting President Allan Kuusisto with a bloody pig's head as he was presiding over a University Senate meeting.

➤ Radical Left-wing attorney William Kunstler spoke to 6,000 on campus on March 5, 1970, raised his fist in the "power to the people" salute, and told his listeners that the movement had progressed from a period of "protest" to a stage of "resistance."

➤ One week later, students, angered over a tenure decision, smashed windows in the administration building.

(Opposite) Dialogue Days took place in March 1970 when Acting President Allan Kuusisto canceled classes following student demonstrations over the University's failure to renew a faculty member's contract and other issues.

➤ On March 19, fifteen students were among twenty-nine arrested for disorderly conduct while staging a four-hour sit-in, blocking the entrance to the Albany Induction Center.

➤ On March 19-20, classes were suspended for two "Dialogue Days." Students and faculty pondered the University's problems in department meetings and a series of workshops. Topics included tenure decisions, 50/50 faculty-student control of the University, racism on campus, "Student as Nigger," and "Anarchy" (no room was scheduled and people were urged not to attend!). Participants produced a long list of recommendations ranging from good teacher awards to 50/50 representation on all University-wide decision-making bodies, to University pronouncements on social, economic and moral issues.

➤ Some black students were involved in a fracas in the dining hall at Colonial Quad; food service workers were assaulted and the dining hall was vandalized. A group of black faculty and staff asserted that the incident was a "response to a long series of real and apparent discriminatory practices and racist attitudes . . ." at the University.

The turbulence reached a peak during May of 1970. On April 30, President Nixon announced that American troops had expanded the Vietnam War by moving into Cambodia. Four days later Ohio National Guard troops fired on and killed four protesting students at Kent State University. The Albany campus like others all over the country exploded in protests. On May 4, students entered the Library, threw books off shelves, dumped others on the ground outside and tried to burn them, and broke windows. Two days later, students from Albany and elsewhere marched downtown to the Capitol, protesting both American involvement in Vietnam and the state of American race relations. The march occurred without violence. But that night on campus Molotov cocktails were thrown at the Administration Building, and fire bombs

Representative Ogden Reid addresses a Vietnam Moratorium, October 15, 1969.

started blazes in both Colonial and Dutch Quads; the former's Flag Room was destroyed. Students struck in an attempt to shut down the University.

The administration organized a "crisis committee," and faculty and staff held nightly fire watches at both academic buildings and residence halls. The SUNY Trustees responded to student strikes by ruling that all campuses were to remain open. Faculty meetings on May 8, 11, and 12 arranged a compromise by which student strikers were given several alternative ways of receiving credit for their courses. Most undergraduate courses ceased operation while students briefly operated a "School of Suppressed Studies;" graduate classes were largely unaffected. Commencement passed without incident, students departed the campus, and Acting President Kuusisto left for a less revolutionary presidency at Hobart and William Smith Colleges.

What had happened? Some euphorically believed that "the revolution," which would transform the flawed world in which they lived, had come. Others gloomily concluded that the University like American society was "coming apart." With the advantage of hindsight we can now understand how several developments came together to disrupt the University in the Spring of 1970.

William Kunstler, speaking on campus to a crowd of 6,000 on March 5, 1970, in the University gym, told students the movement had progressed from "protest" to "resistance."

Albany students became increasingly politicized in the late 1960s. *Campus Viewpoint*, published for incoming students, for the first time in 1968 included a section on "Political Concerns" which listed student political organizations ranging from SDS (Students for a Democratic Society) on the Left to YAF (Young Americans for Freedom) on the Right. The range and number of such organizations testified to the breadth of students' interest in improving their world, and they began to pursue their political goals with an aggressiveness that would have been unthinkable at the old College for Teachers. Albany students (and many faculty) focused on three areas in the late 1960s: race relations,

A March 1970 protest on the steps of the Capitol in support of the Black Panthers. (Photo by Martin Benjamin, '71.)

undergraduate instruction, and Vietnam.

Student concern about race relations dates back at least to the 1940s, but the formation in 1964 of a new civil rights group, "Freedom Council," marked a new surge of interest. Faculty and students in the mid 1960s enthusiastically supported Martin Luther King's movement and the federal legislation that emerged in 1965. Albany students went south to help in sit-ins and voter registration drives. During these years the interest in civil rights at Albany was mostly a white phenomenon, chiefly because there were very few blacks on campus in the 1960s. The assassination of Martin Luther King on April 4, 1968, changed things. The University community was horrified and sought to make a significant gesture to improve educational opportunities at Albany for young blacks. Everyone applauded the establishment of a federally-subsidized Educational Opportunities Program in the Fall of 1968. EOP provided intensive academic help and financial aid to students who would not otherwise be able to attend college. Many of the students were black or Puerto Rican, all came from lower income families, and by 1969-70 enrollments reached about 365.

With the death of Martin Luther King, "black power" challenged "integration" as the goal of the national civil rights movement. The change was reflected on the Albany campus. Black students, organized in the Black Students Alliance, sought an Afro-American studies program at Albany, and on January 10, 1969, confronted President Collins with a sheet containing a series of demands. Collins quickly signed. He subsequently argued that, looking at the substance rather than the rhetoric of the demands, he had concluded that everything the BSA was seeking was already planned. The Department of Afro-American Studies was soon activated. By 1969-70 black militancy merged into the general student protest activities. After the dining hall incident noted earlier, black students responded by compiling a list of thirty-seven allegations of racism on campus, and when white students protested the shootings at Kent State, blacks rallied to protest the concurrent shootings at Jackson State.

A second source of student discontent in the late 1960s was undergraduate curriculum and teaching. By the Spring of 1968 President Collins observed that student concerns had shifted from campus social problems such as dorm hours and alcohol on campus to academic issues such as grading systems and faculty tenure.

Undergraduates worked to change both the grading system and general education requirements. Many students and faculty believed that students should have total freedom to choose their courses. They also argued that replacing letter grades with Satisfactory/Unsatisfactory grades would improve education by transforming the classroom from a competitive to a cooperative environment. S/U grading was approved by the Senate in the Fall of 1969. Proposals to eliminate requirements were a major focus of the "Dialogue Days" of March 1970 and were approved by the Senate a month later.

The tenure issue was more complicated. It was traditionally granted by the institution on recommendation of the faculty. In the 1950s, tenure decisions at Albany were made largely on the basis of the person's teaching performance. But by the late 1960s, good teaching was not enough; tenured professors also had to be productive scholars. Irate students complained that undergraduate teaching was being undermined by general neglect and by the "publish or perish" syndrome.

Students pursued reform using two strategies. First, they fought hard to gain greater student input into the tenure process. The University ultimately required student evaluations of teaching as a part of the dossier necessary for a tenure decision, and in some cases students served on

A September 1971 protest on Alumni Quad against the State's action in the Attica Prison uprising. (Photo by Jay Rosenberg, '73.)

tenure committees. Second, students vigorously protested what they considered to be ill-considered personnel decisions. Non-renewal cases in psychology in the Spring of 1969 and in rhetoric and public address in the Spring of 1970 became *causes celebre* and absorbed enormous amounts of time and attention. The latter case reached a climax in March of 1970 and was debated during the "Dialogue Days."

The third element in the 1969-70 upheaval was, of course, the Vietnam War. As late as the Spring of 1964 the *Albany Student Press* printed two long and sympathetic articles on an Albany sophomore returning to school after a tour of duty with the Special Forces in Laos. But by 1965 the effects of the draft were being felt, and student opinion of the Vietnam War became highly critical. A Student Peace Group was formed in 1966. In the next couple of years there were periodic "teach-ins" and debates over the war. Senator Wayne Morse appeared on campus to oppose it, General Maxwell Taylor defended it. In February of 1968, students demonstrated against recruiting activities on campus by the Dow Chemical Company, manufacturer of napalm; ten students were arrested for disorderly conduct on grounds that they had interfered with University business. SDS mounted a campaign to close the campus to objectionable groups such as Dow Chemical, the CIA and the armed forces, but 92 percent of the 3,000 students participating in a referendum voted in favor of an open campus. The issue of campus recruitment by defense manufacturers remained significant well into the 1970s. By 1969-70, Vietnam had become a major issue; it was a central concern in the "Dialogue Days" of March 1970, and the Cambodian incursion and the Kent State and Jackson State shootings provided the final fuel for the May student uprising. All of these issues were further complicated by the cry of "Student Power!" Student concerns, especially concerning civil rights and Vietnam, often spilled over into the community. Black students protested for educational reform at Albany High School in 1969. In the heady days of May 1970 some

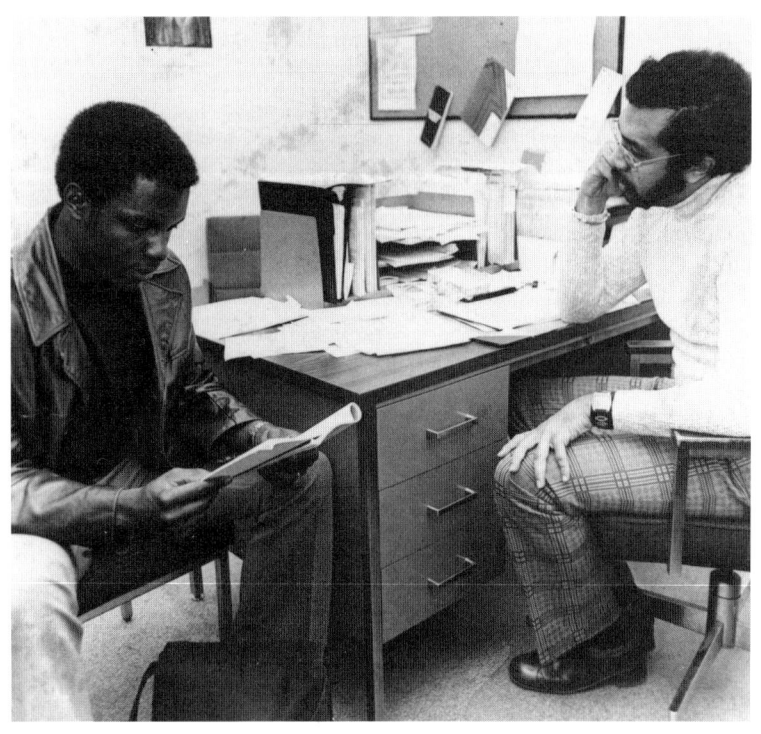

The Educational Opportunities Program was established at Albany in 1968 to provide educational and economic assistance to disadvantaged students. (Below) Carl Martin, right, a counselor in the program, meets with a student. Opposite, graduates of the program from the Class of 1974.

students at Albany and elsewhere contemplated sweeping through northeastern New York to convert Americans to the causes of peace and justice.

Most focused their search for power on the University, particularly the Senate and the academic departments. The Senate had been organized in 1966 as a Faculty Senate, but by 1968-69 students were seeking membership, first on Senate councils, then on the Senate itself. Both goals were achieved by the Fall of 1969. Students sought input and power in departments as well. Their degree of success varied, but for several years proponents of student power continued to argue for 50/50 student/faculty representation on critical bodies such as tenure committees.

Some students and faculty urged the Senate to take positions on the key moral and political issues of the day such as Vietnam. They argued that a university which refused to take such stands risked becoming morally corrupt. Opponents argued that such a step could be fatal by turning society at large against the University and asserted that the function of a university was not to take moral or political positions but to provide an institutional framework within which dialog and learning could take place. Ultimately the faculty in the Fall of 1970 approved a resolution, still in effect today, introduced by Hans Pohlsander and Morris Finder, which stated that "this university . . . [is] dedicated to the search for truth and that in its corporate capacity it does not officially endorse any particular version of the truth be it a matter of political or social philosophy or of scientific theory."

The Spring 1970 vision of a revolution disappeared in the next few months. Instead, students turned to the techniques of single-issue pressure politics. Students remained in the Senate and on its councils, but their presence there was for more than a decade dependent on annual renewal by the faculty. As the Vietnam War wound down in the early 1970s, new issues arose, notably the feminist movement.

The Civil Rights Movement of the 1960s became the on-campus politics of ethnic studies. Faculty in Afro-American Studies were under enormous pressures. They had to work hard to meet requirements for tenure. At the same time, their students often expected the department to become a black cultural center with the faculty attentive to the personal problems of black undergraduates on a predominantly white campus. It was little wonder that the department often led a troubled existence in the 1970s. In the early 1970s, Hispanic students sought and got a Puerto Rican Studies department which became part of a Department of Latin American and Caribbean Studies in the early 1980s.

The educational reforms of 1969-70 had mixed results. S/U grading soon fell victim to the demand of pre-professional students that they receive letter grades required by admissions officers in law and medical schools. The curriculum free from general education requirements lasted about a decade before the faculty pressed for change.

Louis T. Benezet succeeded Evan Collins as President in 1970, following a year-long term by Acting President Kuusisto.

Lengthy debates over how to evaluate teaching ultimately led the University to mandate student evaluations of each class and to require that teaching evaluations play a role in tenure and promotion decisions. Yet students continued to protest individual tenure decisions, leading in 1973 to the appointment of a special committee which clarified and regularized the procedures to be used.

Despite the turbulence of these years, the quality of the University's undergraduate education was recognized in 1973 when Albany was granted a long-sought and highly prized chapter of Phi Beta Kappa, the leading national academic honorary society.

Students focused on gaining membership in the University Senate in 1969. Here, Harry L. Hamilton, professor of atmospheric science, speaks at a Senate meeting.

Three additional educational developments in the early 1970s deserve note. First, the University in the early 1970s launched a new doctoral program, the Doctor of Arts degree. The D.A. program, initiated first in English, emphasized preparing college teachers rather than conventional research specialists. It was a very successful venture, both a culmination of President Collins' long-standing dream of a doctorate designed to train teachers for two-year colleges and a response to the widespread concern over the neglect of undergraduate teaching.

Second, the Fall of 1971 marked the beginning of a community service course through which students could earn academic credit for independent study and collateral work in community agencies. The course institutionalized much student enthusiasm for improving the communities in which they lived.

Third, in the Fall of 1972, Albany launched an important experiment in undergraduate education with the formation of the James E. Allen Collegiate Center, led by Seth Spellman of the School of Social Welfare. Using a $100,000 Carnegie grant for start-up purposes the Allen Center tried to do two things: shorten the length of students' education

163

The James E. Allen Collegiate Center, led by Seth Spellman of the School of Social Welfare, was an important experiment in undergraduate education, designed to shorten the length of study by admitting students after eleventh grade into a high-quality interdisciplinary program. It fell victim to the financial crisis of 1975-76.

by admitting qualified students after eleventh grade, and educate its students through a high-quality inter-disciplinary program. The Allen Center occupied much of the Downtown Campus where students and faculty constituted a close-knit academic community. It was a high-minded experiment undertaken with great energy and enthusiasm. Its final results are still a subject of controversy. Student admissions were disappointing, the faculty had difficulty teaching the interdisciplinary curriculum, and the administration came to regard the Center as unduly expensive. Thus the experiment fell victim to the financial crisis of 1975-76.

The University saw considerable turnover in its top leadership during the 1970s. Collins retired in June of 1969; his Academic Vice President, Allan Kuusisto, served as Acting President through the upheavals of 1969-70. He was succeeded in the Fall of 1970 by Louis T. Benezet, a fifty-five-year-old psychologist with a Columbia University Ph.D. and administrative experience at four private institutions. Benezet served for five years and was succeeded for two years by a Vanderbilt University historian, Emmett Fields, who in 1977 returned to Vanderbilt as president.

Charles O'Reilly from the School of Social Welfare served as acting Academic Vice President from 1969-1971 until Benezet brought in Philip Sirotkin from an administrative post in the National Institutes of Health. There was also turnover in the position of Dean of Graduate Studies. In 1975 the important College of Arts and Sciences was divided into its three component parts (Sciences and Mathematics, Humanities and Fine Arts, and Social and Behavioral Sciences) after a failed two-year search for a new dean.

Benezet and Sirotkin did much to regularize administrative procedures after the almost uncontrolled growth of the 1960s. But the lack of leadership continuity complicated University efforts to deal with the two succeeding crises of these years: the attack on Albany's doctoral programs and the financial crisis and reorganization of 1975-76.

Just as demographics had driven the rapid expansion of Albany in the 1960s, so demographics by the early 1970s suggested a need to slow down. Analysts, predicting a nationwide decline in the number of college-age young people, became concerned about a potential glut of Ph.D.s. In New York the Regents and Commissioner of Education Ewald Nyquist picked up on these concerns, imposed a two-year (1971-73) statewide moratorium on all new doctoral programs, and appointed a Regents Commission on Doctoral Education, chaired by Robben W. Flemming, president of the University of Michigan. The Flemming Commission urged the state to sustain the high quality of established programs rather than try to improve low-quality programs. It also suggested that it would be less costly for the state to subsidize students at private institutions than to provide additional doctoral education for them at public institutions. Accordingly the Regents adopted a program of concentrating programs at a relatively limited number of institutions and undertook to review "the quality of and need for doctoral programs in selected disciplinary areas."

The Afro-American studies department was created in 1969 by President Collins following student calls for courses about the African-American experience. Nathan Wright was among its earliest faculty members and its first chair.

The State Education Department's so-called "Doctoral Project" in 1974 began examining all state doctoral programs in chemistry and history and continued in the following year with astronomy, physics and English. The examinations included departmental self-studies and a site visit and report by two outside consultants. The final decisions were made by a statewide "doctoral council." Albany fared badly in the first two years: the history and English Ph.D. programs received failing grades. One faculty member observed that the site visit had been fair enough; he just hadn't expected the final decision and now understood how students felt when they were "graded on the curve." It was a serious matter; the loss of doctoral programs threatened Albany's ability to fulfill its mission as a university center.

The University responded by pointing out that its Graduate Academic Council in 1970 had begun reviewing its own programs; by 1976 the GAC had assessed all doctoral and master's programs using ninety-eight separate teams of consultants. The University argued that the responsibility for such reviews rested with the institution, not the SED. SUNY decided to mount a legal challenge to the right of the SED to make such decisions, thereby reopening an old issue between SUNY's Trustees and the Regents. SUNY lost in the Court of Appeals, and the history and English programs were de-registered. Meanwhile the University sought to defend its other programs. Internal reviews identified programs unlikely to pass SED scrutiny, and the University itself suspended or eliminated several programs. No other Albany programs were eliminated by the SED.

Philip Sirotkin, Vice President for Academic Affairs, together with Benezet did much to regularize administrative procedures after the growth of the University in the 1960s.

Putting fresh resources into programs coming up for SED review was difficult, given looming financial difficulties. The 1968 Master Plan envisioned a university of perhaps 20,000 to 23,000 students at Albany, and in 1969 faculty and staff were busy planning for a 310,000 square-foot extension to the west end of the academic podium. But 1970-71 brought the first substantial budget cutback in SUNY history, and by March of 1971 Benezet told the academic community that long-term enrollment would likely level off at 15,000 FTE students and that Albany would have to build a first-class university by means other than simply adding more students.

Financial resources became tighter each year. Between 1970 and 1975, Albany's enrollment grew by 15 percent, but the number of faculty declined marginally. Albany's state funding between 1972 and 1974 grew more slowly than the rising rate of inflation. Rapidly growing energy costs became a matter of concern. As one faculty member observed during these years, "The response of the state to inflation is compression." The worsening state fiscal condition in 1974-75 promised actual budget reductions for at least a two-year period. A crisis was at hand.

Benezet, preparing to step down in June of 1975, responded by appointing a "Select Committee on Academic Priorities" to assess the status of the University and develop options for the future. He told the Committee that the resource question "requires us to make hard choices among those programs which are to be advanced, those which are to be held to a minimum, and those which may have to be discontinued at the doctoral level." His charge to the committee foreshadowed the wrenching changes of the next fifteen months. The Select Committee worked very hard for three months and reported in May that the University "simply cannot do everything at once and do it well . . . No institution can possibly be all things to all people . . . programs which are not central to its mission, which have demonstrated an inability to operate effectively, or which have not met the test of quality, must give way to those programs which can meet those tests." In a steadily worsening financial environment, Benezet in June of 1975 invoked retrenchment and made his decisions. Emmett Fields assumed the Presidency in July of 1975, fully briefed by his predecessor and grateful that Benezet had implemented the Select Committee's recommendations. In the fall of that year, Fields charted new directions for the University, urging a "public policy" emphasis in which the University would ally itself with its community and state government. He also made clear that program quality, imbalances in workload, and Albany's unique mission all justified the reallocation of resources to priority departments. New budget cuts in 1976 led Fields to appoint a new Task Force on Programs and Resources. Its immediate

Emmett Fields, second from right, assumed the Presidency in 1975 and charted new directions for the University, including a "public policy" emphasis in teaching and research. Others pictured, from left, Louis Salkever, Vice President for Research and Graduate Studies; unidentified person; John Hartigan, Assistant Vice President and later Vice President for Finance and Business; and John Hartley, Vice President for Finance and Business.

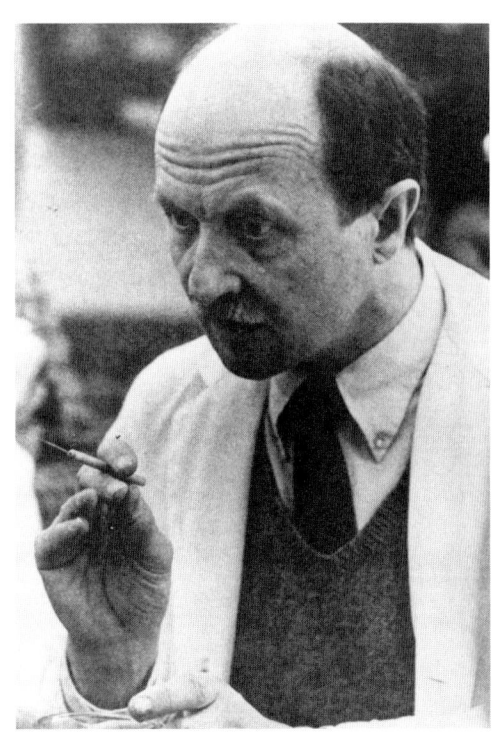

Faculty in the 1970s pursued an active research and scholarly agenda. John Mackiewicz (above) of biological sciences in 1973 became the first Albany faculty member promoted to "Distinguished" rank by the State University Board of Trustees. Kevin Burke (right) and John Dewey (opposite) brought international recognition to the Department of Geological Sciences with their work in plate tectonics.

concern was to identify positions and dollars to be surrendered in the forthcoming budget, but it was equally concerned with resource reallocation. The Task Force completed its work in a month's time and sent its report to the President. On March 15, Fields announced his decisions, terminating programs and closing departments. On April 16, Chancellor Ernest Boyer accepted Fields' recommendations.

In the fifteen-month period from January 1975 through March 1976, two blue-ribbon committees and two presidents had terminated twenty-six degree programs and several academic units, including two schools, three complete departments, and an experimental college; eighty-eight faculty were retrenched, thirty-seven of whom had tenure. There was no question but that budget problems required cuts, but Albany more than any other unit of SUNY used retrenchment to refocus the institution and reallocate shrinking resources.

The pain was substantial. Albany's experiment in undergraduate education, the Allen Collegiate Center, was shut down. The School of Nursing and the Department of Speech Pathology and Audiology

disappeared; both had trained students for high-demand fields. Educational offerings narrowed; there would be only minimal instruction in astronomy and comparative literature with the abolition of those departments.

Concurrently in 1975 the Milne School was closed. A SUNY-wide committee, formed at the behest of Chancellor Boyer, concluded that campus schools were no longer essential to training teachers and recommended closing all of them in the SUNY system. The Milne School, a popular and successful institution which had trained thousands of students, had fallen victim to change. For the first time in 130 years, Albany was without a "model" school.

Many argued that retrenchment and reorganization had been far from fair and equitable. Advocates for discontinued programs had no success in reversing the decisions. Faculty who lost their positions were thrown into a very difficult job market. To some, retrenchment seemed to threaten the tenure system, providing an opportunity to replace troublesome and highly paid tenured professors with more malleable, lower paid individuals. Had that happened? Concerned faculty took the matter to the Association of American University Professors (AAUP), the professional organization that a half century earlier had developed the tenure system to protect faculty members' right to free speech. The AAUP concluded that Albany made consistent provision for a year's notice to faculty being released. But the organization argued that the financial cuts of 1974-76 could have been dealt with through attrition and criticized the practice of employing retrenchment as a tool to achieve institutional reorganization. The AAUP ended by censuring the entire SUNY system.

But the gains were also substantial. Both committees had done their work well; their recommendations were defensible if not palatable. The Task Force had conducted Albany's first comprehensive review of all academic, administrative, operational, and service components, developing a tool that was to become very important in the next decade. Most important, the process reallocated resources to create a stronger University. In the four years from 1976-1980, the University attracted over 250 scholars, about seventy of whom were appointed at the senior level, including seven new deans from other universities. The retrenched individuals were soon gone, but the reallocated resources strengthened

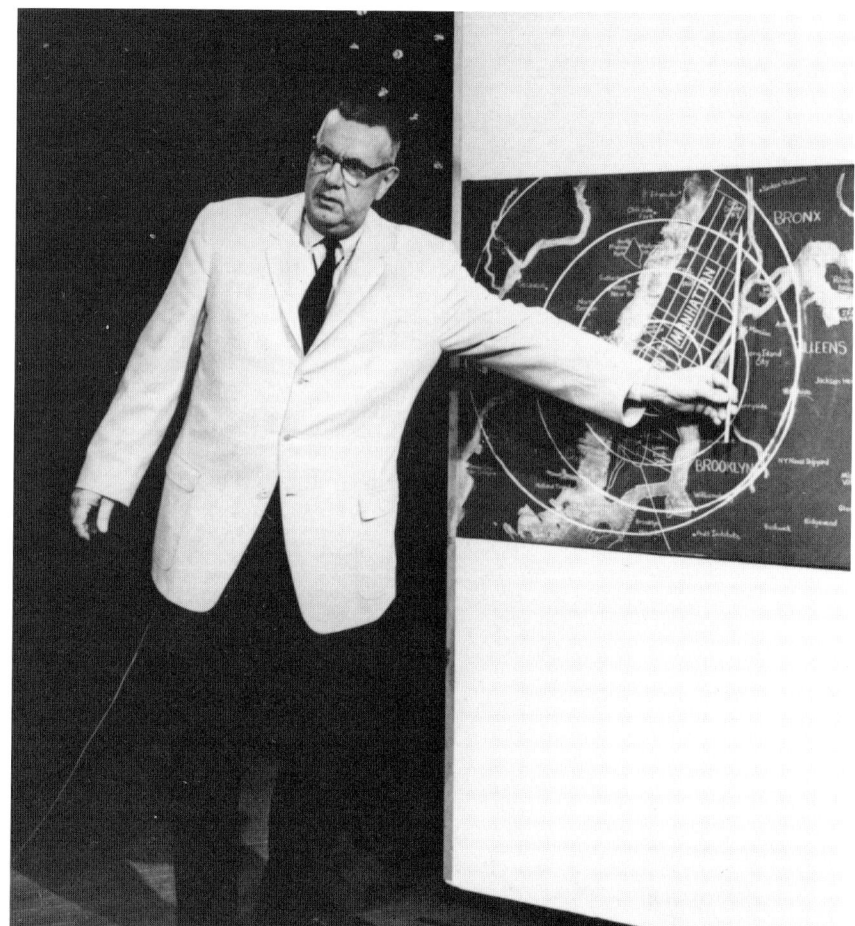

Harry Crull was an innovative teacher of astronomy, a department lost in the financial crises of the late 1970s.

The Institute for Humanistic Studies led the resurgence of the College of Humanities and Fine Arts in the late 1970s. Shown here are Dean John Shumaker; Institute Director M. E. Grenander, Distinguished Service Professor of English; and Deputy Director Hugh Maclean, Distinguished Teaching Professor of English.

retained programs. As one defender put it, the process generated "more winners than losers." The eight years from 1968 to 1976 were turbulent. But the University, pursuing its mission of becoming a public research university, often converted problems into opportunities. Student discontent with undergraduate instruction created opportunities for educational experimentation. If some despaired at quixotic student political activism, others rejoiced in student idealism. The University tenaciously defended its doctoral programs with considerable success. Above all else, Albany met the challenge of the financial crisis of 1975-76, emerging bloodied but stronger.

Professor Marguerite Warren (above) of the School of Criminal Justice, an Albany graduate program of national distinction. Political scientist Bernard K. Johnpoll (above left) was a flamboyant teacher, prolific author, and institutional gadfly.

Ted Fossieck served as principal of the Milne School from 1947 to 1973. The School's closing in 1977 meant that Albany was without a "model" school for the first time in 125 years.

Women's Studies

There are now more than 700 women's studies programs across the country, but the University at Albany's stands out among them. Its seeds were planted early, and it now has reached full status as a *Department* of Women's Studies. In less than twenty years, the concept of women's studies at Albany grew from a single course offering–"Women in Modern Literature," taught in 1971 by English Professor Joan Schulz (pictured)–to a minor field (1973), then a student-initiated interdisciplinary major (1978), followed by a faculty-approved major (1981), and finally a state-approved major in 1989. Departmental status became effective in 1990. The department continues to grow, with its researchers applying feminist perspectives to nearly every academic field. In the 1993-94 academic year it was moved to larger offices in the Social Science building.

In addition to opportunities on the undergraduate level, the department offers a graduate certificate in Women and Public Policy, a master's degree in Liberal Studies, a D.A. in Humanistic Studies, and concentrations on gender in other graduate programs such as sociology, English, and history.

In 1993-94, the Women's Studies roster features twenty faculty members from various departments around campus. The department faculty has also helped create the University's Institute for Research on Women, a research center that sponsors conferences and hosts faculty workshops aimed at observing the new studies on women which are being conducted across discipline boundaries.

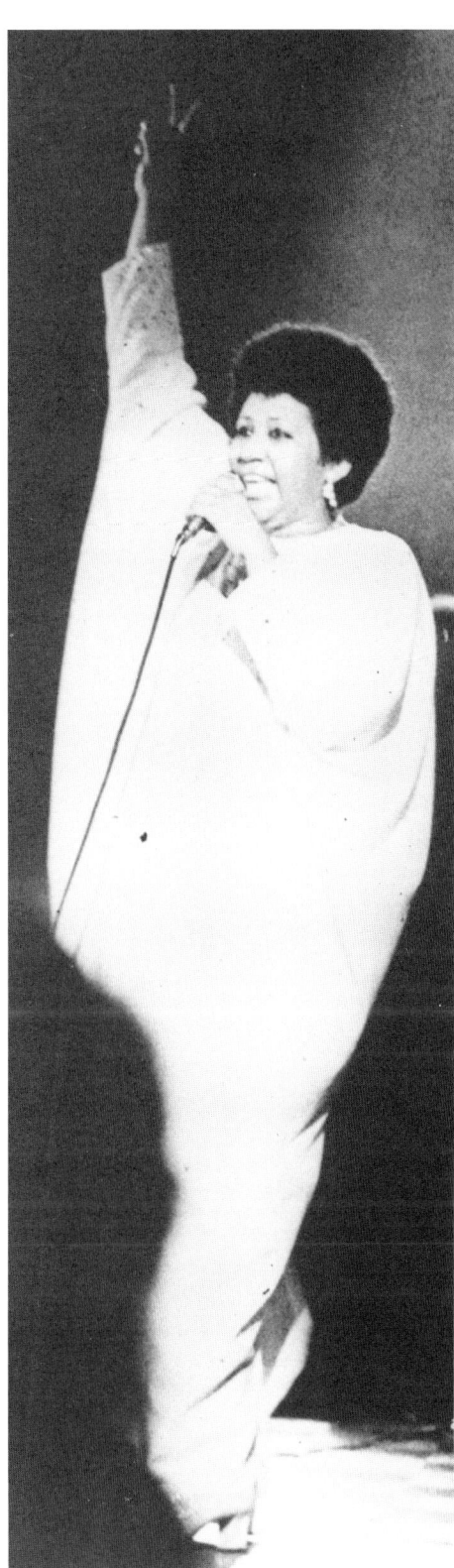

In the 1970s, Albany was a stop for many popular musical acts, including Miles Davis (top left), Aretha Franklin (above), and Eric Clapton (left). (*Torch*.)

Athletics continued to flourish in the 1970s. (Right) Co-captains of the 1977 Great Danes Frederick Brewington, '79, and Ray Gay. Brewington is now a New York City attorney and served as president of the Alumni Association from 1991-1993.

(Above) Michael Lampert, '73, exemplified the new directions of students in the era of the University. He was president of the Student Association for an unprecedented two years from 1971 to 1973. A graduate of Harvard Law School, he became a prominent litigator in New York and New Jersey. A loyal alumnus, he served as president of the Alumni Association from 1979 to 1981.

(Right) Cathy Ladman, '75, a popular stage and nightclub standup comedian, has made frequent appearances on the "Tonight Show" as well as having her own HBO special.

(Left) A performance of *Marat Sade* in 1972 was directed by faculty member Jarka Burian.

(Below) In 1972 the University introduced Community-University Day to encourage more interaction between the campus and the city. Here President Benezet and chairman of the University Council J. Vanderbilt Straub present a "Key to the University" to Albany Mayor Erastus Corning III and Schenectady Mayor Frank Duci. At right is long-time Vice President for University Affairs Lewis P. Welch. At left is Associate Vice President Sorrell Chesin.

CHAPTER VIII
The Emergence of a Mature Public Research University 1976 to 1994

Emmett Fields left the Presidency in the Summer of 1977. His successor, first as Acting President in 1977-78 and then as President from 1978 to 1990, was fifty-three-year old Vincent O'Leary, the first Albany President since John Sayles to be drawn from the faculty and the man who was to have the fifth longest tenure as chief executive in the institution's history.

A California native, O'Leary took degrees at San Francisco State College and the University of Washington, and by the time he was appointed professor in the newly organized School of Criminal Justice at Albany in 1968, he was a nationally recognized expert in the field of parole and probation with extensive experience and an impressive list of publications. O'Leary also brought to the Presidency important personal qualifications. He was immensely energetic and articulate, he was politically astute, and his service as chair of the Select Committee and as a member of the Task Force gave him an unmatched knowledge of the University.

(Opposite) Physics Professor Alain Kaloyeros, a Presidential Young Investigator, is a principal researcher in the University's new Center for Advanced Technology (CAT) for Thin Films and Coatings, approved by Governor Cuomo and funded in 1993 by the New York State Science and Technology Foundation. Here he is pictured with graduate students Cheryl Wyetzner, Greg Braekelmann, Ishing Lou, and Aaron Burke. Burke studied with Professor Kaloyeros as an undergraduate before beginning graduate study at Albany. (Photo by Mark Schmidt.)

Vincent O'Leary was named President in 1978 after serving for a year as Acting President. He was previously Dean of the School of Criminal Justice.

The institution O'Leary presided over in 1977 was far removed in size and mission from the College for Teachers of the 1950s, and as a university Albany had discovered that institutional maturation can be just as harrowing as human adolescence. The challenge of creating a mature public research university in a rapidly changing American society tested the mettle of the University community. The character of undergraduate education had been challenged by the student upheavals of 1970. The quality of Albany's doctoral programs, the heart of any university, had been severely scrutinized. And the fiscal crises of the mid 1970s had threatened the University's ability to respond.

O'Leary proved to be a leader vigorous enough to take on these challenges. He began in the late 1970s and 1980s by recruiting a new management team—vice presidents who constituted a kind of "cabinet" that worked very closely with him. Among them were young leaders possessing strong credentials nationally in scholarship and administration and laying claim to bright futures: Judith Ramaley, a biologist, from 1982 to 1987 served as Albany's first female Executive Vice President, then left for an executive vice chancellorship at the University of Kansas; John Shumaker, Vice President for Academic Planning and Development from 1985 to 1987, later became president of Central Connecticut State University; Warren Ilchman, a political scientist, succeeded Ramaley, and later assumed the presidency of Pratt Institute. Frank Pogue went from Albany's Vice President for Student Affairs to the vice chancellorship of SUNY. Jeanne Gullahorn (Research), Mitchel Livingston (Student Affairs), and John Hartigan (Business) joined holdover Lewis Welch (University Affairs) in refilling those and other vice-presidential posts. Between 1977 and 1981 each school or college got a new dean; seven new deans and ten new department chairs were recruited from other universities. The new administrators brought with them a fund of experience at other institutions that helped guide the University toward maturity.

The single most pressing issue of the 1980s was money, or more accurately the lack of same. While state funding approximately doubled between 1979 and 1989, it hardly kept up with the rate of inflation, and the 1980s saw annual budgetary "mini-crises." O'Leary's response was to elaborate and institutionalize the planning and budgetary processes begun by the Select Committee, the Task Force, and Fields. Every unit of the University developed a plan, the plans were reviewed, and resources were allocated accordingly. Annual "budget panels" of faculty, staff, and students provided valuable input into the process. In addition, SUNY Chancellor Clifton Wharton fought for and in 1986 won some freedom from the burdensome oversight of state government. O'Leary's new system worked. The financial difficulties were controlled, and resources were used prudently. While there was a campus-wide obsession with resource problems, there was also a campus-wide sense that they were being handled in a rational and equitable fashion.

It was becoming clear at the same time that the State of New York was not able to provide all the financial resources necessary for a major public research university. In the 1980s state appropriations (less tuition) constituted less than half of the University's revenues. Hence Albany like other institutions looked for supplemental funding. Tuition and various fees for service increased, although Albany still maintained its position as an excellent "buy" among the nation's colleges and universities. In addition, from 1979 to 1989, external research funding trebled. Finally in 1988 O'Leary recruited Christian G. Kersten as Vice President for University Advancement to undertake a major capital campaign.

In the 1980s, providing an academic infrastructure—space and services—for a large and complex university posed a major challenge. Total enrollments reached about 16,000 by 1980 and hovered around 16,500 thereafter. The University also became increasingly complex. In 1989 it offered forty-eight baccalaureate, sixty-five master's, and twenty-eight doctoral programs and awarded nearly 2,500 bachelor's, more than 1,000 master's, and nearly 125 doctoral degrees.

How did 16,000 students, more than 700 teaching faculty, and several hundred support staff fit on a campus designed for about 10,000 students? To some degree they didn't. Space for every University activity—faculty offices, instruction, research, University Libraries, student activities, and physical education—was always at a premium, many felt cramped, and complaints abounded. The University responded in several ways.

The Uptown Campus was modified to make the most efficient use of existing space. Lounge areas and conference rooms disappeared to make way for faculty offices and laboratories. The Library installed

Jeanne Gullahorn has been Vice President for Research and Dean of Graduate Studies since 1986; Frank Pogue was Vice President for Student Affairs from 1983 to 1987. (Photos by Edward Wozniak)

In 1983 the University officially inaugurated the Rockefeller College of Public Affairs and Policy with a convocation and processional along State Street. Grand Marshal Eugene McLaren of chemistry leads the processional, followed by Rockefeller College founding Provost Warren Ilchman and Alice Rivlin, former director of the Congressional Budget Office and convocation speaker.

more compact shelving. When student demand for on-campus housing declined, some residence hall units were converted to faculty offices. Research centers often moved off campus to rented space.

The Downtown Campus was completely rehabilitated to become the home of the Graduate School of Public Affairs and other professional schools. A refurbished Page Hall became a popular venue for lectures, films, and musical performances. The Thomas E. Dewey Library for Public Affairs and Policy occupied the old Hawley Library. The new occupants of the Downtown Campus had mixed feelings about these developments. Some felt isolated from the Uptown Campus, and faculty who attended meetings or taught classes on the Uptown Campus were not enthralled with the three-mile "commute." Still, the professional schools were in close physical proximity to state offices with which they often worked, and the handsome buildings of the College for Teachers were preserved and used.

The long-term space problem could be eased only with new construction; that, however, came very slowly and used both state and private funds. Alumni House, financed by alumni and others, was completed in 1976 and provided facilities for the Alumni Association as well as attractive space for meetings and conferences. A 1991 addition housed the ever-more-active University Advancement program. Freedom Quadrangle, a 410-bed apartment-type residence facility designed for graduate and advanced undergraduate students, was opened in 1988. To ease the shortage of physical education facilities, the University in 1986 erected a $500,000 vinyl-nylon "bubble" and in 1992 opened a handsome 4,800-seat Recreation and Convocation Center equipped with basketball, squash, racketball, and handball courts, an indoor track, and high-tech training rooms. A privately financed Albany Collegiate Inter-Faith Center (the "New Chapel House"), located on the edge of the Uptown Campus, was opened in 1988; it offered students a place for worship and was often used as well for small conferences by University groups.

The computer transformed every aspect of University life during the 1970s and 1980s. Courses were first available on the campus in the mid 1960s, and by 1983 the Department of Computer Science was offering a Ph.D. The computing power available on the campus increased exponentially. Central mainframes, which in 1983 could handle three million instructions per second, increased their capabilities ten times by 1990. During the 1980s, offices converted from typewriters to a word-processing system, and student user rooms appeared in both academic buildings and residence halls. Personal computers sprang up like spring flowers in faculty offices and student residences; all had easy access to the University Computing Center, other University offices, and national data bases and computing facilities through networking.

Administrative and academic information flows were similarly transformed. Student academic records were computerized. By 1987 students had access to a computerized degree-audit system that enabled them to track their way through Albany's degree requirements. The following year the Student Information Retrieval System (SIRS) gave University personnel on-line access to student records.

The implications for research and instruction were profound. At one end of the spectrum, scientists gained access to super computers; at the other end, undergraduates found that word processors greatly enhanced their writing. Everywhere there was emphasis on something loosely called "computer literacy" and on quantitative studies.

The University Libraries, too, were affected both by financial stringencies and by the advent of the computer. The extraordinary growth rate of collections in the 1960s was reduced by half in the 1970s and 1980s, and acquisitions policies were redesigned to support curricula and graduate research. Since 75 percent of the acquisitions budget was represented by serials, by 1990 the rapidly

(Top) In 1986, ground was broken for apartment-style residence halls across Fuller Road from the main campus. Albany Mayor Thomas M. Whalen III, former chair of the University Council, joined President O'Leary and Alan V. Iselin, chair of the University Council between 1982 and 1990 before becoming a State University of New York Trustee. (Photo by Edward Wozniak)

(Bottom) In 1980 the Campus Center's Assembly Hall was converted into a Middle Eastern room for scenes from the motion picture thriller *Rollover*, starring Kris Kristofferson and Jane Fonda.

Faculty through the 1980s and 1990s earned national reputations for their research and teaching and played an important role in the life of the University and the community at large. They included Margaret Stewart (top), Distinguished Teaching Professor of Biological Sciences, well known for her environmental work; and Distinguished Service Professor of Physics James Corbett (bottom, at left), one of the pioneering faculty members in that department in the area of advanced materials. Corbett is pictured with physics Professor William Lanford, right, the son of Oscar Lanford, the Dean of the College in the 1950s.

escalating cost of journals forced an actual reduction in the number of periodical subscriptions. The computer made possible an integrated catalog, circulation, reserve and acquisition on-line system and gave users access to local data bases and to collections in the Association of Research Libraries (1975) and the Research Libraries Group (1984).

The millionth volume was added in 1982, and by 1989 that number had grown to 1.3 million, with an additional 2.4 million microform items, 400,000 government publications and 7,000 periodical subscriptions. By then the main library building was simply too small to support the collections and their heavy use. A library "annex" plan developed in the 1990s would ease problems by housing a state-of-the-art electronic library focused on information storage and retrieval.

At the heart of the University were its faculty members. They supervised the educational program, taught the students, both undergraduate and graduate, and did the research that distinguished a university from a college. Most had been recruited during the great growth spurt of the 1960s. Their numbers stabilized, then declined slightly during these years. Most counts reported between 600 and 700 full-time and varying numbers of part-time faculty.

Improved faculty quality—essential if Albany was to mature as a research university—was difficult to accomplish when there were almost no new positions to fill, the faculty was relatively highly tenured, and turnover rates were low. The two keys to improving the faculty in these years were tenure and promotion decisions and effective recruiting.

By 1980 the University had in place a rigorous system of faculty review for tenure and promotion which sought to guarantee procedural due process, openness and equity. Not all agreed that those laudable goals had been achieved, but the highly publicized and controversial tenure cases so characteristic of the late 1960s and early 1970s slowly disappeared.

When openings occurred by virtue of resignation, retirement, or tenure actions, the University was better positioned to recruit well than it had been earlier. It was better known, recruitment was conducted far more systematically, and salaries remained very competitive. An Albany position looked very attractive to a young scholar facing a nationwide academic depression.

Two generalizations suggest that the quality of Albany faculty improved. First, as we shall see, there was a significant improvement in Albany's graduate programs, and faculty quality was always a key element in such judgments. Second, SUNY established a series of distinguished professorships in the early 1970s. Successful candidates received special titles and salary increases, but only after passing external scrutiny. At this writing, Albany faculty members had won ten Distinguished Teaching Professorships, twelve Distinguished Service Professorships, and nine Distinguished Professorships.

The faculty also became more diverse during these years. There were more women and minorities on the faculty in the 1990s than there had been two decades earlier. Women made up nearly half of the faculty in the mid 1930s but only about 15 percent by the mid 1980s; the figure rebounded to 24 percent in 1992-93 as a result of vigorous affirmative action efforts. The faculty counted about eight percent of its numbers from minority groups in 1993.

University faculty continue the tradition of service to the University and the community: Edward Cowley (below right) began in the Milne School before becoming the third art professor in the University's history. He was founding chair of the Department of Art, whose faculty have been central to the development and sustenance of the art community in the region; two Collins Fellows, so honored for their service and devotion to the University are: music Professor R. Findlay Cockrell (below), well known in the Capital Region as an ambassador of music, performing frequently throughout the area, and psychologist Shirley C. Brown (right), who has served two terms as a member of the New York State Board of Regents.

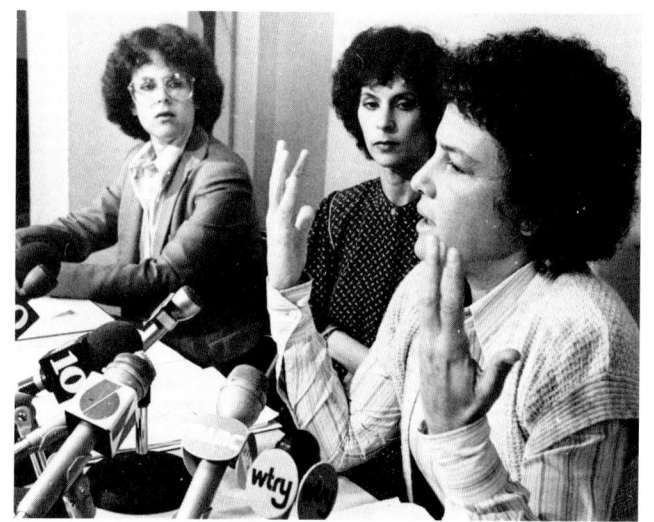

The Center for Women in Government, established in 1978 by Linda Tarr-Whelan and Nancy Perlman with support from the Ford Foundation, works to identify and remove barriers to equal employment opportunities for women in the public sector. In 1983 the Center conducted a Comparable Worth Study, commissioned by the Governor's Office of Employee Relations and the Civil Service Employees Association, which served as the basis for New York's pay equity plan to eradicate sex and race-based discrimination in setting salaries in the State system. (Left) Announcing the study are, from left, Ronnie Steinberg, director of research and implementation for the Center, Perlman, who was its executive director, and Karen Burstein, Commissioner of Public Service.

The faculty as a whole was responsible for overseeing the educational programs of the University through a Faculty Senate created in 1966. But the spirit of inclusiveness abroad in the late 1960s and 1970s converted the Faculty Senate into a University Senate. At various times students, librarians, and non-teaching professionals became members. For a time in the early 1970s, members of the classified civil service, ranging from custodians to secretaries, also participated in the governance system.

Many faculty were unhappy with what they perceived as the erosion of their educational prerogatives. Faculty interest and participation in the Senate declined, and Senate meetings often seemed devoted to trivial issues ("pets, pistols and parking," as one senator put it). The nub of the matter was student participation. Some argued that students had their own political structure in Student Association, that the Senate should be left to the faculty, and that students should be removed. Others, however, saw the Senate as a useful institution representative of the University as a whole. Consequently in 1981 a compromise was worked out in which students gained continuing membership while faculty senators gained separate access to the President and the right to have a separate count of faculty votes on certain educational issues. During the 1980s both the size of the Senate and the relative numbers of students were reduced in an effort to create a more effective and deliberative body. Still, the governance system as a whole continued to work, mostly because of conscientious and well-staffed Senate councils.

In the 1980s, Albany succeeded in establishing strong graduate programs, and new initiatives were undertaken despite severe financial

Research centers, organized in interdisciplinary fashion around specific study areas, proliferated in the 1980s. They included the Center for Stress and Anxiety Disorders, directed by Distinguished Professors of Psychology David Barlow, and Edward Blanchard (above). The Center is the top-funded center of its kind in the nation, and Barlow has been honored by the National Institute of Mental Health with a Merit Award, which provides up to ten years of federal support for his research.

constraints. Between 1980 and 1989 the University added twenty-seven new graduate programs. Some resources for graduate programs became available from the retrenchments of 1975-76 and the University's termination of four additional graduate programs during the 1980s. New money came with the New York State-funded Graduate Research Initiative begun in 1987; GRI funding enabled Albany to create thirty-five new faculty positions and eight postdoctoral associate positions in several targeted areas.

Departments faced program reviews in the late 1980s with far more confidence than a decade earlier. The ninety-one reviews conducted between 1980 and 1989 were directed more to program improvement than to possible termination. Rating graduate programs and departments became a major national enterprise during the 1970s and 1980s. By the end of the 1980s several Albany programs—atmospheric sciences, accounting, sociology, psychology, criminal justice, Germanic languages, public administration, social welfare and the D.A. in English—had achieved national recognition using indices ranging from reputation to scholarly productivity and professional contributions.

The quality and reputation of graduate programs were closely tied to faculty research, and success in research was often measured by the level of external funding. Research funding doubled between 1975-76 and 1979-80 and trebled again by 1988-89. By 1989 external research and training support of over $38 million was equal to nearly half of the campus's state appropriation, comparable to that of the centers at Buffalo and Stony Brook, and four times that of Binghamton. Albany had joined the ranks of the top one hundred institutions in the nation in federally-funded research and development.

Graduate student enrollment reached about 4,500 during the 1980s. Close to 40 percent of the graduate students were full-time, the Schools of Business and Education having particularly heavy part-time enrollments. The arts and sciences colleges and the School of Education each had about 30 percent of the graduate students; the other 40 percent were distributed among the professional schools. The quality of Albany's graduate students was in general quite high, with high-demand programs such as clinical psychology receiving applications the equal of any in the nation.

Richard Nathan, Distinguished Professor of Public Policy and Provost of the Rockefeller College since 1989. (Photo by Joseph Schuyler.)

Political activism returned in the 1980s, including protests to encourage the State University of New York to adopt a policy of divestment of holdings in companies doing business in South Africa until apartheid was eradicated. (Photo by Student Photo Service.)

Challenged by a description in a national college guide that Albany students lacked "school spirit," Student Association leaders Patty Salkin, '85, and Ivan Shore, '85, organized the world's largest game of musical chairs to put the University at Albany in the *Guinness Book of Records*. 5,060 students and faculty turned out for the game, ultimately won after four hours by Pete Serafi, '86, of Scarsdale. (Photo by Hai Do, courtesy of the Albany *Times Union*.)

Albany's research and graduate programs developed a distinctive "public policy" orientation during these years. In the 1960s there was a general assumption that Albany, given its location, might logically develop such an emphasis. But it was President Emmett Fields who articulated the goal of forging an alliance between the University and the community in the 1970s. The boundaries of the University were to become the boundaries of the state. Policy studies were to occupy a position of special prominence.

The new direction was not greeted with universal enthusiasm. Some thought it ill-advised to put scarce resources into a new initiative. Others feared political interference. But O'Leary had faith in the University's ability to conquer new research territory, and enthusiastically supported the new orientation with resources. Between 1977 and 1980 all but two of fifteen departments judged to be in a position to engage in policy analysis received additional and/or upgraded faculty positions.

Michael Corso, '83, '84, was elected President of the Student Association in 1982-83.

In order to strengthen policy-oriented educational and research programs, O'Leary in 1981 clustered Criminal Justice, Social Welfare, Information Science and Policy, and the Graduate School of Public Affairs into a new unit, the Nelson A. Rockefeller College of Public Affairs and Policy, headed initially by Warren Ilchman and later by Richard Nathan. Closely related was the Nelson A. Rockefeller Institute of Government, a SUNY-wide institute located near the Downtown Campus. It worked closely with faculty in Rockefeller College, and was headed by the same individual who was Provost of Rockefeller College.

The University had no medical school. But in 1985 Dr. David Axelrod, New York's Commissioner of Health, helped bring about a collaboration between the University and the New York State Department of Health, resulting in the establishment of the University's School of Public Health. It coupled the resources of the nation's largest and most sophisticated state health research facilities, the Wadsworth Laboratories, with the campus's strength in science and its commitment to public policy. Three years later the Albany Medical College became a partner in the endeavor. Soon over 150 jointly-appointed faculty and a core of independently recruited full-time faculty were developing graduate programs in public health.

Richard "Doc" Sauers, Albany's basketball coach and faculty member in Physical Education since 1956, marked his 600th career victory in 1992, making him the winningest coach in National Collegiate Athletic Association Division III history.

In the late 20th Century much of the best research and instruction was often found in interdisciplinary and problem-oriented centers and institutes. Such clusters of faculty and students were not new at Albany, but they proliferated in the 1970s and 1980s; a 1990 report listed forty-eight, supporting a wide range of services and research interests.

One of the most visible was the New York State Writer's Institute, established in 1983 by Pulitzer Prize-winning novelist and Albany faculty member William Kennedy. He used some of his MacArthur Foundation "genius" grant to get the Institute started, and it soon received state funding. It gained additional national recognition by helping recruit novelist Toni Morrison for a prestigious Schweitzer Chair at the University, and maintained a high public profile by hosting campus visits by outstanding authors, sponsoring conferences (notably one on non-fiction writing featuring Norman Mailer, Garry Wills, and others), and producing a nationally syndicated "Bookshow" on public radio, hosted by the Institute's associate director, Professor of English Tom Smith.

The international dimensions of the University's teaching and research blossomed during these years. By 1990 the Albany campus administered study-abroad programs in fourteen countries. Linkages were developed with a number of foreign universities. Two of the most notable examples were in China: a joint Ph.D. program in Sociology with Nankai University, and School of Business faculty exchanges with Fudan University. Albany faculty became well-traveled: to Indonesia, improving that country's educational system; to Somalia, educating managers; and to Brazil, helping develop budgeting systems and merit-selection procedures for its civil service system.

Some other centers of graduate instruction saw major changes. The well-established School of Education reinvented itself in the late 1970s and 1980s, shifting its focus from teacher preparation to graduate education and discipline-based educational research, often with a public policy emphasis. The College of Humanities and Fine Arts, which felt the brunt of the late 1970s program-pruning (four doctoral programs and two departments lost, reduced enrollments and resources) bounced back. Enrollments stabilized, new interdisciplinary programs were established (Chinese Studies and Women's Studies, for example), and a second D.A. program in Humanistic Studies was added in 1984.

Graduate study and research were reshaped by the new public policy orientation and by the emphasis on improving quality. But the institution never forgot that it was a *university* and could remain one only if it offered advanced graduate study and research in fields central to the definition of a university, particularly the liberal arts and sciences. Hence in the late 1980s the University sought to reestablish doctoral programs in history, English, French studies, and philosophy.

In the late 1960s, undergraduates had complained of neglect. A decade later they

Intercollegiate and intramural athletic programs continued to be strong through the 1980s and new ones were added in both men's and women's sports. (Above) Albany Crew, a club sport, makes use of the nearby Hudson River and participates in the city's Knickerbocker Regatta. Zoraida Davis, '91, (left) recorded the most triples of any player ever in Division III women's softball and finished her sophomore season as the team's leading batter. As a junior she was named to the All-Championship Team when the Lady Danes won the New York State Women's Collegiate Association Championship.

began to receive new attention. Since SUNY budgets were enrollment driven, Albany's funding depended on its ability to recruit and retain a strong undergraduate student body. But recruiting some 2,000 quality freshmen and another 1,000 transfer students annually became more difficult in the 1980s as the number of New York high school graduates declined.

Yet the caliber of incoming undergraduates remained very high. "Traditional freshmen," that is the 70 percent of entering freshmen students admitted under conventional standards, were very able indeed. The SAT scores of such students entering in 1987 and 1988 ranked Albany ninth nationally among public doctoral universities, behind Virginia, Michigan and Berkeley but ahead of the University of North Carolina, the University of Wisconsin, and UCLA.

Albany students came overwhelmingly from New York; a quarter of the 1986 freshman class came from New York City, nearly a third from Long Island, and about a seventh from the Capital District. Most Albany students were no longer "first generation" college students; over half of the arriving freshmen in 1986 had at least one parent holding a bachelor's degree. Entering students were primarily middle class, although a quarter came from families with incomes of more than $50,000 and another quarter from families with incomes of less than $20,000. There was a

(Top) In 1986 President O'Leary welcomed Governor Cuomo and New York State Sen. Kenneth LaValle were on hand for the University's Commencement and the graduation of their daughters Lisa LaValle (above) and Madeline Cuomo (left). The Governor offered the Commencement address and Senator LaValle received the Medallion of the University for his service to education.

notable increase in the number of "non-traditional" undergraduates, particularly older students (faculty found them particularly well-motivated). And by 1993 the student body was becoming significantly more diverse ethnically and racially.

Undergraduates in the 1960s had been relatively confident in their ability to move into well-paying jobs upon graduation and hence enjoyed the luxury of participating in the counter-culture or working for social change. Students in the 1970s and 1980s, observing the changed economic circumstances in America, became markedly career-oriented. Hence the programs they chose changed with the market for college graduates. Beginning in the early 1970s students began to flood the School of Business, and during the 1980s a third of entering freshmen announced their intention to major in business or accounting. Students perceived career opportunities in other areas as well: psychology, computer science, social welfare, and even teacher education. And it sometimes seemed as if everyone wanted to become a lawyer!

Popular areas became greatly overcrowded; the School of Business had to limit enrollments, for example. But the University was able to convert crowding from a problem into an opportunity. Students initially denied admission to courses or majors of their choice were directed into other fields where they often discovered both a vocation and the virtues of a liberal arts education. As students proceeded through their four years, their aspirations for graduate study increased, careers became less important, and liberal education seemed more significant.

In the 1970s, when Albany had no general education requirements, the breadth of an individual's education depended on how well he or she chose from among the wide range of courses available. A substantial minority of students were taking few courses outside the college of their major field, sometimes too safely navigating the minefields of degree requirements and academic regulations.

For this and other reasons meant to re-instill the ideal of liberal arts education, general education requirements returned in the 1980s. An experimental program was offered to about 300 students in 1980, and two years later a full-blown General Education Program came into being. It required students to take two courses each in six rubrics of general education. A "Writing across the Curriculum" component,

The computer has transformed every aspect of the University's life since the late 1970s, including providing an on-line catalog in the University Libraries. The University will begin construction in 1994 of an "electronic" library that will provide information-retrieval capabilities and instructional technology. (Photo by Joseph Schuyler.)

added in 1986, required every academic department to offer "writing intensive courses" integrating writing with the subject matter of the course. A "human diversity" requirement was added in 1989, but by that year the whole program was under review. Freshmen entering in the Fall of 1993 were responsible for a revised set of requirements, striving toward a more coherent, critical and active engagement with the core disciplines.

The whole issue of undergraduate teaching was systematically reevaluated. While Albany students and alumni were generally satisfied with the quality of instruction, they complained about being closed out of courses. For their part, faculty pointed to rising student/faculty ratios and to increased research and administrative obligations. Everyone agreed that teaching could always be improved and that incentives for good teaching as compared with research should be enhanced. Student course evaluations were taken more seriously in tenure and promotion decisions; if outstanding teaching did not guarantee tenure, teaching competence became a prerequisite for it. The creation of the rank of Distinguished Teaching Professor in 1972 and other SUNY and campus awards for teaching excellence added further incentives.

In the late 1980s the University also tried to connect more closely the academic and non-academic life of undergraduates. Some classes were conducted in the residence halls, and a few faculty lived there, interacting with students and providing special programming. Special-interest housing was revived, giving undergraduates with similar academic interests an opportunity to live together. In 1993 there were twelve such housing areas including such interests as Romance languages, business and economics, honors, science, and the visual and performing arts.

The University became more attentive to the special needs of students at opposite ends of the academic spectrum. Students in academic difficulty could find "peer" tutors (for a fee), could attend study groups in any of eighteen freshman/sophomore level courses in ten areas, and, in the

Turning renewed attention to the undergraduate experience in the 1980s, the University instituted initiatives such as a Presidential Scholars program and University Honors, as well as academic support services to assist those experiencing difficulty. Sung Bok Kim, Dean of Undergraduate Studies, (top) and Carson Carr Jr., Associate Dean and Director of the Educational Opportunities Program, (bottom) have been instrumental in developing many of these programs.

case of freshmen, were assigned faculty mentors who helped them adjust to University life. Some departments had their own academic support services, and a Writing Center offered assistance to those having difficulties developing writing skills. The academically talented also received attention. They were encouraged to participate in the University's honors programs, beginning with special honors general education courses in the first two years and continuing with departmental honors programs.

The results were generally good, as measured by one of the most highly praised self-evaluative systems in the nation, run by the Office for Institutional Research. Retention and graduation rates at Albany were typically better than at the other three university centers, and the three-year retention rates at Albany were among the highest in the nation for public universities. Albany students also proved very successful in competing for admission to graduate schools and law schools. In a long series of "outcomes" studies, both alumni and undergraduates expressed a high level of satisfaction with their Albany education. Most of the alumni reported that they would come to Albany if "they had it to

An aerial view looking south of the University at Albany in 1981. With Washington Avenue and the main entrance in the foreground, the four residential quadrangles, clockwise from top left are Indian, Dutch, Colonial and State, named for the periods of New York State history. Following the initial construction of the Uptown Campus, there was no additional expansion at the University through the 1970s and most of the 1980s despite marked increases in enrollment. (Photo by Gary Gold, '70)

do all over again." Undergraduate education at Albany was far from perfect, but the University had good reason to be proud of its success.

The Student Association for more than a half century had provided a focus for student culture. It remained influential in the 1970s and 1980s, in part because it elected students to the Senate, but more because the mandatory student tax, through the '80s, was generating more than $1 million dollars annually. The SA budget was a fiscal lifeline to many of the ninety to 160 student organizations recognized on campus.

But student interest in the association waned. Turnouts for SA elections were usually low. An attempt in the 1980s to bring graduate students into SA (with its built-in mandatory tax) failed. Periodic referenda to renew the mandatory character of the student tax often came dangerously close to failure because of low student turnout. And surveys of student opinion showed a decline in satisfaction with student government between 1978 and 1988.

Student living arrangements varied. Demand for residence hall and off-campus housing fluctuated with their relative costs and convenience. Residence halls were crowded between the mid 1970s and the mid 1980s; on occasions there was doubling and even tripling-up. The overflow was housed in facilities such as the old Wellington Hotel in downtown Albany. In the 1980s, students, often pursuing greater personal freedom, began moving off campus in larger numbers.

Most off-campus students settled in areas close to the bus line connecting the two campuses. The combination of their numbers and lifestyles generated "town-gown" tensions. Year-round residents often complained of the consequences of crowding and student life styles: noise, parties, trash, and parking.

The City of Albany had in 1974 passed a so-called "grouper law," limiting

Dr. David Axelrod, New York State Commissioner of Health from 1979 to 1991, was instrumental in bringing about the establishment of a School of Public Health at the University in 1985. The School is a unique collaborative agreement that combines the academic resources in science education at the University with one of the nation's largest and most sophisticated health research laboratories. Here Axelrod addresses the 1990 Commencement after receiving the Medallion of the University.

Following the 1986 Commencement ceremony, Governor Cuomo took a few minutes to chat with the student members of Purple and Gold.

apartment occupants to no more than three unrelated persons. But the law was largely ignored until the mid 1980s, when a University study estimated that about 1,500 students were living in violation of it. In the Fall of 1989 a University-city task force examined the situation and urged the city to enforce its regulations aggressively, while asking the University to clearly inform its students of acceptable behavior. It also sought the creation of a mediation service to deal with specific problems.

Social activities remained a central element of undergraduate student culture. Indeed, Albany gained some reputation as a "party campus;" the 1991 *Princeton Review College Guide* asserted that Albany students "fall into the 'party away your free time' rut." Dress, like social life, remained informal.

The Greek societies had traditionally played a major role in undergraduate social life, but had almost disappeared during the 1970s. In 1980 the University identified only three Greek groups on campus, and none were noted in that year's *Torch*. But during the 1980s they made an astonishing comeback; in 1991 the University counted at least twenty fraternities and eight sororities whose total membership included

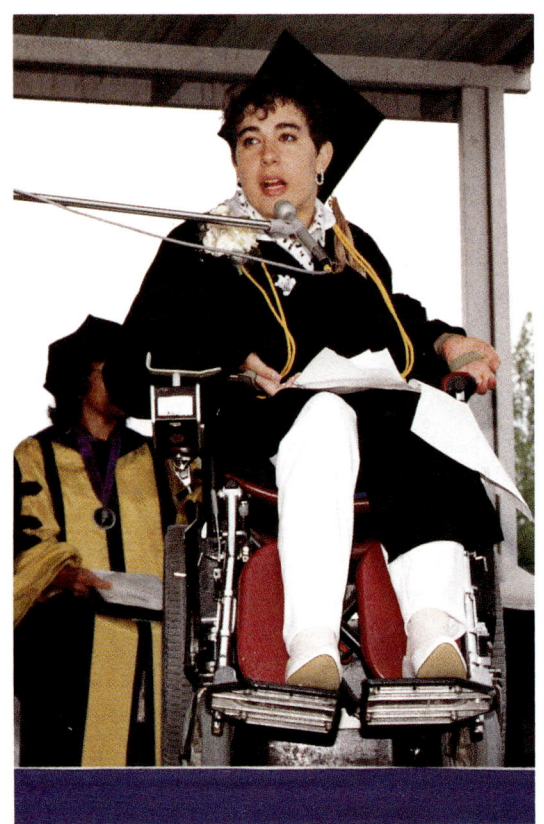

Efforts to provide access and support for disabled students through the 1980s and 1990s have led to increased participation by students with disabilities in all aspects of University life. Sheri Dinkelsohn was Commencement student speaker in 1989.

one out of four Albany undergraduates. Some were local, more had national affiliations (the SUNY ban on such groups had been rescinded in 1976). Some occupied space in the residence halls beginning in 1985; others operated "unofficial" houses from downtown residences.

Many areas of student life reflected larger cultural changes occurring in American society. The sexual revolution of the 1960s became more complicated in subsequent decades. The fear of AIDS introduced a new cautionary note. The emergence of the women's movement changed the terms of male-female relations. By the late 1980s, "date-rape" became a significant issue on college campuses. Many more gays and lesbians came out of the closet and joined organized advocacy groups.

Student use of "recreational" and other drugs had been a major cause for concern in the 1960s, but it is very difficult to track their use in subsequent years. A 1991 campus study suggested that nearly half of those Albany students surveyed had used marijuana at least once in the previous year, and some estimated that 8 to 10 percent of the student body used cocaine or other "hard drugs."

But the "drug of choice" for Albany students was clearly alcohol. Public expectations of teachers meant that Albany students before the 1960s either were teetotalers or consumed their alcohol in private. But the 1960s brought changes: fewer students aimed to become teachers, the cultural shifts of the decade emphasized personal freedom and experimentation, and the University loosened its traditional regulation of student life. Thus alcohol played a central role in the public social life of the campus in the 1960s and 1970s.

The problem became more complicated when between 1983 and 1985 the state raised the legal age for purchase of alcohol from eighteen to twenty-one. Since the vast majority of undergraduates were under twenty-one, the University sharply restricted alcoholic beverages at public functions and attempted to limit their use in the residence halls. Alcohol usage went underground and off campus, but probably did not decline much. The University's multi-faceted substance abuse prevention effort promised to test the University's educational expertise as much as more traditional academic issues.

Idealistic student political activism declined in the 1970s but then revived in the 1980s around different issues. The right of Albany students to cast their votes in polling places on the campus was a heated issue in 1983. Other student activists concentrated on apartheid in South Africa and the civil war in Nicaragua. The large Jewish student population made itself heard on Middle Eastern issues and on the plight of Soviet Jewry. Most political activists were vaguely liberal, but diverse voices were heard in the political arena; forty student members of The Coalition Against Pornography protested the University Cinema's presentation of an X-rated film on campus in 1985.

Student groups appealed to almost every imaginable interest. On a page headed, "Here's Where to Get Involved," the '87-'88 *Viewpoint* listed more than 120 student organizations. They ranged from the Accounting Club to the Young Americans for Freedom, from the Amateur Radio Club to the Taikwon Do Club, from the Dance Council

After nearly disappearing in the 1970s, Greek life at Albany experienced an astonishing resurgence in the 1980s, as was evident at 1991's Fountain Day. About one in every four undergraduate students was a member of one of forty-nine Greek organizations. (University Photo Service.)

to the Pre-Chiropractic Club. Some, such as the *ASP* or Theatre Council, had a long history on campus. Others, such as the Water Polo Club or Don't Walk Alone (the latter with a emphasis on campus security), embodied newer concerns.

All-University activities were relatively scarce but spirited. An April 1985 game of musical chairs involving 5,060 students, faculty and staff put Albany for the first time into the *Guinness Book of Records*. The annual "Fountain Day" enabled the campus community to celebrate the coming of warm weather and the play of decorative fountains. Purple and Gold, a new honor and service organization, performed some of the functions of the defunct Myskania. Torch Night became a moving ritual for nearly all graduating students.

Intercollegiate athletics grew, particularly with the addition of women's teams. In 1993 Albany fielded ten women's and eleven men's squads. Their fortunes, of course, varied from year to year, the mid 1980s being especially successful. In 1985-86 all eight winter sports participated in some kind of post-season play. Women's gymnastics finished fourth in the ECAC tournament in 1985. The 1984 women's basketball team compiled a 23-4 record and the following year had a 24-game win streak, only to lose in the quarter-finals of the NCAA championships. The wrestling team had an impressive 17-2 season in 1985-86 and often sent individual wrestlers to national and international

(Above) The fifteenth President of the University, H. Patrick Swygert, was appointed in 1990. (Photo by Joseph Schuyler.)

(Opposite) Ed Lemon, '94, from Ossining in a 1993 football game against St. Lawrence. (Photo by Steve Lobel, '70.)

meets. The track and cross-country teams boasted several top-ten NCAA team finishes and a hoard of All-American individuals in the late 1980s.

"Doc" Sauers continued his winning ways and became one of the most successful Division III coaches in NCAA history. 1991-92 marked the thirty-seventh consecutive non-losing season for Sauers-coached teams at Albany (still unbroken) and brought him his 600th varsity basketball win. Football coach Bob Ford, in his first sixteen years at Albany, compiled the highest winning percentage of any Division III coach in the nation. The 1985 football team was ECAC champion. Both Sauers and Ford sent assistants on to head coaching positions at other institutions.

The University in 1989 considered moving to NCAA Division I in all sports except football. While a campus committee reported that Albany was well positioned for such a move by virtue of size, academic quality, aspirations and facilities, the process was suspended in 1991 when fiscal challenges from the state again threatened University programs. By most criteria, the University had developed a highly successful

Purple and Gold is an honorary service society that continues the traditions of Myskania. Here members of the organization in 1991 join President Swygert and Mrs. Sonja Swygert.

sports program. Yet it never became the focus of University life that some people hoped for and others feared.

The University presided over student activities through its student affairs office. That function had been downgraded in the 1970s with the end of *in loco parentis*. The Middle States visitation team in 1980 thought that student services had been short-changed and urged the University to recreate the position of Vice President for Student Affairs. Consequently in August of 1983 Frank Pogue, a sociologist who had for a decade chaired the Department of African and Afro-American Studies, was appointed to the position.

Pogue and his successor, Mitchel Livingston, sought to provide direction and leadership in all facets of student life. Their most notable goal was to improve the quality of life in the residence halls and reconnect it with academic concerns. But the division also oversaw a variety of student support services such as the University Health Center, Middle Earth, and counseling personnel.

Rules governing student behavior were outlined in a brochure called *Student Guidelines*. Enforcement was in the hands of Student Affairs and a student judicial system developed in the late 1960s. The student-run system worked well in the area of residential life, but dealing with academic dishonesty cases was more complicated. Faculty/student panels heard such cases, but often struggled to find appropriate sanctions. A failing grade in the course in which cheating occurred sometimes seemed too lenient while suspension or expulsion often seemed too harsh.

Distinguished Service Professor Edna Acosta-Belen, (top) '69, Ph.D. '77, is a member of the Department of Latin American and Caribbean Studies, one of several new departments established to teach and research issues in ethnic and cultural studies. Anthropologist Dean Falk (bottom) has received national attention for her theories about the evolution of the human brain. (Acosta-Belen photo by Gary Gold, '70. Falk photo by Joseph Schuyler.)

(Above) Each fall President Swygert honors members of the University faculty who have edited journals or authored books during that year at the Authors and Editors Recognition Program, where the works are displayed. (Opposite) Tom Smith, professor of English, associate director of the New York State Writers Institute and host of the nationally syndicated public radio program "The Book Show," is the featured speaker. (Photos by Deborah Neary.)

When Institutional Research surveyed students on their level of satisfaction with their Albany experience, academic areas fared well. But students in 1991 were less satisfied with college social activities, the bus service, financial aid services, campus food, recreation and intramurals, parking, and the bookstore than their counterparts had been thirteen years earlier.

Americans have had great confidence in education. In the 1840s the Normal School was asked to train teachers who, through the common schools, would eliminate all of the social vices of the day. In the 1960s, students and faculty looked to the university for a solution to Vietnam. The issue of the 1980s and 1990s was "diversity." Optimists believed the university had an opportunity to solve within its own community one of the world's most perplexing problems. Pessimists feared that the competing interests and values so central to diversity could destroy the university as an institution.

"Diversity" refers to the emergence in American society of self-conscious cultural groups who challenge the dominant culture. On the Albany campus such groups began to appear in the late 1960s. The earliest were African-Americans influenced by the "black power" movement, but they were quickly joined by other ethnic groups: Hispanics, Italians, and Jews. By 1975-76 there were on campus nearly a dozen student organizations with an ethnic or national identification. Racial and ethnic groups were joined by feminists and gay and lesbian activists.

All of these interests cultivated group self-consciousness; some showed separatist tendencies. Traditionally African-American Greek societies appeared on campus, and in 1985 a black sorority sponsored the First Annual Minority Homecoming Pageant, complete with minority homecoming king and queen.

The new cultural groups raised an important educational issue. Whose culture is to be transmitted to the next generation? Over a period of a quarter century the new cultural groups gained access to the undergraduate curriculum. New departments appeared: Africana Studies, Puerto Rican Studies (subsequently part of a merger that created Latin American and Caribbean Studies), Judaic Studies, Women's Studies, and Hispanic and Italian Studies. In addition, new undergraduate general education requirements included a "diversity" component.

The University embraced diversity as a positive principle that gave voice to new groups and enriched the fabric of university life. The academic calendar began to observe the Jewish holidays. Affirmative action programs brought more women and minorities to the faculty. Albany took justifiable pride in its efforts to provide access to the physically handicapped and special help to students with learning disabilities. Everyone rejoiced when Michael Corso, a blind communications major and honors student, was elected Student Association president in 1982. Diversity committees explored "all avenues for increasing diversity . . ." In the late 1980s the University undertook a successful campaign to recruit minority undergraduates in such numbers that the composition of the student body would ultimately resemble that of New York's population.

Programs to minimize group tensions and help the University's diverse population live together were also developed. Incoming freshmen in the Fall of 1988 read Toni Morrison's novel, *Beloved*, concerned with racial issues, and those the following year read Jonathan Kozol's moving report on the plight of New York City's homeless, *Rachel and Her Children*. The annual World Week celebrated a range of international cultures. Sexuality Week, begun in 1983, presented a variety of lectures and workshops. In 1986, Gay and Lesbian Pride Week offered speakers, workshops, and films in addition to a candlelight vigil for victims of AIDS. Speech and behavior that offended the sensibilities of "minority"

A newer Albany tradition since 1978 has been "Fountain Day," originally conceived by Student Association Vice President Fred Brewington, '79 to celebrate the Human Awareness Program (HAP) with "HAP Day." The celebration marks the day in spring when the University's Main Fountain begins operating again. Virtually the entire University community gathers for the noon-time festivities. Pictured (above) are a view of the fountain as the water went on in 1992, and (opposite) spectators on the podium in 1993. (Photos by Joseph Schuyler.)

groups were frowned on, a forerunner of the 1990s debate about laudable attempts to persuade people to avoid offensive language versus infringement upon the academic freedom and free speech of others.

Vincent O'Leary announced his resignation as President in 1989. His successor in the following year was forty-seven-year-old H. Patrick Swygert. The University's first African-American President had received an A.B. (1965) and a J.D. (1968) from Howard University. Apart from successful ventures into U.S. government service during the Carter administration, he had spent most of his career at Temple University, first as a law school professor and later in administrative positions culminating with that of executive vice president. He came to Albany with the requisite combination of academic credentials, administrative experience, energy, and sense of direction.

Swygert's early years as President emphasized continuity, but he also began to put his own impress on the University. When he arrived in Albany he announced that his first priority was "restoring undergraduate

The University at Albany New York State Legislative Delegation was organized in 1993 under the leadership of Senator Hugh Farley, '58, of Niskayuna and Assemblyman John McEneny of Albany. Gathered at the State Capitol in April 1993 were (front row) Assemblymen Robert D'Andrea of Saratoga Springs and Ronald Canestrari of Cohoes; Senator Farley; Assemblymen James Tedisco of Schenectady and Pat M. Casale of Troy; (back row) University Vice President for Finance and Business Carl P. Carlucci; John P. Berry, director of the Senate Finance Committee Office of Budget Studies; University Vice President for Student Affairs Mitchel Livingston; Assemblyman McEneny; President Swygert; Vice President for Academic Affairs Karen Hitchcock; Assemblyman Anthony J. Casale, '69, of Herkimer; and Vice President for University Advancement Christian G. Kersten. Unable to attend the event were Vice President for Research and Graduate Studies Jeanne E. Gullahorn and Senators Joseph L. Bruno of Brunswick, Howard C. Nolan Jr. of Albany, Stephen M. Saland of Poughkeepsie and Ronald B. Stafford of Plattsburgh; and Assemblymen Arnold W. Proskin, '61, of Colonie and John J. Faso of Kinderhook. (Photo by Joseph Schuyler.)

Members of the University Council, 1993-94: Seated, from left, Athena C. Kouray, Esq.; The Honorable John E. Holt-Harris, chair; Martha W. Miller, MA '67; Standing, from left, Steven N. Fischer, Vivian Hillier Thorne, '48, representing the alumni(ae), A. Rita Chandellier Glavin, Esq.; Athena V. Lord; Professor Joan Schulz, representing the faculty; Carolyn Gillis Wellington and John J. Poklemba, Esq. Not present when photo was taken were Karima Wilkins, '94, representing the students, and Richard A. Hanft, Esq. (Photo by Mark Schmidt.)

The 1993 Alumni(ae) Leadership, from right to left: kneeling, Roberta Greenbaum Bastow, '81, president; Jason J. Friedman, '85, vice president; Frederick K. Brewington, '79, immediate past president. Second row: Lorna Reamer, Alumni Office; Board members Teresa Kerwin Lehr, '60; Diane DiGiorgio, '80, '85; Barry Z. Davis, '74; Kristin Lang, '92; and Esther Siegel Hoffman, '37, '40; Nadine Weltman Lahan, '70, Gold Coast Florida Chapter; Board members Maria Maglione, '88; and Victor K. Looper, '70; Susan Mindich McCullough, '84, Metro New York Chapter; Board members Annette Gardiner DeLyser, '49, '55; Claire F. Deloria, '56, '59. Back row: Amy Doig Cullen, M.A. '90, Alumni Office; Board member Winsome Foderingham-Herard, '89, '92; Helen E. Adams, M.S., '90, Alumni Office; Carol Livingston, Director of Alumni Affairs; Board members Robert S. Peterkin, '66, '76; Kenneth T. Doran, '39; and Stephen J. Colucci, '76, '79, '82, chair Council of Classes; Konrad W. Maier, '54, Western New York Chapter; Board members Paul D. Piccininni, '77; and Arthur N. Collins, '48; Matt Necon, '83, Los Angeles Chapter; Jonathan D. Waks, '90; Andrew Paul, '81, San Francisco Chapter; Board member Patty E. Salkin, '85; Andrew Fox, '88, Metro New York Chapter; Robert Giuffrida, '72, Capital District Chapter; Board members Michael Olin '85, '86; and Harold C. Hanson, '63; Jack Krull Jr., '79, Nation's Capital Chapter, Board member David A. Gellman, '78, '79. (Photo by Magic Photo.)

Since 1991 the University has held its Commencement exercises at the Knickerbocker Arena, Albany County's civic center. Pictured here is the 149th Commencement on May 16, 1993. The University will award its 100,000th degree at the Sesquicentennial Commencement in 1994. (Photo by Joseph Schuyler.)

instructional resources and improving the quality of the undergraduate experience." But he also made clear that the University's commitment to achieving racial and cultural diversity and helping diverse groups live together remained undiminished. Maintaining and improving the quality of the faculty and graduate programs and continuing and enhancing programs of service to the surrounding community were also on his agenda.

As usual, the issue of money intruded itself into University aspirations. In Swygert's first two years, state appropriations for Albany declined nearly 10 percent. Only by 1993 did the financial pressures appear to ease a bit. The search for private money became even more important. The Campaign for Albany, the major fund-raising effort of the University, had set a goal of $25 million by the Sesquicentennial year, 1994.

William Kennedy, Professor of English, (below) put Albany on the map in the early 1980s with his series of novels set in his native city. Following receipt of a MacArthur Foundation "genius award" in 1982 and the Pulitzer Prize for Fiction in 1983, Kennedy established a Writers Institute at the University, now funded by the New York State Legislature with a statewide mission. In 1987 the film based on *Ironweed* was filmed in the city and premiered at Albany's Palace Theater. (Photo by J. S. Carras, *Troy Record*.)

The University began celebrating its international dimensions in the 1980s with World Week, (above) a series of events and activities featuring students and faculty from other nations.

Novelist Toni Morrison, (below) who received the Governor's Arts Award in 1986 from Gov. Cuomo, joined the University at Albany faculty from 1985 to 1989 as the holder of a prestigious Schweitzer Chair in the Humanities, funded by the New York State Legislature. While she was at Albany, Morrison published the novel *Beloved*, for which she received the Pulitzer Prize for Fiction. In 1993 she was awarded the Nobel Prize for Literature.

Faculty through the 1980s and 1990s earned national reputations for their research and teaching and played an important role in the life of the University and the community at large. Ronald A. Bosco (above), Distinguished Service Professor of English, also served two terms as chair of the University Senate in the 1980s and co-chaired the Mission Statement Task Force of 1991-92; Shirley Jones (right), was named Distinguished Service Professor of Social Welfare in 1993. (Photos by Joseph Schuyler.)

Swygert retained that goal but in a daring move extended the drive to century's end and raised the final target to $55 million, the largest such campaign in the history of any SUNY institution.

Under Swygert, resourcefulness and increased dialogue with and support from the state government helped the University begin to address pressing needs and aspirations. Construction began in 1993 on a two-pronged extension to the Campus Center to provide more room for student services, and the University hoped by the Sesquicentennial to break ground directly south of the Campus Center for a digital-based, computer program and storage addition to the University Libraries. The most pressing need remaining was space for organized research, and in early 1993 the University announced plans to construct a 75,000 square-foot Center for Environmental Studies and Technology Management that would house the ASRC and National Weather Service,

Fuerza Latina, a student group, celebrates Hispanic heritage and culture with a celebration on the podium. (Photo by Matt Glynn, University Photo Service.)

Revitalized Greek life on campus is reflected in this portrait of the 1993 Pan Hellenic Council. Front: Raymond Lewis, Kevin Coleman. First row: Carlos Melendez, Deborah Plaskett, Tisa Howard, Bryan Carlen, Refina Bautista; Quamin Ellis, Nichole Michaels, Claudett Bazile, DeAnna Baker, Tanya Morrissey, Marsha Bastien, Kimberly Smith, Darryl Thorpe. Back row: Paul Buckley, Ian Ashe, Talim Lessane; Anthony Parker, Nickki Gant, Valerie Malland, Darrell Penn, Jamie Knight, Kelsel Thompson-Feliciano, Fateema Jones, Renee McNeal, Johnny Pacheco, Felicia Richardson, Michael Williams, Alexandra Guerrero, and Tardis Johnson, council president. (Photo by Sean Sime, University Photo Service.)

the Center for Advanced Technology, X-ray optics research, and high-tech business development and incubation programs—the project to be funded through a $10 million grant from the Legislature.

Resignations and retirements gave the new President an opportunity to make some administrative appointments and at least one important organizational change. Karen Hitchcock joined the University as its new Academic Vice President in 1991. She was a cell biologist who came with extensive administrative experience from a post as vice chancellor for research and dean of the graduate college at the University of Illinois-Chicago. Other administrative appointments included Carl P. Carlucci, former secretary of the New York State Assembly Ways & Means Committee, as Vice President for Finance and Business, Judy Genshaft as dean of the School of Education, and Richard Hughs as dean of the School of Business. Perhaps most important, a College of Arts and Sciences was reconstituted in the Fall of 1993 with Judith Gillespie as its dean.

Some of the most welcome academic news came in 1992-93 with the

(Right) On December 10, 1991, the University launched a $55-million "Campaign for Albany," the most ambitious ever undertaken by a SUNY institution. President Swygert was joined on the occasion by, from left, Assemblyman Ed Sullivan of New York, chair of the Assembly Higher Education Committee; Gary R. Allen, '70, chair of the campaign, Assemblyman Anthony J. Casale, '69, and J. Spenser Standish, chairman of Albany International and president of The University at Albany Foundation. The Sesquicentennial year goal is $25 million, with the balance to be raised by the end of the decade. (Photo by Edward Wozniak.)

Homecoming 1990 included presentation of the first President's Outstanding Young Alumni Service Award to Patty E. Salkin, '85, center left, and Frederick Brewington, '79, center right. President Swygert, left, and Alumni Association President Susan VanHorn Shipherd, '64, join Salkin and Brewington and their spouses Howard Gross and Adrienne Brewington.

(Top) Mary Anne Crotty, MPA, '82, is Governor Cuomo's Director of State Operations. (photo by Joseph Schuyler.)

(Above) A distinguished alumnae, Susan Molinari, '80, '81, is the first Albany graduate ever elected to Congress, now a second-term member from Staten Island.

(Right) In 1991 President Swygert presented a University chair to Barry and Nina Wagman of Wantagh at the President's Recognition Dinner in appreciation of their two years of service as national chairs of the Parents' Fund. The Wagmans have three daughters who attended Albany—Tracey, '91, Julie, '92, and Shari, '94—and through their involvement in generating support for the University represent a tradition of parental involvement. They currently serve as National Parents' Chairs for the "Campaign for Albany."

long-sought approval to reestablish the history, English, French studies and philosophy Ph.D.s. It marked an important milestone in the history of the institution. Doctorates central to the definition of a research university were once again offered at Albany, signifying a renewed emphasis on traditional academic disciplines.

Between 1977 and 1993 the University at Albany matured. The faculty steadily improved. Graduate programs were solidly established and, in some cases, developed national and international reputations. Research activities expanded several-fold and became an integral part of the campus. First-rate students received a quality undergraduate education. The report of the Middle States Association accreditation team in 1990 offered a resounding endorsement of the University's decade of full maturation, concluding that "Albany has made remarkable progress in becoming a high quality center for undergraduate study and an impressive graduate/research university in areas of public policy."

The future directions of the University were articulated in a new *Mission Statement* in 1992, prepared by a faculty committee—chaired by

Student leaders from the 1990s: William Weitz, '92, (below) was President of the Student Association in 1992, and was elected Student Trustee to the SUNY Board of Trustees in 1993-94. Derek Westbrook, '92, (left) was president of ASUBA, a student assistant in the Educational Opportunities Program, and the Commencement 1992 student speaker. He also won the 1990 National Council of Black Studies Creative Writing Competition in the undergraduate division.

Distinguished Service Professor of English Ronald A. Bosco and Graduate School of Public Affairs Dean Frank Thompson—at Swygert's initiative. It reaffirmed the traditional goals of a public research university: the advancement of knowledge, teaching, and public service. But it added several special emphases. The University, it said, should foster the ideals of justice, hold fast to the ideals of freedom of thought, inquiry, and expression, and seek to profit intellectually from differences of opinion and of culture. The document also made clear that the University was a comprehensive public research university whose programs in the arts and sciences and the professions reinforced one another and whose graduate programs and research activities reinvigorated undergraduate instruction. Finally, the *Mission Statement* reiterated the University's responsibility to build partnerships with academic, business, cultural and governmental organizations.

As Albany approached its Sesquicentennial, it could look back with pride on 150 years of contributions to public higher education. As a Normal School in the 19th Century it was a leader in training teachers for New York's common schools, and as a College for Teachers in the 20th Century it became one of the nation's premier institutions for preparing secondary school teachers. In 1962 the institution entered a new era, charged with becoming a modern public research university, and by 1994 that transformation had been completed with distinction.

In their first 149 years, the Normal School, Normal College, College for Teachers, and University had awarded 99,651 degrees. A total of 94,798 alumni(ae) were still living and contributing both to the institution from which they had graduated and to the larger societies of which they were a part.

Torch Night continues as one of the most enduring student traditions at Albany. It was renewed and enlarged in the 1980s.

Just as the members of the University community could look back with pride on their past, so they could look forward to their future with hope and confidence. The University in 1994 was well placed to achieve even greater distinction. The motto of the institution—*Sapientia et sua et docendi causa*, "Knowledge both for itself and for the sake of teaching"—held firm.

Chancellor of the State University of New York D. Bruce Johnstone presents the Presidential Medallion to H. Patrick Swygert at the President's Inauguration on April 5, 1991.

Appendix

The University at Albany Council 1993-94

The Honorable John E. Holt-Harris, Chairman, Albany
Steven N. Fischer, Albany
A. Rita Chandellier Glavin, Esquire, Waterford
Richard A. Hanft, Esquire, Troy
Athena C. Kouray, Esquire, Schenectady
Athena V. Lord, Albany
Martha W. Miller, Glenmont
John J. Poklemba, Esquire, Glens Falls
Carolyn Gillis Wellington, Schoharie
Vivian Hillier Thorne, Delmar, representing the alumni/ae
Joan E. Schulz, representing the faculty
Karima Wilkins, '94, representing the students

Officers of the University at Albany 1993-94

H. Patrick Swygert, President
Carl P. Carlucci, Vice President for Finance and Business
Jeanne E. Gullahorn, Vice President for Research and Dean of Graduate Studies
Karen R. Hitchcock, Vice President for Academic Affairs
Christian G. Kersten, Vice President for University Advancement
Mitchel D. Livingston, Vice President for Student Affairs
Meredith A. Butler, Dean of Library Faculty
David O. Carpenter, Dean of Public Health
David E. Duffee, Dean of Criminal Justice
Judy L. Genshaft, Dean of Education
Judith A. Gillespie, Dean of Arts and Sciences
Richard E. Hughs, Dean of Business
Sung Bok Kim, Dean of Undergraduate Studies
Richard P. Nathan, Provost of Nelson A. Rockefeller College of Public Affairs and Policy
Frank J. Thompson, Dean of the Graduate School of Public Affairs
Lynn Videka-Sherman, Dean of Social Welfare

Trustees of the State University of New York 1993-94

Chairman Frederic V. Salerno, Rye
Vice Chairman Arnold B. Gardner, Buffalo
Richard A. Berman, New York City
Roderick G.W. Chu, New York
D. Clinton Dominick, Newburgh
Judith Lasher Duken, Plattsburgh
Hazel N. Dukes, New York
John L. S. Holloman, Jr., East Elmhurst
Alan V. Iselin, Albany
Miles L. Lasser, Jamestown
Thomas Dixon Lovely, Garden City
Nancy H. Nielsen, Orchard Park
Rosemary C. Salomone, Rye
N. Theodore Sommer, Binghamton
William F. Weitz, '92, Albany
Chancellor D. Bruce Johnstone

Distinguished Professors
The highest professorial rank in the State University of New York

Edna Acosta-Belen, Distinguished Service Professor, Latin American and Caribbean Studies, 1993
Manuel Alvar, Distinguished Professor, Hispanic and Italian Studies, 1991
Charles Luther Andrews,* Distinguished Teaching Professor, Physics, 1976
David H. Barlow, Distinguished Professor, Psychology, 1989
Edward B. Blanchard, Distinguished Professor, Psychology, 1989
Ronald A. Bosco, Distinguished Service Professor, English, 1992
Stephen C. Brown, Distinguished Teaching Professor, Biological Sciences, 1986
Donn E. Byrne, Distinguished Professor, Psychology, 1991
James W. Corbett, Distinguished Service Professor, Physics, 1981
William N. Fenton,* Distinguished Professor, Anthropology, 1974
Harry L. Frisch, Distinguished Professor, Chemistry, 1978
Eugene K. Garber, Distinguished Teaching Professor, English, 1989
Walter M. Gibson, Distinguished Service Professor, Physics, 1988
Josiah B. Gould, Distinguished Teaching Professor, Philosophy, 1990
M.E. Grenander,* Distinguished Service Professor, English, 1986
Richard H. Hall, Distinguished Service Professor, Sociology, 1989
William K. Holstein, Distinguished Service Professor, School of Business, 1991
Mauritz Johnson,* Distinguished Service Professor, Program Development and Evaluation, 1982
Shirley J. Jones, Distinguished Service Professor, Social Welfare, 1993
John Mackiewicz, Distinguished Teaching Professor, Biology, 1973
Hugh N. MacLean,* Distinguished Teaching Professor, English, 1974
Bruce B. Marsh,* Distinguished Teaching Professor, Physics, 1989
Richard P. Nathan, Distinguished Professor, Rockefeller College, 1990
Robert Rienow (deceased), Distinguished Service Professor, Political Science, 1979
Warren F. Roberts, Distinguished Teaching Professor, History, 1984
Seth W. Spellman (deceased), Distinguished Service Professor, Social Welfare, 1984
Margaret M. Stewart, Distinguished Teaching Professor, Biology, 1977
Edward S. Thomas, Distinguished Teaching Professor, Mathematics, 1985
Hans H. Toch, Distinguished Professor, Criminal Justice, 1985
Bernard Vonnegut,* Distinguished Professor, Atmospheric Science, 1983
Douglas M. Windham, Distinguished Service Professor, Education, 1991

*Retired

Collins Fellows

Honored for "extraordinary devotion to the University at Albany"

Edna Acosta-Belen, Collins Fellow, Latin American and Caribbean Studies, Hispanic and Italian Studies, and Women's Studies, 1988

M. I. Berger, Collins Fellow, Educational Administration and Policy, 1990

Kendall Birr,* Collins Fellow, History, 1985

Christine E. Bose, Collins Fellow, Sociology, Latin American and Caribbean Studies, and Women's Studies, 1992

Shirley Brown, Collins Fellow, Psychology, 1987

Harold Cannon (deceased), Collins Fellow, Accounting, 1986

Frank Carrino,* Collins Fellow, Hispanic and Italian Studies, 1984

Richard Clark,* Collins Fellow, Educational Psychology and Statistics, 1989

R. Findlay Cockrell, Collins Fellow, Music, 1987

Arthur Collins,* Collins Fellow, English, 1985

Stephen E. DeLong, Collins Fellow, Geological Sciences, 1991

Helen Desfosses, Collins Fellow, Public Administration and Africana Studies, 1992

Margaret Farrell,* Collins Fellow, Teacher Education, 1986

Judith Fetterley, Collins Fellow, English, 1990

Francine W. Frank, Collins Fellow, Linguistics and Cognitive Science, 1993

Helen Horowitz,* Collins Fellow, Economics, 1984

Sung Bok Kim, Collins Fellow, History, 1993

Eugene McLaren,* Collins Fellow, Chemistry, 1988

Donald J. Reeb, Collins Fellow, Economics, 1992

Joan E. Schulz, Collins Fellow, English, 1991

Harold Story,* Collins Fellow, Physics, 1989

*Retired

Index

A

Academic Administration, 26 (photo), 27, 29, 69 (photo), 69-70, 94-95, 131, 136 (photo), 137 (photo), 166 (photo), 167 (photo), 177-79, 179 (photo), 185 (photo), 187, 192 (photo), 205, 212
   Centers and Institutes, 136, 140 (photo), 170 (photo), 184 (photo), 188
   Departments and Programs, 55, 168
   Schools and Colleges, 129-130, 168, 178, 180 (photo), 185, 185 (photo), 187, 188, 194 (photo), 212
Acosta-Belen, Edna, 201 (photo), 218, 219
Academic programs, *see* Instruction, Undergraduate and Graduate Study and Programs
Adams, Harriet Dyer, 151 (photo)
Admissions, Undergraduate, 23, 33-34, 56, 71-72, 136-137, 190
African-Americans, 35, 105, 114 (photo), 158-159, 158 (photo), 162, 165 (photo), 205
Albany, City of, 15, 17, 52, 124
Albany Country Club, 123 (photo), 124
Albany Student Press, *see* Student Culture, Publications
Alden, Joseph, 28-30, 29 (photo), 38 (caption)
Allen, Gary R., 213 (photo)
Allen, James E., 146
Allen, Robert, 139 (photo)
Alumni(ae), 17 (photo), 21 (photo), 26 (photo), 30-32 (photo), 35 (photo), 34-40 (photo), 43 (photo), 46 (photo), 54 (photo), 59 (photo), 61 (photo), 62 (photo), 65 (photo), 69 (photo), 82 (photo), 115 (photo), 122 (photo), 150 (photo), 151 (photo), 213 (photo), 214 (photo), 216
   Association, 40, 74-75, 138-139, 207 (photo)
   Memorial Window, 39-41, 42 (photo), 51
   Reunions, 40, 80, 90 (photo)
Alvar, Manuel, 218
Andrews, Charles Luther, 69, 218
Architects, *see*
   Stone, Edward Durell
   Ross, Albert R.
   Wright, Frank P.
Arbit, Bernard, 90 (photo)
Arey, Oliver, 28, 29 (photo)
Aspinwall, William, 54 (photo), 59 (caption), 69
Athletics and Physical Education, 29, 55 (photo), 60-61, 70, 72 (photo), 80, 82, 109 (photo), 143, 147 (photo), 174 (photo), 180, 188 (photo), 198 (photo), 199-200, 201
Axelrod, David, 187, 194 (photo)

B

Barlow, David, 184 (photo), 218
Barnard, Henry, 21
Barnard, Phoebe Ann, 21 (photo), 32
Bastow, Roberta Greenbaum, 207 (photo)
Bayley, David H., 218
Beaver, Ralph, 69, 132
Benezet, Louis T., 162 (photo), 164, 166-167, 175 (photo)
Berger, M.I., 139 (photo), 219
Berman, Richard A., 218
Bickel, Theodore, 142
Birchenough, Harry, 55, 85 (photo)
Birr, Kendall, 139 (photo), 219, 224, 224 (photo)
Bishop, M. Harriet, 54 (photo)
Bishop, Marjorie, 89 (photo)
Blanchard, Edward, 184 (photo), 218
Blue, Leonard, 69, 69 (photo)
Board of Trustees, *see* Governing Bodies

219

Board of Visitors, *see* Governing
    Bodies
Boroff, David, 105, 116
    (caption), 141, 144
Bosco, Ronald A., 210 (photo),
    215, 218
Bose, Christine E., 219
Bouck, William C., Governor,
    13, 15
Boyer, Ernest, 168, 169
Brett, Henrietta, 122 (photo)
Brewington, Frederick, 174
    (photo), 204 (caption), 207
    (photo), 213 (photo)
Brimmer, Bertha, 59 (photo)
Brown, Shirley C., 183 (photo),
    219
Brown, Stephen C., 218
Brubacher, Abram, 62 (photo),
    63, 64-66, 68, 71, 74, 75,
    83, 84, 84 (photo), 146
Budgets and Finance, 26, 96,
    129, 166-170, 178-179,
    208
Building and Campuses, 71
    (photo), 74, 74 (photo)
    State Street, 11, 16 (photo),
        17
    Lodge and Howard Streets,
        26, 27 (photo)
    Uptown Campus, 118,
        123-128, 123-125
        (photos), 127 (photo),
        141, 153 (photo), 179,
        180, 181 (photo), 193
        (photo), 211
    Western and Washington
        Avenues, (Downtown
        Campus), 52-54, 56
        (photo), 70, 71
        (photo), 97, 117, 180
    Willett Street, 39, 41-42
        (photos), 48 (photo),
        49, 50, 51
Bulger, Paul, 79 (photo)
Burian, Jarka, 175 (caption)
Burke, Arvid, 79 (photo)
Burke, Kevin, 168 (photo)
Burstein, Karen, 184 (photo)
Butler, Meredith A., 218
Byrne, Donn E., 218

C

Cady, Jean, 86 (photo)
Canestrari, Ronald, 206 (photo)

Cannon, Harold, 219
Carlson, William, 120
Carlucci, Carl P., 206 (photo),
    212, 218
Carpenter, David O., 218
Carr, Carson, Jr., 192 (photo)
Carrino, Frank, 219
Casale, Anthony J., 206 (photo),
    213 (photo)
Casale, Pat M., 206 (photo)
Centennial (1944), 86, 91
    (photo)
Center for Advanced Technology
    (CAT), 176 (photo), 212
Center for Environmental
    Studies and Technology
    Management, 211
Cheatum, Mary, 105
Chesin, Sorrell, 175 (photo)
Chu, Roderick G. W., 218
Civil War, 32 (photos), 34
Clapton, Eric, 173 (photo)
Clark, Richard, 219
Cleveland, Grover, 9 (photo)
Cochran, David H., 28 (photo)
Cockrell, R. Findlay, 183 (photo)
Collins, Arthur, 105, 122
    (photo), 139 (photo), 219
Collins, Evan Revere, 94-96, 96
    (photo), 118 (photo), 122,
    126, 129, 131-133, 145
    (caption), 146, 146
    (photo), 153 (photo), 158-
    159, 162 (caption), 163
Collins, Judy, 142
Collins, Virginia, 96 (photo)
Commencement, 9 (photo), 49
    (photo), 128 (photo), 131
    (photo), 190 (photo), 208
    (photo)
Common Schools, 12-13
Computers, 181, 191 (photo)
Conklin, Mary E., 87 (photo)
Cooper, Hermann, 65, 86
Corbett, James W., 182 (photo),
    218
Corning, Erastus, III, 124, 124
    (photo), 127 (photo), 175
    (photo)
Corso, Michael, 187 (photo),
    203
Council, *see* Governing Bodies
Cowley, Edward, 183 (photo)
Crotty, Mary Anne, 214 (photo)
Crull, Harry, 170
Cuomo, Madeline, 190 (photo)

Cuomo, Mario M., Governor,
    190 (photo), 195 (photo),
    209 (photo)
Curriculum, Undergraduate, *see*
    Instruction, Undergraduate

D

D'Andrea, Robert, 206 (photo)
Davis, Miles, 173 (photo)
Davis, Zoraida, 189 (photo)
de Beer, Anna Boocheever, 59
    (photo)
De Cicco, Dorothy, 112 (photo)
DeLong, Stephen E., 219
Departments, *see* Academic
    Administration
Desfosses, Helen, 219
Dewey, John, 169 (photo)
Dewey, Thomas E., Governor,
    84, 99 (photo), 120
Dinkelsohn, Sheri, 196 (photo)
Dippikill, Camp, 102
Discipline, *see* Student Body,
    Behavior and Discipline
Diversity Issue, 202, 203, 208
Doctoral Program Reviews, *see*
    Graduate Study and
    Programs
Dominick, D. Clinton, 218
Donehue, Vincent, 81
Dormitories, *see* Student Body,
    Housing
Douglas, Gertrude, 86 (photo)
Draper, Andrew Sloane, 40, 46,
    47 (photo), 49, 51, 61, 121
Duci, Frank, 175 (photo)
Duda, Betty, 115 (photo)
Duken, Judith Lasher, 218
Dukes, Hazel N., 218
Dunham, George H., 20
    (caption)
Dwight, Francis, 17

E

Earle, Kathy, 129
Educational Opportunities
    Program, 158, 160-161
    (photos), 192 (photo)
Ely, Donald, 114 (photo)
Enrollments/Graduates, 23, 29,
    45, 49, 56, 63, 93, 128-
    129, 179, 185, 216
Epstein, Jacob, 122 (photo)
Erskine, John, 86, 91 (photo)
Eson, Morris, 139 (photo)

Executive Committee, *see*
    Governing Bodies
Experimental School, *see*
    Practice School
Extension Programs, *see*
    Graduate Study and
    Programs

F

Faculty, 23, 26 (photo), 32, 32
    (photo), 33, 38 (caption),
    39-40 (photos), 50 (photo),
    54 (photo), 62 (photo), 64
    (photo), 68-69, 70 (photo),
    81 (photo), 84-85, 85-88
    (photos), 97-98, 104-105
    (photos, 111 (photo), 116
    (photo), 132, 137-140
    (photos), 138-139, 153
    (photo), 163 (photo), 165
    (photos), 168-172 (photos),
    176 (photo), 182-184, 182-
    185 (photos), 188 (photo),
    201-203 (photos), 210
    (photo)
    Governance, 96, 130, 161,
        162, 163 (photo), 184
    Tenure, 97, 163, 169, 182
Faculty-Student
    Association, 102
Falconer, Ray, 136, 140 (photo),
    141
Falk, Dean, 201 (photo)
Farley, Hugh, 206 (photo)
Farrell, Margaret, 219
Fenton, William N., 218
Fetterley, Judith, 219
Fields, Emmett, 164, 167, 167
    (photo), 177, 187
Finder, Morris, 162
Fischer, Steven N., 207 (photo),
    218
Fiser, Webb, 136 (photo)
Flinton, Edgar, 95, 98 (photo),
    133
Fonda, Jane, 181 (photo)
Ford, Robert, 143, 200
Foreign Students, *see*
    International Students
Foreign Study, 137, 188
Fossieck, Ted, 171 (photo)
Founding, 11, 12, 13
Frank, Francine W., 219
Franklin, Aretha, 173 (photo)
Fraternities and Sororities, *see*

Student Culture:
Fraternities and
Sororities
Frederick, Robert, 85 (photo)
Freedman, Ira, 90 (photo)
French, Florence Smith, 7, 86
French, William Marshall, 7, 86
Friedlander, Leonard E., 114 (photo)
Friedman, Jason J., 207 (photo)
Frisch, Harry L., 218
Fund-raising
Alumni Memorial Window, 39-43
Capital Campaign, 179, 211, 213 (photo)
Dormitory Campaign, 74-75, 76 (photo), 77
Futterer, Agnes, 80, 81, 81 (photo), 94, 103, 111 (photo)

G

Garber, Eugene K., 218
Gardner, Arnold B., 218
Gardner, Randolph, 139 (photo)
Gay, Ray, 174 (photo)
Genshaft, Judy L., 212, 218
Gibson, Walter M., 218
Gillespie, Judith A., 212, 218
Glavin, A. Rita Chandellier, 207 (photo), 218
Goodwin, Edward J., 49
Gould, Harold, 81, 103, 111 (photo)
Gould, Josiah B., 218
Gould, Samuel, 120
Governing Bodies, 15, 65, 207 (photo)
Graduate Study and Programs, 47, 67, 68, 98, 133-134, 163, 165-166, 185, 187-189, 212, 214
Graduates, see Enrollments/Students
"Great Dane," The, 129 (photo)
Green, Mattie, 85 (photo)
Green, Mordaunt, 38
Greenberg, Sol, 90 (photo)
Grenander, M. E., 170 (photo), 218
Griffin, Dorothy Griffin, 82 (photo)
Gullahorn, Jeanne A., 178, 179 (photo), 218

H

Hall, Richard H., 218
Hamilton, Harry L., 163 (photo)
Hamilton, Thomas, 119 (photo)
Hanft, Richard A., 207 (caption), 218
Hanson, Harold, 207 (photo)
Harriman, W. Averell, Governor, 120, 124
Harrison, Wallace, 124
Hartigan, John, 167 (photo), 178
Hartley, David, 95
Hartley, John, 167 (photo)
Hartlief, Dale, 140 (photo)
Hastings, Harry, 75, 153 (caption)
Hastings, Louise Clement, 153 (caption)
Hathaway, Merlin, 138 (photo)
Hawley, Gideon, 12 (photo)
Heald, Henry, 121
Heald Commission, 121
Henry, Joseph, 17, 21
Hilton, Florence Linindoll, 122 (photo)
Hispanic-Americans, 162, 211 (photo)
Hitchcock, Karen R., 206 (photo), 212, 218
Holloman, John, L. S., Jr., 218
Holstein, William K., 218
Holt-Harris, John E., 207 (photo), 218
Hoover, Herbert, 84
Hopkins, Vivian, 104 (photo), 106 (caption)
Horner, Harland Hoyt, 62 (photo), 69
Horowitz, Helen, 7, 138 (photo), 219
Horton, Edward B., 35 (photo)
Hughes, Charles E., 54
Hughs, Richard, 212
Hulburd, Calvin T., 13
Humphrey, Friend, 15 (photo)
Husted, Albert N., 32, 32 (photo), 33, 40, 40 (photo), 55
Hutchins, Ruth, 85 (photo)
Hutchinson, David, 62 (photo)
Hyde, Aurelia, 46 (photo)
Hyde, Mary F., 38 (caption), 39 (photo)

I

Ilchman, Warren, 178, 180 (photo), 187
Instruction, Undergraduate, 18-23, 29-30, 47-50, 50-51 (photos), 55, 65-67, 68 (photo), 86 (photo), 100, 107 (photo), 159, 162-163, 164 (photo), 172, 189-192, 192 (photo), 193-194, 205, 208
International Students, 35, 35 (photo), 106 (photo), 137, 188, 209 (photo)
Irvis, K. Leroy, 82 (photo)
Iselin, Alan V., 181 (photo), 218

J

James E. Allen Collegiate Center, 163-164, 164 (photo), 168
Jennings, John, 105, 114 (photo)
Johnpoll, Benard K., 171 (photo)
Johnson, Mauritz, 218
Johnstone, D. Bruce, 217 (photo), 218
Jones, Louis, 86, 87 (photo)
Jones, Shirley, 210 (photo), 218
Jones, William, 30 (photo)
Joplin, Janis, 142, 145 (photo)

K

Kaloyeros, Alain, 176 (photo)
Kendall, Richard, 139 (photo)
Kennedy, William, 188, 209 (photo)
Kersten, Christian G., 179, 206 (photo), 218
Kim, Sung Bok, 192 (photo), 218, 219
Kimball, Rodney, 32, 32 (photo)
King, Martin Luther, Jr., 157
Knotts, Walter, 139 (photo)
Koch, Audrey, 113 (photo)
Kodzu, Senzaburo, 35, 35 (photo)
Koriyama, Naoshi, 106 (photo)
Kouray, Athena C., 206 (photo), 218
Kozol, Jonathan, 203
Kristofferson, Kris, 181 (photo)
Krizka, Helen, 78

Kunstler, William, 155, 157 (photo)
Kuusisto, Allan, 137, 154 (photo), 155, 157, 164

L

Ladman, Cathy, 174 (photo)
Lampert, Michael, 174 (photo)
Lanford, Oscar, 95, 97 (photo), 136, 182
Lanford, William, 182 (photo)
Larney, Violet, 138 (photo)
Latina, Fuerza, 211 (photo)
LaValle, Kenneth, 190 (photo)
LaValle, Lisa, 190 (photo)
Lemon, Ed, 198 (photo)
Lennig, Arthur, 111 (photo)
Libraries, 17-18, 70, 97, 136, 153 (photo), 181-182, 191 (photo), 211
Livingston, Mitchel D., 178, 201, 206 (photo), 218
Lord, Athena V., 207 (photo), 218
Lovely, Thomas Dixon, 218

M

Mackiewicz, John, 168 (photo), 218
MacLean, Hugh N., 170 (photo), 218
Mailer, Norman, 188
Mann, Horace, 13, 13 (photo), 18, 26
Marsh, Bruce B., 218
Martin, Carl, 160 (photo)
McClelland, Mary, 38 (caption), 39 (photo), 55
McGee-Russell, Samuel, 139 (photo)
McEneny, John, 7, 206 (photo)
McLaren, Eugene, 180 (photo), 219
Merrit, Edna, 69 (photo)
Metzler, William Henry, 70
Milk, Harvey, 115 (photo)
Miller, Martha W., 207 (photo), 218
Milne School, see Practice School
Milne, William J., 45, 46, 47 (photo), 48, 49, 49 (photo), 52, 59 (caption), 61, 67
Minerva, see Student Culture, Traditions

Mission of the Institution, 29, 45, 98, 121-123, 214-216
Model School, *see* Practice School
Molinari, Susan, 214 (photo)
Morrison, Toni, 188, 203, 209 (photo)
Morse, Wayne, 160
Moving Up day, *see* Student Culture, Traditions
Munsey, R. Keith, 97
Murphy, Alice Hastings, 153 (photo)
Myskania, *see* Student culture, Government
Mysliborski, Judith, 150 (photo)

N

Names of the Institution, 11, 45, 47, 61, 119
Nathan, Richard, 185 (photo), 187, 218
Native American students, 34 (photo), 35
Nelson, Milton, 70, 85 (photo), 94, 95
New York State Writers Institute, 188, 203 (photo), 209 (photo)
Newell, Gladys, 79 (photo)
Nielsen, Nancy H., 218
Nixon, Richard M., 156
Nyquist, Ewald, 165

O

O'Leary, Vincent, 177, 178, 178 (photo), 181 (photo), 187, 190 (photo), 205
Olson, Milton, 137 (photo)
One Hundred and Twenty-Fifth Anniversary, 146
O'Reilly, Charles, 164
Otlinger, Albert, 84

P

Page, David Perkins, 10 (photo), 12, 18, 21, 22, 23, 25, 27, 29
Parker, Caroline G., 34 (photo)
Parker, Nicholson Henry, 34 (photo)
Passow, Harry, 90 (photo)
Passow, Shirley, 87 (photo)
Paul, Thurston T., 88 (photo)
Paxton, Tom, 142

Payne, Clyde, 105
Perine, Eunice, 7 (photo), 65
Perkins, George R., 12, 26 (photo), 28-29, 37
Perlman, Nancy, 184 (photo)
Persico, Joseph, 115 (photo)
Peterkin, Robert, 150 (photo), 207 (photo)
Pettit, Paul Bruce, 103 (photo)
Phelps, William, 11, 17 (photo), 21, 26 (photo), 35
Phi Beta Kappa, *see* Student Culture, Honoraries
Phinney, Josiah, 105 (photo)
Physical Education, *see* Athletics and Physical Education
Pierce, Anna Eloise, 46 (photo), 55, 58, 62 (photo),65, 73, 74, 76 (caption), 77 (photo), 83, 95
Pogue, Frank, 178, 179 (photo), 201
Pohlsander, Hans, 162
Poklemba, John J., 207 (photo), 218
Potter, Alonzo, 13 (photo), 18
Potter, Edward Eldred, 18, 65 (photo)
Practice School, 21, 30, 67, 98, 169, 171 (photo)
Presidents, *see*
    Alden, Joseph, 1867-1882
    Waterbury, Edward P., 1882-1889
    Milne, William J., 1889-1914
    Brubacher, Abram, 1915-1939
    Sayles, John, 1939-1947
    Collins, Evan Revere, 1949-1969
    Benezet, Louis T., 1970-1975
    Fields, Emmett, 1975-1977
    O'Leary, Vincent, 1977-1990
    Swygert, H. Patrick, 1990
    see also Principals
Primary School, *see* Practice School
Principals, *see*
    Page, David Perkins, 1844-1848
    Perkins, George R., 1848-1852

    Woolworth, Samuel B., 1852-1856
    Cochran, David H., 1856-1864
    Arey, Oliver, 1864-1867
    see also Presidents
Privett, Zollie, 89 (photo)

R

Ramaley, Judith, 178
Rappleyea, Clarence, 115 (photo)
Reeb, Donald J., 219
Reid, Ogden, 156 (photo)
Reilly, Joan, 112 (photo)
Religion, 60, 76 (photo), 79-80, 112 (photo), 181
Research, 98, 134-136, 176 (photo), 185, 187
Residential halls, *see* Student Body, Housing
Retrenchment (1975-76), 166-170
Richardson, Leonard Wood, 62 (photo)
Rienow, Robert, 88 (photo), 218
Risley, Adna Wood, 55, 62 (photo), 70 (photo)
Rivalry, *see* Student Culture, Traditions
Rivlin, Alice, 180 (photo)
Roberts, Warren F., 218
Rockefeller, Nelson A., Governor, 118 (photo), 119, 120, 121-122, 123 (caption), 124-126, 124 (photo), 131 (photo)
Roosevelt, Eleanor, 105
Roosevelt, Franklin D., 84
Rosenberg, Haskell, 90 (photo)
Ross, Albert R., 54

S

Salerno, Frederic V., 218
Salkever, Louis, 167 (photo)
Salkin, Patty E., 186 (caption), 207 (photo), 213 (photo)
Salomone, Rosemary C., 218
Sanderson, Miriam, 103
Saturday Review Article of the College, 105, 116 (photo)
Sauers, Richard "Doc," 102, 188 (photo), 200

Sayles, John, 55, 62 (photo), 67, 74, 76 (caption), 84, 87 (photo), 91 (photo), 94, 177
Schaefer, Vincent J., 136, 140 (photo), 141
Schools and Colleges, *see* Academic Administration
Schulz, Joan E., 172, 172 (photo), 207 (photo), 218, 219
Secondary Schools, 45, 49
Select Committee on Academic Priorities, 167
Semi-Centennial (1894), 38, 40
Senate, *see* Faculty Governance
Serafi, Pete, 186 (caption)
Sesquicentennial, 216
Seward, William, Governor, 13, 34
Shaver, Elizabeth, 44 (photo)
Shiperd, Susan Van Horn, 213 (photo)
Shore, Ivan, 186 (caption)
Shumaker, John, 170 (photo), 178
Signum Laudis, *see* Student Culture, Honoraries
Sirotkin, Philip, 164, 166 (photo)
Smith, Donnal, 86
Smith, Jack, 87, 89 (photo)
Smith, Sigmund, 114 (photo)
Smith, Tom, 188, 203 (photo)
Sommer, N. Theodore, 218
Spellman, Seth W., 163, 164 (photo), 218
Staley, Harry, 139 (photo)
Standing, Ted, 105
Standish, J. Spencer, 213 (photo)
State College News, *see* Student Culture, Publications
State University of New York, 119-121
Steinberg, Ronnie, 184 (photo)
Steinhauer, Robert, 122 (photo)
Stevenson, Adlai, 104
Stevenson, John, 112 (photo)
Stewart, Margaret M., 182 (photo), 218
Stewart, Watt, 87 (photo), 90 (photo)
Stoddard, George, 86, 91 (photo)
Stokes, Ellen, 76, 95, 98 (photo)
Stone, Edward Durrell, 124-128

Stoneman, Katherine, 31, 31 (photo), 33
Story, Harold, 219
Straub, J. Vanderbilt, 175 (photo)
Student Association, *see* Student Culture, Government
Student Body
    Behavior and Discipline, 37, 73-74, 83, 143-146, 196, 201
    Finances, 36, 56, 76 (photo), 78, 94, 120 (photo)
    Housing, 24 (photo), 36-37, 55 (photo), 56, 58, 67 (photo), 74-75, 74-76 (photos), 93, 94-95 (photos), 96-97, 99-103 (photos), 132-133 (photos), 140, 146, 149 (photo), 180, 181 (photo), 192, 194, 195
    Profile, 33-35, 56, 71-73, 100-101, 140, 190-191
Student Culture, 37-38, 58-61, 75-83, 93-94, 101-104, 138-146, 149 (photo)
    Campus Queen, 112 (photo)
    Dress, 103, 145, 195
    Fountain Day, 197 (photo), 199, 204 (photo)
    Fraternities and Sororities, 38, 52-53 (photos), 59, 82, 90 (photo), 103-104, 110 (photo), 140, 152 (photo), 195-196, 197 (photo), 212 (photo)
    Freshman Camp, 108 (photo)
    Freshman Week, 76
    Government, 66 (photo), 75-78, 101-102, 104-105, 114 (photo), 141, 143, 194, 215 (photo)
    Guinness Day, 186 (photo)
    Honoraries, 64, 79, 163, 195 (photo), 199, 200 (photo)
    Minerva, 48 (caption), 116 (photo), 140
    Moving-Up Day, 66 (photo), 76
    Music, 80, 102-103, 142, 145 (photo), 173 (photos)
    Organizations, 36 (photo), 38, 80, 142, 194, 197, 199, 211 (photo)
    Political and Social Views, 83-84, 104-105, 142-143, 148 (photo), 155-157, 158-159 (photos), 160-162, 196, 197
    Publications, 44 (photo), 58, 78, 102, 141-142, 144 (photo)
    Rivalry, 76, 108 (photo), 114 (photo), 121 (photo)
    School Colors, 59
    School Mascot, 129 (photo)
    Social Life, 59, 67 (photo), 71 (photo), 78 (photo), 82, 83 (photo), 95 (photo), 110 (photo), 145-146, 149 (photo), 195, 196
    Telethon, 142, 148 (photo)
    Theater, 58 (photo), 80, 81, 81 (photo), 111 (photo), 175
    Torch Night, 76, 114 (photo), 130 (photo), 199
    Traditions, 76, 139-140, 199
    World Week, 209 (photo)
Sullivan, Ed, 213 (photo)
Summer Session, 68
Swygert, H. Patrick, 199 (photo), 200 (photo), 202 (photo), 205, 206 (photo), 208, 211, 212, 213 (photo), 214 (photo), 215, 217 (photo), 218
Swygert, Sonja, 200 (photo)

T

Tarr-Whelan, Linda, 184 (caption)
Task Force on Programs and Resources, 167-168
Taylor, Maxwell, 160
Teachers' Institutes, *see* Graduate Study and Programs
Teaching, *see* Instruction, Undergraduate and Graduate Study and Programs
Tedisco, James, 206 (photo)
Teevan, Richard, 139 (photo)
Telethon, 148 (photo)
Thant, U, 143 (photo)
Thomas, Edward S., 218
Thompson, Frank J., 215, 218
Thorne, Clifton C., 137 (photo)
Thorne, Vivian Hillier, 207 (photo), 218
Tibbets, Ralph, 104 (photo)
Tisdale, Walter, 126, 126 (photo)
Toch, Hans H., 218
Truman, Harry, 104
Tucker, Harriet, 128 (photo)
Tuition, 29, 68, 120 (photo), 121, 129
Twoguns, Harriet E., 35

V

Valentine, Gertrude C., 64, 64 (photo)
Van Buren, Martin, 16
Van Liew, Marion Syddum, 6 (photo), 74 (caption)
Vaughn, Harold "Sparky," 114 (photo)
Videka-Sherman, Lynn, 218
Vietnam War, 155-156, 156 (photo), 158, 160-161
Vonnegut, Bernard, 218

W

Wagman, Barry, 214 (photo)
Wagman, Nina, 214 (photo)
Walker, Adam, 55
Wallace, Edith O., 69, 116 (photo), 138
Warnock, George, 104
Warren, Marguerite, 171 (photo)
Waterbury, Edward P., 28-29, 31, 40, 43 (photo), 45-46
Wayne, Marvin, 112 (photo)
Weitz, William F., 215 (photo), 218
Welch, Lewis P., 175 (photo), 178
Wellington, Carolyn Gillis, 207 (photo), 218
Westbrook, Derek, 215 (photo)
Wetherby, David, 112 (photo)
Whalen, Thomas M., III, 181 (photo)
Wharton, Clifton, 179
Wheeler, Paul, 139 (caption)
Wickham, Jenny Warnham, 43 (photo)
Wilkins, Karima, 207 (caption), 218
Willkie, Wendell, 84
Wills, Garry, 188
Windham, Douglas M., 218
Wolkonsky, Catherine, 138 (photo)
Wolner, Louis, 114 (photo)
Women
    Minorities, 183
    Students, 24 (photo), 34-35, 56, 100
    Women's Studies, 172
Woodward, Clifford Ambrose, 62 (photo)
Woolworth, Samuel B., 28, 28 (photo)
World War I, 63-65, 64-65 (photos)
World War II, 84-87, 88 (photo), 89 (photo), 93-94
Wright, Nathan, 165 (photo)
Wright, Silas, Governor, 26

Y

Young, Samuel, Col., 11, 13, 33

Z

Zambelli, Drew, 151 (photo)

About the Author

Kendall A. Birr, Professor Emeritus of History, joined the faculty of the New York State College for Teachers in 1952. His interest in history and his service to the University did not abate with his "retirement" in 1990. His research and writing of this Sesquicentennial history began a year ago and he continues to teach regularly, including a recent seminar on the "History of the University at Albany."

The consummate "University Citizen," Professor Birr has won virtually every service award offered by the University and its related organizations, including the 1993 University Citizen Award. He was one of the earliest faculty members chosen as a Collins Fellow, an award that recognizes "extraordinary devotion to the University." Over several decades, he has played a central role in academic development and faculty governance.

Professor Birr earned his B.A. from Cornell College, Iowa, and his M.S. and Ph.D. from the University of Wisconsin, concentrating on U.S. history and American studies. In this book he traces Albany's founding and growth from a state normal school to its present eminence as a public research university. The institution's history is enriched by his rich portrait of life for its faculty and students over the past 150 years.

The Willett Street building, home of Albany Normal School, 1885–1906